# INTERPRETATIONS
# OF SHAKESPEARE

# INTERPRETATIONS OF SHAKESPEARE

BRITISH ACADEMY
SHAKESPEARE LECTURES

*Selected by*
KENNETH MUIR

CLARENDON PRESS · OXFORD

Oxford University Press, Walton Street, Oxford OX2 6DP
London New York Toronto
Delhi Bombay Calcutta Madras Karachi
Petaling Jaya Singapore Hong Kong Tokyo
Nairobi Dar es Salaam Cape Town
Melbourne Auckland
and associated companies in
Beirut Berlin Ibadan Mexico City Nicosia

Oxford is a trade mark of Oxford University Press

Published in the United States
by Oxford University Press, New York

British Library Cataloguing in Publication Data
Interpretations of Shakespeare: British
Academy Shakespeare lectures.
1. Shakespeare, William—Criticism and
interpretation
I. Muir, Kenneth
822.3'3        PR2976
ISBN 0–19–812952–1

Library of Congress Cataloging-in-Publication Data
Interpretations of Shakespeare.
Includes index.
1. Shakespeare, William, 1564–1616—Criticism and
interpretation. I. Muir, Kenneth.
[PR2976.I58 1986]      822.3'3      86–12761
ISBN 0–19–812952–1 (pbk.)

set by Set Fair Limited
and printed in Great Britain
at the University Printing House, Oxford
by David Stanford
Printer to the University

# CONTENTS

# INTRODUCTION

There have been two previous selections of the British Academy Shakespeare lectures, by J. W. Mackail in 1933 and by Peter Alexander in 1964. Both are out of print; but, though I was free to choose any of the twenty-four in those two volumes, I have chosen only one.

The lectures have been delivered, almost without a break, since 1911, when the series was inaugurated by J. J. Jusserand, a choice which avoided the necessity of choosing between English candidates. The second lecture was given by A. C. Bradley, who repaired one of the omissions in *Shakespearean Tragedy* by speaking on *Coriolanus*. Since then most well-known Shakespeare scholars of the past seventy years have contributed to the series. There have been several surprising omissions; but the lectures as a whole give a fair idea of the changing face of Shakespeare criticism. We may regret the absence of stage directors (with the sole exception of Harley Granville Barker), of dramatists (with the same exception),[1] of dramatic critics, and of poets, except Lascelles Abercrombie. But an Academy naturally gives preference to the academic; and it is pleasant to observe that the term could be stretched to include Émile Legouis's amusing fantasy that the Bacchic element in Shakespeare reflected the poet's own struggle against alcoholism.

Most of the early lecturers tackled large and unspecialized topics—'Shakespeare and Germany', 'Shakespeare in America', 'Shakespeare after Three Hundred Years'—and they were addressed, for the most part, to audiences equally unspecialized. Although these lectures were sometimes finely phrased, their content has inevitably become dated, sometimes embarrassingly so. Walter Raleigh, for example, devoted much of his 1918 lecture to ritual attacks on Germany; Mackail in 1916 cheerfully asserted that research had done away with 'the old

---

[1] Bernard Shaw proposed a vote of thanks after Granville Barker's lecture and, to the alleged annoyance of the second Mrs Barker, took the opportunity of lamenting that he had deserted the stage to become an academic.

thoughtless idea that the body of work passing under
Shakespeare's name' was all his; and Canon Beeching could
deplore that Shakespeare chose to write on such an indelicate
subject as Venus and Adonis. On the other hand, reacting
against supposedly Victorian ideas on the desirability of
uplift, several lecturers declared that Shakespeare was not a
moral teacher. 'He lets morality take care of itself,' declared
Mackail. But before they finished their discourses, the
disclaimers of moral purpose admitted perforce that the plays
did have a moral effect. 'It obliges human hearts to melt,' said
Jusserand; 'it teaches them pity'. Shakespeare improves us by
fighting our egoism. 'What he sets before us', said Mackail, 'is
life.' Shakespeare depicts vices and virtues, 'but they are
neither approved nor condemned, they are only displayed, as
causes with their effects'. Beeching similarly spoke of the
uplifting tendency of the plays, partly by 'their profound
intuition into the springs of conduct' and partly, in Pauline
phrase, by 'the love they inspire in us for whatsoever things
are true and honest and just and pure and lovely and
gracious'.

Later lecturers sometimes chose topics as broad, but most
of them exemplify the increased specialization of Shakespeare
scholarship and criticism, and their confidence that their
audiences would be more than literate. When J. C. Maxwell
and Ernst Honigmann spoke on *Measure for Measure*, they
could take it for granted that their auditors would be
acquainted with R. W. Chambers's famous lecture on the play
and, indeed, the continuing controversy stemming from it, to
which all the best-known critics and stage-directors have
contributed during the last forty-five years. Was Isabella a
saint or a self-centred prig? Was the Duke a symbol of power
divine or an incompetent busybody? Was Lucio to be equated
with Lucifer or was he a spokesman for common sense? Was
the play an allegory or a satire on providential government?

Some of the best lectures have been rendered obsolete by
their very success. After Charles J. Sisson's lecture on 'The
Mythical Sorrows of Shakespeare' (1934), no responsible critic
would be able to argue that there was a direct connection
between Shakespeare's tragic period and his private life:

Shakespeare was not stung into tragedy by any Dark Lady. He was not depressed into tragedy by the fall of Essex, who threatened revolution and chaos in England . . . He did not degenerate into tragedy in a semi-delirium of cynicism and melancholy . . . Shakespeare *rose* to tragedy in the very height and peak of his powers, nowhere else so splendidly displayed.

Fifteen years earlier, A. W. Ward, in 'Shakespeare and the Makers of Virginia' (1919) had parenthetically issued a similar warning:

We should always remember that Shakespeare is the greatest of dramatic artists, and that whatever principle, maxim or experience finds utterance in his plays should be read in the light of the dramatis personae from whom it proceeds . . . It is they who speak—and think—in the first instance, and not the author of their being.

It was not Shakespeare—to take a notorious example—but Gloucester who compared the gods to cruel and wanton boys.

Sir Edmund Chambers, who in his austere volumes, *William Shakespeare: A Study of Facts and Problems* (Oxford 1930), wantonly dallied with the idea that the poet had suffered a breakdown after *Timon of Athens*, had earlier destroyed another fashionable heresy in 'The Disintegration of Shakespeare' (1924). He attacked what he called 'certain critical tendencies which, in their extreme manifestations, offer results hardly less perturbing than those with which the Baconians and their kin would make our flesh creep'. He was referring to the attempt to allocate large parts of Shakespeare's plays to other dramatists.[2]

A few years later, Lascelles Abercrombie's 'Plea for the Liberty of Interpreting' (1930) tackled the problem from a different angle. He stressed the fallibility of 'scientific' method when applied to great poetry, and argued that even if Shakespeare took over material from Marlowe ( in *Henry VI*) or Kyd (in *Hamlet*), he converted it to his own uses.

---

[2] Not merely *Henry VI* and *Titus Andronicus*, which remain suspect with some critics, but even plays as late as *Julius Caesar* and *Troilus and Cressida*. T. S. Eliot's essay on *Hamlet* had been influenced by the disintegrating theories of J. M. Robertson.

Abercrombie was aware that liberty could easily develop into absurdity. He condemned 'ungovernable subjectivism', the imposition of modern notions on an Elizabethan poet—such as the notion that Imogen was corrupt and that she nearly succumbed to Iachimo's advances, or that Hippolyta was the most lascivious wöman in the canon.

The lectures so far mentioned would necessarily be included in a collection designed to illustrate the history of Shakespeare criticism in the first half of this century; but the present selection is made from those lectures concerned with literary and dramatic topics. That purpose also excludes such famous lectures as Caroline Spurgeon's exposition of Shakespeare's imagery, partly because it was not concerned with the more valuable side of her work—her analysis of the dominant imagery of individual plays[3]—and partly because her pioneering work has been refined and modified by later critics.

A number of informative lectures were concerned with editorial and textual questions. Pollard, one of the founders of the new bibliography, spoke on 'The Foundations of Shakespeare's Text' (1923); Greg brilliantly exemplified 'The Principles of Emendation' (1928); McKerrow, who was to have edited the Oxford Shakespeare, spoke on 'The Treatment of Shakespeare's Text by his earlier Editors' (1933); Peter Alexander, the editor of one of the best one-volume editions, discussed 'Shakespeare's Punctuation' (1945); and Alice Walker gave an account of 'Edward Capell and his Edition of Shakespeare' (1960). Admirable as these lectures are, they represent, one may say, only a prelude to literary criticism.

Even when we have excluded the lectures already mentioned, there are still left fifty to choose from, and it would be easier to pick twenty than ten. Twelve of the more recent lecturers have concentrated on a single play, and even on a single scene,

---

[3] e.g. the sickness imagery in *Hamlet*, the kitchen imagery in *Troilus and Cressida*. R. Tuve, *Elizabethan and Metaphysical Imagery* (1947), questioned whether the field from which imagery is drawn is as significant as Caroline Spurgeon believed. Several critics have argued that to concentrate on a single iterative image, merely because of its numerical predominance, can distort the meaning of a play. See, for example, *This Great Stage* by R. B. Heilman (Baton Rouge, 1948), *Shakespeare's Roman Plays* by Maurice Charney (Cambridge, Mass., 1961), and *Shakespeare the Professional* (London, 1973) by Kenneth Muir.

as J. I. M. Stewart's analysis of the assassination scene in *Julius Caesar* (1971). Rather than choose pieces on six or seven different plays, it seemed better to give contrasting views of only two plays. This could have been Chambers, Maxwell, and Honigmann on *Measure for Measure* or G. L. Bickersteth and Philip Brockbank on *King Lear*, but in the end I opted for two on *Hamlet* and two on *Othello*, all excellent in their different ways. There is, regrettably, nothing on the comedies, nothing on actors and audiences, nothing directly on questions of style, and nothing on Shakespeare in the new world, where the Shakespeare industry has been flourishing throughout the period. What is written on most of these topics is liable to be overtaken by new ideas.

During the twenty-five years following the publication of Bradley's *Shakespearean Tragedy*, doubts were raised about his methods. It was pointed out that he was insufficiently aware of the theatrical conditions under which Elizabethan dramatists wrote; it was alleged that he concerned himself with such details as Hamlet's age, or the question of Lady Macbeth's children, which would not occur to a member of an audience; that he tended to apply modern psychological theories to the cruder characterization of the sixteenth century; and that he treated the plays as though they were novels by George Eliot. In fact, Bradley was an ardent playgoer and he was well aware of the differences between a prose narrative and a poetic drama. But critics on both sides of the Atlantic pooh-poohed the idea that Shakespeare's characterization was based on a profound, if instinctive, knowledge of human psychology. Robert Bridges, assuming that Shakespeare was prevented from being as great an artist as he was a poet by the crude taste of the groundlings, asserted that the Macbeth depicted in the play could not possibly have murdered Duncan—Bernard Shaw concurring[4] —that Angelo was not the sort of man to lust after a novice, and that the plot of *Othello* was absurd since Desdemona had no opportunity to commit adultery with Cassio—much less a

---

[4] *Shaw on Shakespeare*, ed. E. Wilson (Harmondsworth 1969), p. 139: 'The incongruity of the ferocious murders . . . with the humane and reflective temperament of the nervous literary gentleman whom Shakespeare thrust into his galligaskins.'

thousand times.[5] Edgar Elmer Stroll argued[6] that the Moor
depicted in the first two acts could not have become the
jealous maniac of Acts III and IV, but that Shakespeare
obtained some of his most thrilling theatrical effects in
defiance of psychological reality, by the maximum of contrast
between the dreadful deed and the noble doer of it. L. L.
Schücking showed[7] that Shakespeare often made his heroes
and heroines talk out of character, using the unrealistic device
of self-explanation for the information of the audience, as
when Lear says 'I should e'en die with pity / To see another
thus.' William Archer could even argue that modern dramatists
such as Pinero and Galsworthy were better playwrights than
those of the seventeenth century, including by implication
Shakespeare.[8] G. Wilson Knight, though claiming that he was
in the Bradley tradition,[9] nevertheless seemed to subordinate
the characters to themes and images; and L. C. Knights, who
did not share Knight's involvement in acting major Shakespearian roles, attacked the Bradleian concentration on character in *How Many Children Had Lady Macbeth?* (1933). He
declared that *Macbeth* was more like *The Waste Land* than a
prose play by Ibsen and, unconsciously echoing Bradley's own
words, he pronounced that a Shakespearian tragedy was a
dramatic poem. He was surprised to find that he was preaching
to the converted.

The British Academy lectures often deal directly or indirectly with the question of character, either subordinating it to
other dramatic qualities or regarding it as of paramount importance. When C. S. Lewis spoke on *Hamlet* (1942: No. 7),
for example, he argued that the character of the Prince was
not of central importance, and he explained the differences
between the critics on that character by arguing that he was
not a specific individual, but Everyman, burdened with
original sin and the thought of the undiscovered country from
whose bourn no traveller returns. To which it was retorted

[5] Robert Bridges, *The Influence of the Audience* (1927) cf. *Othello*, v. ii. 215.
[6] Edgar Elmer Stoll, *Othello* (Minneapolis 1915).
[7] L. L. Schücking, *Character Problems in Shakespeare's Plays* (New York and London, 1922).
[8] *The Old Drama and the New* (London, 1923), *passim*.
[9] G. Wilson Knight, *The Wheel of Fire* (edn. London, 1949), p. v.

that just as Coleridge's Hamlet was a self-portrait, one who 'lost the power of action in the energy of resolve', and just as Freud's Hamlet inevitably suffered from the Oedipus complex, so the Lewis Hamlet reflected the theological interests of the author of the *The Screwtape Letters* and *The Problem of Pain*. His Hamlet, however strangely drained of personality, may be usefully contrasted with the Hamlet who emerges in Harold Jenkins's lecture on 'Hamlet and Ophelia' (1963: No. 8)—a brilliant forerunner of his splendid Arden edition.

Meanwhile, Una Ellis-Fermor had argued that 'The Art of the Dramatist' consisted precisely in his ability to create life-like characters, Shakespeare outshining all his rivals in this respect. The lecture was intended as the first chapter of a book she did not live to complete. Other chapters dealt with themes and imagery, but she regarded such matters, however important, as subsidiary.[10] L. C. Knights, by the time he delivered his lecture in 1957 (No. 5), had modified his position on characterization.[11] Although he was primarily concerned with Shakespeare's poetic and political wisdom, he considered that it was embodied in his characters.

The two lecturers on *Othello* arrive by very different routes at approximately the same interpretation. Helen Gardner, disagreeing with both Bradley and Granville Barker, who had found the play ultimately depressing, and disagreeing more strongly with T. S. Eliot and F. R. Leavis, who had argued that Bradley had sentimentalized the play by shutting his eyes to the hero's faults,[12] proclaims by her title that Othello is 'The Noble Moor' (1955: No. 9). She justifies the title by her sensitive analysis of many passages in the play. G. K. Hunter's strategy (1967: No. 10) is different. By a wide-ranging account of contemporary superstitions, nurtured on theological and racial prejudice, he shows that the original audience would have expected a moor to be devilish, but that

---

[10] *Shakespeare the Dramatist*, ed. Kenneth Muir (London, 1961). This is an edition of the unfinished book referred to above.

[11] See L. C. Knights, 'The Question of Character in Shakespeare', *Further Explorations* (London, 1965), *passim*.

[12] Leavis in his Retrospect to the reprint of *Scrutiny* regarded that journal's dethronement of Bradley as one of its major achievements. It certainly had the effect of making people question Bradley's concentration on character.

Shakespeare upsets their expectations by making the white Iago devilish and the black Othello, notwithstanding the evil into which he falls, fundamentally virtuous.[13] Both Helen Gardner and George Hunter stress the recovery of the hero's nobility in the final scene. Unlike the wife-murderers in Calderón's tragedies—*A secreto agravio, secreta venganza* and *El médico de su honra*—Othello executes judgement on himself.

Romantic ideas of Shakespeare's unquestioned perfection have given way to a sober realization that to work in the theatre is to involve oneself in makeshift decisions and regrettable compromises. This realization is the more positive result of the excessive reactions to Bradley's *Shakespearean Tragedy*. Molly M. Mahood's title, 'Unblotted Lines' (1972: No. 4), is an allusion to the boast of Shakespeare's fellows that there were no blots in his manuscripts, and to Jonson's famous retort 'Would he had blotted a thousand!'. (In the commendatory verses in the First Folio, however, Jonson allowed that Shakespeare had sweated and revised.) Although readers may question the validity of some of Professor Mahood's examples, she shows convincingly that Shakespeare's inspired carelessness revealed the presence of an exploring and adventurous mind. It was a mind, moreover, that thought in terms of the theatre and relied on the responses of a heterogeneous audience.

One method by which Shakespeare ensured the responses at which he aimed is the subject of Muriel C. Bradbrook's 'Shakespeare's Primitive Art' (1965: No. 3)—his use of icons from *Titus Andronicus* to *The Tempest* as a means of ensuring a collective response to the situations in his plays.

Philip Edwards, like L. C. Knights, dealing with Shakespeare's treatment of politics (1970: No. 6), starts from the paradox that although he 'was preoccupied' with 'the mind and the heart of the individual' he 'should have written a group of plays unmatched in any literature for their political

---

[13] Rymer's attack on the credibility of the play, and particularly on the character of Iago—since soldiers were notoriously honest—misses the point. Shakespeare relies on the stereotype of 'honest soldier' to get the other characters to believe Iago. The matter is discussed by Nigel Alexander in 'Thomas Rymer and *Othello*', *Shakespeare Survey*, xxi (1968), 67–78.

content'. In a closely packed argument, Edwards considers the relation between the self or the person and public or official life. He discusses this in relation to a number of plays, especially *Richard II*. In the end he makes it clear that Shakespeare's treatment of politics is so impressive because he is aware both of the person and of the office.

The last lecture, chronologically, is Michel Grivelet's subtle meditation on the artist as Proteus (1975: No. 2). In it he ranges from Coleridge to Joyce by way of William Richardson, Ovid, Homer, and Keats, with interesting comments on the character of Proteus in *The Two Gentlemen of Verona* and on Shakespeare's genius in identifying with a wide range of characters. The lecture, therefore, touches on the same theme as Una Ellis-Fermor's.

# 1. SHAKESPEARE THE DRAMATIST

By U. Ellis-Fermor

In speaking today of Shakespeare the dramatist I propose, with your permission, to consider one question: To what degree and in virtue of what quality in his genius is Shakespeare a dramatist? What, in other words, constitutes the specifically dramatic quality in his writing and how nearly is that the native habit of his mind? For it is evident that, in the Elizabethan period, when conditions fostered the art of drama, many writers became practising dramatists who in another age would have sought another medium; Ben Jonson was almost certainly one of these and so, in some degree, were Marlowe on one hand and Webster on the other. Just so, during the nineteenth century, many poets as evidently diverted their imaginations from the drama, which offered them only an incomplete and inhibited form of artistic communication. Was dramatic expression, then, partly induced in Shakespeare, as it was in Marlowe, Jonson, and Webster, by the favourable conditions, the prevailing mood of the age? Or was it essential to his genius, innate in him, profiting no doubt by the coincidence of man and moment, but not prompted, as in some of his contemporaries, by the demands of that moment? May we, as a first step towards answering this (and so my initial question), look for a moment at the nature of drama, or, more precisely, at the nature of dramatic genius?

Clearly we are not concerned here with the obvious characteristics of the literary form that we call drama; these, though derivative from, are not the essential manifestation of, dramatic genius. If we remind ourselves of them briefly it is rather that, having so recalled them, we may set them aside before beginning to look for the generic and then the differentiating qualities of the art and of the artist. We are not likely to meet with disagreement, to need to justify ourselves, when we say that in a play which shows competent craftsmanship as a play, we expect to find at least three things: action, or a reasonably clear and coherent plot; characters, themselves the sources of this action, who convince us that they are human beings, such as we meet or might expect to meet; speech, the dialogue through which plot and character are revealed, which satisfies us that it is such speech as these men, meeting these events, might use. If one or other of these three is notably defective, we find a piece of work which fails as a play, whether or not it has in it fine poetry, subtle thought, or firm design. There is some noble poetry in W. B. Yeats's *Shadowy Waters*, but there is not enough action, in outward event or inner experience, to give it the vigour and immediacy of drama. There is subtle and sometimes searching thought in much modern drama, but such a play as Denis Johnston's *The Old Lady Says No* fails to move the audience—as a play—because the central figures are not imagined primarily as human beings. There is firm design and some understanding of character in Browning's *Strafford*, but the words do not strike upon our imaginations as they would if they were instinct with the life of speech at any level of experience. If, however, all these ends are duly served, the play will be at least a workmanlike piece of craftsmanship (it may, of course, be much more), even though the emphasis be laid on the action, as in *The Spanish Tragedy*; on the revelation of character, as in Maeterlinck's *Aglavaine et Sélysette*, or on verbal wit, as in Etherege's *Man of Mode*.

To determine, then, what dramatic genius is in its essence, we must look below these formal characteristics, these outward signs of dramatic thought, and ask what are the innate powers of mind which lead a poet to apprehend life in terms of dramatic experience which, if they are not thwarted by circumstance or conditions, will certainly direct his artistic expression to dramatic, rather than to any other, literary form. We are not concerned, that is, with the nature of the average play (which, like the average novel, need not be a work of art at all) but, first, with the nature of dramatic art, and then with that of dramatic genius; the first of these may best be learned from the study of the major drama; the second can only be so learned.

And so, setting aside technical and formal considerations,

we examine first the generic qualities which the great
dramatist shares with certain other major artists and then
those qualities or powers which differentiate the dramatist
and drama. We call in evidence such dramas as, while
fulfilling the technical demand, so inform it with the universal
and the enduring that, when what is temporal and perishable
has lost its meaning, an imperishable and eternal significance
shines through, and Aeschylus speaks to men of today, not as
an Athenian of two thousand years ago, but as a man whose
essential experience is still ours. Passion, thought, and poetic
imagination, unchanging even in the wreckage of the civiliz-
ations they worked upon, survive event and circumstance and
reveal man's kinship with the indestructible spirit of which
great art is an image. And it is somewhere here that we shall
find our starting-point. Passion, thought, and poetic imagination are, I think, the generic characteristics of dramatic
genius and we can trace their manifestation in the substance of
drama, and, if we wish, in the form, through the work of all
the greatest dramatists. How, then, do these manifest
themselves in drama, and what is Shakespeare's portion here?

It is perhaps upon the passion and intensity with which the
dramatist apprehends the world of experience that great
drama depends, in the first instance, for its power and its
immediacy; though passion is, in the last analysis, inseparable
from thought and poetic imagination, and these from each
other. It is the intensity, first of his imaginative experience of
the world about him, then of his artistic experience—the act
of transmuting this into a work of art—that gives to the great
dramatist his power to move men; to touch the depths of their
imaginations; to free them, and to set at work the powers of
life. Nor are there any narrow limits to the shape this mighty
force may take when it informs the characters in a great
drama. It may be released, or may appear to be released,
almost without guidance, as in the terrifying whirlwinds of
madness in a Lear or a Timon. It my be stifled, or appear to be
stifled, in the marmoreal calm of the Chorus Leader in the
*Oedipus at Colonus*: 'Not to be born at all Is best,[1] or in the

---

[1] *Oed. Col.* 1225–8:

μὴ φῦναι τὸν ἅπαντα νικᾷ λόγον · τὸ δ' ἐπεὶ φανῇ,
βῆναι κεῖθεν ὅθεν περ ἥκει
πολὺ δεύτερον, ὡς τάχιστα.

deceptively prosaic utterance of Middleton's or Ford's tragedies, of Ibsen's late plays. A Macbeth, an Agamemnon, a Jocasta may, as men do in actual life, hold it with difficulty in some kind of restraint; a Clytemnestra, a Lady Macbeth, seemingly with less difficulty, may hide it altogether. A Medea, an Othello, a Borkman may, without crossing the border-line of madness, release a part of what is shattering the mind. It is the presence of the passion, not the mode or the extent of its expression, that matters, and it is our awareness of forces beyond our own imagination that strikes us into awe and receptivity in the presence of the *Agamemnon*, the *Oedipus*, *Othello*, *Lear*, or *Timon*. Whether it appears to be revealed or seems to be hidden is really of less moment than we think, for our subconscious minds, wiser in this than 'meddling intellect', recognize and respond to the hidden as swiftly as to the manifest.

This power is not the prerogative of the dramatist; it will be found in varying kinds and degrees in all great artists. But though diffused or mitigated passion, though moments only of concentration are compatible with the highest reaches of art in other kinds, the dramatist depends upon it as the very matter of his. We recognize its working in the debates in the second book and in other isolated passages in *Paradise Lost*; but *Samson Agonistes* is instinct with it throughout. In Dante and in Goethe it is again intermittent, giving place to description, to meditation, to reasoned reflection, even to satire; in Wordsworth there is still less direct expression; it is diffused in the underlying groundwork of the thought; the solemn exultation of the music, in his major poems, its only outward sign. But in the great dramatists it is sustained and seemingly inexhaustible; Marlowe, Webster, Racine (in this among the greatest) suffer no dilution and little or no intermission. The power and comprehensiveness of their passion would alone distinguish the great masters of drama from all but the ocasional companionship of their fellows. And here Shakespeare, as our instinctive choice of plays suggests, is with Aeschylus and Sophocles.

But the great forces set at work by passion are not undirected. 'God spoke to Job out of the whirlwind', and over the passion evoked by the intensity of his apprehension presides, in the major dramatist, the directing thought which gives us what has been called the logic of poetry.[2] The operation of thought, the effect of the continual discipline of contemplation or reflection, is harder to discern in drama than in many forms of art. And this we should expect, for it is inseparable from the differentiating quality of drama (of which we shall have to speak later), that preoccupation with the life of man, doing and suffering, which affords—except in rare instances—but little opportunity for the direct expression of reflection. Such revelation as there is is therefore implicit and can often be consciously abstracted only by a deliberate consideration of the total effect of action, character, and sentiment interrelated within a given play held whole in the mind of the critic.

This is, in effect, to say that in some plays it cannot be abstracted at all, for nothing but the total play will give us its 'meaning'. What, after all, is the meaning of *Much Ado*? Or for that matter, of *Antony and Cleopatra*? A governing idea, a sequence of thought, can, it is true, be traced in *Troilus and Cressida* or the group *Richard II*, *Henry IV*, *Henry V*, but even here thought and content are more nearly co-terminous than it is always convenient to admit. The 'logic of poetry' remains, in fact, the logic of *poetry*, and thought is revealed, in each aspect of the play, precisely by the presence of the excellence proper to that aspect; if we consider the characters, we find in it the depth of Shakespeare's understanding of motive and human experience; if the structure, it is in the flawless relation of the form to its subject. If we look for a theme in Shakespeare's plays, we find none, other than the bottomless and endlessly extending wisdom that asks of his readers a lifetime's consecration to explore. The operation of thought, then, is easier to discern than the resultant thoughts; a man must be blind to whom Shakespeare's architecture spells nothing, but he would fall into as great a folly if he assumed that the operation of this governing and presiding intelligence must necessarily give indications which can be abstracted and restated as the conclusions of a philosopher, a historian, a moralist, or a psychologist. The dramatist's is an

---

[2] I am partly indebted for this phrase to Mr C. Day Lewis, who, in his recent work *The Poetic Image* (London, 1947), discusses in chapter V the function of poetic logic, referring back to the use, by W. P. Ker, of the term 'poetical logic'.

impersonal art; its ways are secret and his thoughts are often hidden in those ways. But the sign of thought, in profound and powerful, sometimes in prophetic, form, is in the strength and majesty of the work of art itself and each fresh exploration teaches us to recognize here the conscious and unconscious intellectual control of passion.

So it is (with reservations which will be noted later) with the thought of Aeschylus and with that of Sophocles, Euripides, Ibsen. It is true that in these a part (a progressively diminishing part) is explicitly stated in the commentary of the chorus or an equivalent modern agent; but the total thought remains co-terminous with the content of the play, of which this is itself a part. And it is too easily forgotten that in the first and second and, in some degree, in the third of these dramatists there are formal and aesthetic relations between the choric odes and the rest of the play which reveal in terms of another mode some part of the theme and are indispensable to full conscious or unconscious apprehension of it.[3]

In all of these poets, then, the major dramatists of litera-ture, the forces evoked by passion are directed by thought, serving to express it, as it in turn expresses them.

And so we 'enter that state of grace which is called poetry',[4] a mode of experience, a condition of mind which is inherent in and yet partially distinguishable from passion and from thought as they are from each other. By 'poetry' in this sense I would be understood to mean that apprehension of beauty which irradiates the mind of the poet, presenting order or form as an aspect of truth, and distinguishing it at that point from the mind of the philosopher or of the saint. This radiance, this sense of glory in things seen or felt or imagined and of the ultimate and underlying truth of which they in turn are images, is communicated to us in ways which again differ widely in each of the greatest dramatists. It is at work in the major lines of design which give form to structure and to character and in the details of expression—imagery and verbal music. It is the ever-present sense of significance in all

---

[3] On the relations between the choric ode of Aeschylus with the form on the one hand and the theme on the other, see H. A. F. Kitto, *Greek Tragedy* (London, 1939).

[4] See again C. Day Lewis, *The Poetic Image*, p. 58.

things, of some hidden reality in them ever about to become manifest. Its clarity is at its height in the work of Aeschylus, of Sophocles, of Shakespeare, where design and detail are alike instinct with it; it is intermittent in certain dramatists second only to the greatest; though always there, it burns low and sometimes almost invisibly in Ibsen. Like passion, the poetic apprehension of the universe may reveal itself in drama clearly or more obscurely. From the time of his full maturity it never fails in Shakespeare's authentic work; in Ibsen, at the opposite extreme, it is sometimes so deep buried as to leave us blind to its working. Yet the imagery of *Antony and Cleopatra* springs, though with fuller potency, from the same faculty as the occasional overtones of beauty in *Rosmersholm*, and the secret kinship of the two is revealed by the solemn yet continuous presence of such overtones, side by side with clear and distinctive imagery, in such a play as the *Oedipus at Colonus*.

Such, then, are the genetic forces that we discover if we look below the outward characteristics of drama presented to us by a normally constituted play and inquire what is the essential attribute of dramatic genius. But these, being generic qualities, are shared in varying degrees and relations by all great literature. What, then, differentiates drama from other forms of literature and the dramatists from other writers?

The nature of this differentiation has already been indicated in some of the suggestions we have made. Put briefly, it consists in this, that the dramatist (with whom up to this point we must be prepared to admit a certain kind of novelist) is concerned with the life of man acting and suffering. Here and here only can he rightly find his material. However far he may make universal his implicit theme, his subject remains man's experience, and all that he says or implies must be said in terms of this medium. From this there follow, almost as corollaries, two inferences. First, that the dramatist's mood, his attitude, will itself show a characteristic differentiation, which we may think of as sympathy. He enters into the minds of his characters (ideally into the minds of all of them) and speaks, as it were, from within them, giving thus a kind of impartiality to his picture of life, sorrowing with him that sorrows, rejoicing with him that rejoices. In certain rare cases this may take the form of an equidistant detachment from, rather than active participation with, all his characters,[5] but this, for our purpose, is a distinction without essential difference. It is the equality of his relations with them all that is the essential feature. And in close conjunction with this inference we may draw a second. The dramatist's primary concern being man's life, acting and suffering, and his relation to this basic material being one of sympathy, the mode which offers him the fullest expression is direct revelation by the agents themselves. No other means will allow him so to concentrate upon the essentials of his subject, no other will present so economically the passions and thoughts of men as to leave men themselves, under due safeguards, to present them. And from what has been said of the nature of that sympathy which is a differentiating characteristic of dramatic genius, it follows that the genuine dramatist meets no obstruction in expressing his passion thus mediately instead of immediately, as the passion of his characters, not as his own; not in the fact that his reading of life can only be expressed indirectly and by implication (in such ways as we have already indicated), and that even his sense of the poetry that irradiates his universe is at the mercy of the people of his drama.

Now, just as the different dramatists, though fundamentally akin, differ somewhat in the balance and relation of these generic qualities we began by considering, so, it will be found, do they differ in respect of this differentiating characteristic of dramatic sympathy and the technical mode that follows from it. Dramatists differ in their power, or their desire, of maintaining equidistant relations with their characters; at one extreme we find Marlowe, who, in *Tamburlaine* and in *Faustus*, identifies himself with one or at most two characters and enters only intermittently into the others; at the other

[5] This is extremely rare in drama, even in comedy. (It is not to be confused with what is extremely common in most dramatists below the greatest, an imperfect distribution of sympathy, so that some of the characters, but not all, are treated objectively.) Middleton alone appears to preserve this attitude in tragedy and that only in the main plots of his two major tragedies. Ibsen occasionally seems to achieve it, but this is generally found, on closer inspection, to be either a momentary failure of sympathy in one direction or the result of a deceptive concealment of an underlying but passionate sympathy.

extreme we find Shakespeare, who speaks from within each of his creatures as it speaks. So also do they vary in the extent to which they express directly their own passion, their own perception of poetic truth, and make explicit or keep implicit their reading of life. Marlowe again is at one extreme in the first of these and Shakespeare at the other; in the second the extremes may be illustrated by Aeschylus on the one hand and Shakespeare again on the other. So far as his characters allow him, a dramatist may express with a measure of directness his emotion and his poetic delight. But those larger inferences from his experience which we call his reading of life can only, as we have said, be expressed implicitly, in terms of character and event and the relation between the two. In so far as he does in fact depart from this law, itself an inference from the differentiating chracteristics of drama, in so far does he depart from the strict dramatic mode. This divergence, here possible to dramatists, may be briefly illustrated by the different methods of revealing thought through or independently of character and action. (Since, as has been indicated, the problems in the dramatic revelation of passion and of poetic experience are less crucial, the divergence in practice is less wide there and calls the less for illustration.)

Aeschylus, as is obvious, gives us in twofold form his comment on the world of his play; in one form it is implicit and dramatic, lying wholly within the dialogue; in the other, in the choric odes, it is explicit and to that extent non-dramatic, sometimes almost a direct statement of a theme. The two are complementary and in complete harmony, but each is dependent upon the other and neither alone would render fully his interpretation. This is true to a less degree of Sophocles. Euripides, perhaps simply because he came later in the tradition which had bequeathed the choric ode, but more probably because he instinctively laid more emphasis upon action and suffering, revealed his reading rather by the indirect, implicit method. More than any modern of comparable stature, Ibsen renders parts of his interpretation in terms of direct commentary, though he is dramatist enough to put suitable characters in charge of the operation.[6] Of the greatest

---

[6] Here the modern convention of dramatic plausibility may be partly responsible. Certain of the Elizabethans, who were not subject to the naturalistic convention,

dramatists of the world's literature, one alone, so far, has used the dramatic mode, and only the dramatic, for the revelation of his underlying thought. It is Shakespeare who baffles impertinent conjecture and unimaginative exegesis alike by affording us no re-expression of his implicit, dramatic utterance in terms of explicit commentary. The reading of life revealed by his plays cannot, as we have already noticed, be abstracted, for it is co-extensive with the plays themselves and can only be learnt by a lifetime spent in their world.

If, now, we look again at the properties of the resulting 'kind', those outward characteristics which, taken together, constitute the conventional forms of drama, can we discover anything more? I think we can, by this means, add something to what we have already said of the operation both of those generic forces and of those differentiating qualities which are at work in the mind of a dramatic genius. We may observe that they can transmute, not only traditional and conventional forms but even the limitations imposed not by convention but by the nature of the kind itself, and make both subservient to significant form.

When a traditional or conventional form comes into the hands of a dramatist of genius, when passion, thought, and poetic imagination have there expressed themselves in terms of sympathy and by means of direct presentation, we find the elements of a play (action, character, dialogue) transformed, so that each fulfils more than the bare functions necessary to make of the work drama rather than some other literary kind. Through the operation of those powers the relation between these elements becomes more fruitful; action or plot becomes significant form, itself an aspect of the play's meaning or thought; the revelation and grouping of character becomes the spatial aspect of the play's structure,[7] and dialogue or

though poets of great dramatic force, availed themselves of the relative freedom of their dramatic form to use the equivalent of brief choric commentary without undue regard to the characters to whom it was assigned. Webster is adept at inducing his reader to accept this without realizing it.

[7] The spatial aspect of structure and the relation between spatial and temporal form in drama are discussed in detail in G. Wilson Knight's *The Wheel of Fire* (London, 1930). 'A Shakespearian tragedy is set spatially as well as temporally in the mind. By this I mean that there are a set of correspondences which relate to each other independently of the time-sequence which is the story' (p.3). (The theory is developed in the first chapter, 'On the Principles of Shakespearian Interpretation'.)

speech the vehicle not merely for our necessary knowledge of action and character, but of much upon which depends our understanding of the relations between the world of the play and the wider universe of which that world is a part. Contrast between scene and scene becomes in *Troilus and Cressida* an image of disjunction, in *Antony and Cleopatra* of synthesis; in the first play the theme is the discord of the universe, in the second it is the conflict in Antony's mind between an empire and a mistress, and the vastness of that empire images the magnitude of the conflict. The grouping of characters in each play serves the same end, somewhat as does the relation of colour and shape in pictorial composition; and imagery directly and verbal music indirectly relate the significance thus revealed within the play to that of the wider, surrounding universe.

When we consider such drama as this, which has passed beyond mere adequate craftsmanship to take its place among the great art-forms, we find that it, like all other arts, meets and conflicts with the limitations imposed by its form and seeks out means of transcending them. And it is the major dramatists, with whom we have been all along concerned, who discover and reveal to their fellows the possibilities inherent in the form, which can, paradoxically, enable them to transcend its limitations. Their discoveries may be defined by their followers or imitators, by those who are consciously or unconsciously taught by them, sometimes as branches of technique, sometimes almost as technical devices; but in the hands of the original masters they are the findings of far-reaching imaginative exploration. It is Aeschylus, so far as our knowledge allows us to judge, who perceives a further function of the choric ode, using it to refer outward, beyond the boundaries of the play's actual content, to a moral and spiritual universe of which his chosen portion of life is a significant part. But this is the least innately dramatic of all the modes of transcending limitation in scope, and what we have already said would lead us, even if we had not studied his work, to expect that Shakespeare would not use it. In fact, he does not. But since to remain in subjection to the limitations of a form is to write a work of art which may be the poorer for its submission, he finds his own ways to enlarge the content of his play, to deepen its significance, and to reach out beyond a given pattern of character and event to a universe of thought and experience of which they are but a representative fragment. Certain of the means by which he does this we can in part discern, though our description of their working must necessarily be imperfect. The soliloquy (very differently used by most of his predecessors and contemporaries and by many of his successors down to the present day) allows him to let down a shaft of light into the hidden workings of the mind, to enable us to overhear its unspoken thought without in effect suspending the outward movement of the action or breaking the impression of the immediacy and reality of the dramatic world. The imagery in his dialogue, for which, again, the Elizabethan habit gave him precedent, allows him, without extending the body of the speech, to let those same words which convey to us our necessary knowledge of feeling, thought, or event convey simultaneously many other things which our subconscious minds apprehend even if our conscious thought does not, deepening and extending our perception, now of the mood of the play, now of the nature of a character, now of the significance of the action, now of the relation of the whole to that wider universe which surrounds it. The verbal music, all that we include in the effects of rhythm and pitch inherent in the words and disengaged from our language by Shakespeare's blank verse, have a similar function and work simultaneously with imagery to similar ends. He, moreover, can evoke, by rare and exquisite use of what may be called the overtones of speech and action,[8] something other than, yet simultaneous with, the words, images, and music which yet continue in their appointed functions. Each of these powers latent in the medium of dramatic dialogue was known to one or other of Shakespeare's contemporaries; Shakespeare alone uses them all, and, at the height of his power, simultaneously, and he alone to all the ends I have suggested. Of the great moderns, Ibsen is a master

---

[8] This use of what may be called the dramatic overtones, though it is as old as dramatic art itself, being akin on one side to irony and on another to the significant use of silence, is peculiarly skilful in some modern plays. The French Théâtre de Silence depends in part upon it for its effects; in Thornton Wilder's *Our Town* it is, if I am not mistaken, the principal vehicle of the theme.

of the first and of the last; of the soliloquy which reveals the hidden thought of his characters and of the art which evokes from speech the overtones that reveal something related to, yet other than, that speech. But imagery tends with him, as never with Shakespeare, to pass over into the less dramatic mode of symbol, and verbal music is limited (though never destroyed) by his later dedication to the prose medium.

It is perhaps at this point that we realize how often and how nearly we have approached to begging the question in saying: 'This writer (or his method) is more nearly dramatic than that.' Can we now attempt some such statement without falling into that fallacy? Can we say that if, from our chain of hypothesis and deduction, we can abstract for ourselves an idea of what constitutes the innately dramatic mind, the mind that finds its expression in a mode which is fully and strictly dramatic, then such and such dramatists approach most nearly to this ideal? I think we can.

Clearly enough it has been to Shakespeare that we have been so often tempted to point. Even in a brief and cursory survey of the obscure movements of the great genetic powers, we find, and I think we find justly, that Shakespeare, in the possession of the primal forces from which drama derives, is with the greatest. Yet already there, and still more when we pass to the differentiating characteristics of the art, he sometimes seemed to stand a little apart. We suspected, again somewhat in anticipation of the argument, that it is he alone who uses no modes but the dramatic; he alone who never steps out of his play to speak, disguised or undisguised, in his own person. Can we, with that in mind, point to any distinctive characteristic and say that this carries an artist to the heart of the dramatic experience and gives to his work full dramatic quality? Is there, in fact, in his approach to his material anything which sets apart the genuine dramatist, the man whose art is wholly dramatic from the first moment of its conception to the last detail of communication? Is there a faculty which makes possible for him a special mode of artistic experience,[9] and that mode the dramatic?

[9] I assume here the distinction between artistic and aesthetic experience drawn by Lascelles Abercrombie in *Towards a Theory of Art* (London, 1926), and now generally accepted, the artistic experience being that involved in the act of artistic creation.

If we look again at the distinction we drew between the dramatic and the other forms of great poetic art, we shall find at the same time both the explanation of our conviction that Shakespeare's art is the most consistently dramatic and the answer to this last question. The method of a given artist, while derived primarily from his instinctive choice of material, is immediately determined by his approach to it, and Shakespeare's method reveals the approach distinctive of the dramatic artist, a limitless sympathy with man acting and suffering. Because of this sympathy, the passion, thought, and poetic imagination which inspire all artists are, in the dramatist, determined towards the distinctive dramatic method, the direct revelation by those who themselves act and suffer. And when these primal forces of art are so determined they infuse the principle of life that transmutes convention and transcends limitation, preserving the art from sterility and renewing it phoenix-like from age to age.

When we apply our minds to the understanding of a character in a great play, attempting to enter into it with our imaginations as a great actor does in preparing to act it, what is it that we find? We find that the dramatist has so wholly imagined his character that what he has revealed within the framework of the play seems to be only a part of what he knows, just as what a man reveals of himself in any one series of his actions is but a part of what he is. We are accustomed to say that the dramatist has identified himself with Agamemnon, with Oedipus, with Agavé, with Macbeth, with Hjalmar Ekdal. We can, if we will, amuse ourselves by transporting the character to other periods of situations, back into childhood or away into some other series of events and actions, and this frivolity is not without its use if it teaches us something of the fullness of that original imagining. We find, by degrees, that we can do this most often with the characters of Shakespeare's plays, for it is his practice to give us hints, not so much of events as of formative influences in the lives of an Edmund, an Iago, a Hamlet, even of so early a figure as Richard III. And so, returning to our study of the actual content of the play before us, we may trace the processes of the mind, as the actor must and does, through scenes in which the continuum of speech is interrupted and find again that the

guidance given us is enough because Shakespeare's understanding of the mind was whole. We can, if we use our
imaginations faithfully in the interpretation of the clues that
are given us, follow the thought of Bolingbroke through the
scene before Flint Castle and the deposition scene, in both of
which, but for a brief speech or two, he is silent through long
periods; just so we may divine the links between the broken
phrases in Lady Macbeth's speech in the sleep-walking scene,
and relate each utterance to some moment in the foregoing
action, the memory of which now calls it forth. All this we
can do with the central figures in Shakespeare's plays as with
many other dramatists (for some who are not the greatest
treat in this way their central figures).

But can we now, disengaging Shakespeare's work again
from the matrix of great drama we have been studying,
discover anything more? What if the actor or the reader
change his part from Macbeth to Lady Macbeth, is not what
we have said still true? Obviously it is. Then is it true also of
Duncan, of Banquo, of Macduff—even of the unfortunate
Malcolm, encumbered as he is by the third scene of the fourth
act? We must, I think, agree that it is. And are there not two
murderers, men who appear but for a brief moment or two to
plan with Macbeth the assassination of Banquo? Are we not
given just enough indication of the world they live in to arrive
at a momentary understanding of the springs of their motives
and to remain convinced that though only a slender arc of
each personality enters the frame of the play, the circle is
complete beyond it, living full and whole in the poet's
imagination? And so we might pursue the investigation
through all the authentic plays of Shakespeare's maturity. In
all of them we find this imaginative sympathy, this identification
of the poet himself with every character in his drama.

But this is not the end. We said a moment ago that the
thought of Bolingbroke in certain scenes of *Richard II*[10] was
potentially revealed to us even in those passages where he is
silent and other men are speaking, and that we, while they
speak, can continue to identify ourselves with him. And we
can, if we wish, make each of these other men in turn the

[10] *Richard II*, ii, and iv. i.

centre of our attention and then, when they in their turn are silent, their thought will similarly be revealed to us while others speak. It is not a matter merely of Shakespeare's identifying himself with each in turn, with each man as he comes to life in speech, but with each man's momentarily hidden life for so long as he is within the framework of the play and, if necessary, beyond it. The self-identification with each and every character is not only whole but simultaneous. This, I submit, is the genuine dramatic mode of thought, the fundamental quality which reveals the innate dramatic genius, and it is this, I believe, which distinguishes the essentially dramatic from all other kinds of genius. How rare this is, a moment's reflection will assure us.

If this is true, then we have in Shakespeare not only a dramatist but *the* dramatist, the only one in the great company of dramatic poets who is wholly and continuously dramatic. The only one, that is to say, in whom there are to be found, in the highest degree and uncontaminated with other modes of thought, both the generic powers and differentiating qualities of dramatic genius, and a resultant art whose mode and whose methods are wholly dramatic.

The artistic experience of the essential dramatist thus differs from that of other artists at a point very near its roots, and the response of human beings of many races and of most recorded ages indicates the depth of the relation between common human experience and the best-loved of the arts. For the paradox inherent in the dramatist's attitude to man, his subject, is also the source of his power. In his vast, impersonal sympathy lies one solution of the problem so long familiar to mystics: 'Teach us to care and not to care.' And the dramatist having, like the great mystic, in some measure solved this problem, speaks as one having authority.

For the communication thus made is distinguished from that of the imperfectly dramatic by a factor whose significance it is almost impossible to over-estimate. 'This even-handed justice', this universal sympathy which has at once the balance of impersonal detachment and the radiance of affection, gives to the record made and to the reading of life implied a power of assurance beyond that of any utterance short of the affirmation of the mystic. Convinced at once of the depth and of the range of Shakespeare's experience through his imaginative understanding of the passions and thoughts of men, we are convinced no less of the truth of his perception through this single quality, the universal sympathy of the genuine dramatist. For it is this which, operating without bias, reveals in the mind of a man the shadow of the divine attribute of simultaneous immanence and transcendence. The confidence felt by generations of men of many races in the reading of life implicit in the total body of Shakespeare's plays depends in the last resort on the fact that not merely did he know what is in man, but that he knew it as a dramatist. 'If this is true', it was once said of a concerto of Bach, 'all is indeed well.' Because, in the man whose genius is wholly dramatic there is no prepossession, no prejudice, no theory, because no matter of common experience is left out of the account, his ultimate assumption, still implicit because still dramatic, will carry the same assurance as the revealed vision of the mystic, and will carry it in times and in the places the mystic does not touch. This is the supreme function of the dramatist. That Shakespeare has fulfilled that function beyond all others is only to say in another form that he, beyond all others, is wholly a dramatist.

# 2.   A PORTRAIT OF THE ARTIST AS PROTEUS

By Michel Grivelet

The idea of picturing Shakespeare as Proteus was conceived in circumstances which will not recommend it to most critics of our day. Chapter xv of *Biographia Literaria*, which deals, as the author's summary indicates, with 'the specific symptoms of poetic power elucidated in a critical analysis of Shakespeare's *Venus and Adonis* and *Lucrece*', concludes, somewhat unexpectedly, on a brilliant visionary parallel. Seeing the playwright seated 'on one of the two glory-smitten summits of the poetic imagination, with Milton as his compeer, not rival', Coleridge writes:

> while the former darts himself forth and passes into all the forms of human character and passion, the one Proteus of the fire and the flood; the other attracts all forms and things to himself, into the unity of his own ideal. All things and modes of action shape themselves anew in the being of Milton; while Shakespeare becomes all things, yet for ever remaining himself.[1]

The insistence on character is perhaps a little surprising in a critical analysis of two non-dramatic poems. But Coleridge, though he acknowledges no debt, seems to be here directly inspired by a predecessor. Some forty years before, in 1774, William Richardson, the author of *A Philosophical Analysis and Illustration of some of Shakespeare's Remarkable Characters*, had formulated the same idea in support of the view that human nature can nowhere be studied better than in Shakespeare. For the moralist, as the serious and reasonable student of humanity that he is, finds himself confronted with a dilemma: he cannot dispense with the living, intimate knowledge—of the passions especially—which actual experience provides; but, on the other hand, as Richardson puts it with some ingenuity:

---

[1] *Biographia Literaria*, ed. J. Shawcross (Oxford, 1958), ii. 20.

by what powerful spell can the abstracted philosopher whose passions are all subdued, whose heart never throbs with desire, prevail on the amorous affections to visit the ungenial clime of his breast, and submit their features to the rigour of his unrelenting scrutiny?[2]

It is therefore most fortunate that there should be a great dramatist thanks to whom, not only the amorous affections but also others that are less amiable, indeed all the affections of the human heart are, without improper risks, submitted to the analyst. For, Richardson declares:

the genius of Shakespeare is unlimited. Possessing extreme sensibility, and uncommonly susceptible, he is the Proteus of the drama, he changes himself into every character, and enters easily into every condition of human nature.[3]

The transcendental view of the poet which Coleridge and the other Romantics have done so much to establish was thus, at its birth, associated with and perhaps dependent upon what would now be mostly regarded as one of the worst superstitions of Shakespeare criticism: the vulgar error of taking characters in a play for real people, for 'fellow humans with ourselves', as Ellen Terry once said.

It will, I am afraid, seem very ungracious and very unwise of me to propose this pursuit of Proteus—the symbol in any case of elusiveness—in answer to the great honour of being invited by the British Academy to give the Shakespeare lecture for the present year. An honour which, to me, is all the more impressive as few of my countrymen have received it, and the last of them (nearly fifty years ago) was no other than Émile Legouis, one of the Founding Fathers of English studies in France.

Some secret compulsion—to use the language of psychoanalysis—must have forced upon me the choice of so ill-advised a subject. Yet I am persuaded at the same time that, if properly understood, the idea which it propounds is not inadequate, not irrelevant to the questions of our time. It is even one, I shall venture to say, that the poet himself invites us to consider.

[2] Edinburgh, 1774, p. 16.
[3] Op. cit., p. 40.

When Richardson, or Coleridge, or Hazlitt after them,[4] tell us that Shakespeare is another Proteus, they take it for granted that what they say is nothing if not flattering. But then they must be forgetting that the dramatist's one brief reference to the figure of classical mythology occurs, early in his career, as one more touch added to the self-portrait of a determined villain. Drawing up a list of all the deceitful mischief-makers he intends to emulate in order to 'get a crown', Richard, Duke of Gloucester, finally exclaims:

> I can add colours to the chameleon,
> Change shapes with Proteus for advantages,
> And set the murderous Machiavel to School.[5]

A notorious fraud, Proteus is not out of place in such detestable company. He is the worst of seducers. Such is at least the assumption which the author of *King Henry VI* seems to share with most of his contemporaries.

The probable source for this conception is Ovid's first book of *The Art of Love*, at the end of which the teacher of the art gives the following instructions to his pupil:

I was about to end but various are the hearts of women; use a thousand means to waylay as many hearts. The same earth bears not everything; this soil suits vines, that olives; in that, wheat thrives. Hearts have as many fashions as the world has shapes; the wise man will suit himself to countless fashions, and like Proteus, will now resolve himself into light waves, and now will be a lion, now a tree, now a shaggy boar.[6]

The most typically protean of the high deeds of Gloucester is, in *Richard III*, the wooing and winning of Anne—a victory achieved, as he comments exultantly, against God, her conscience, and her 'extremest hate', yet with no friends on his side but 'the plain devil and dissembling looks'. Richard proves in this more capable than many of his changeful kind. More capable, for instance, than the Proteus of Spenser, in

---

[4] 'On Genius and Common Sense', *The Complete Works*, ed. P. P. Howe (London 1930–4), viii. 42.
[5] *King Henry VI, Part 3*, III. ii. 191–3.
[6] Ovid, *The Art of Love and other poems*, translation by J. H. Mozley (The Loeb Classical Library, London, 1962).

Book III of *The Faerie Queene*, where this 'Shepheard of the seas of yore' rescues Faire Florimell from the clutches of the lustfull Fisherman only to assail her chastity with more cunning—but all in vain. More capable, too, than Volpone, the Magnifico of Venice, who boasts to Celia that, for her love, 'in varying figures' he would have contended 'with the Blue Proteus' and tries, though with no success, to tempt her to a riot of erotic encounters under an infinity of fabulous shapes.

We are invited, by John Manningham in his diary, to believe that at the time when they performed *Richard III*, Burbage in the main role, Shakespeare was not above cheating his fellow out of an amatory conquest he had made and jesting that it was only right for him since 'William the Conqueror was before Rich. the 3'.[7] But if it is hard for us to imagine that the shameless seducer is a type in which the young poet would have recognized himself, who can deny, on the other hand, that between the dramatist and his villainous hero there is a real sort of intimacy. 'Shakespeare himself', says a critic, 'was obviously fascinated by Richard.'[8] The relationship is one in which intense absorption goes along with hatred and fear. Richard is a prodigious player, an actor, and as such he owes a great deal to the author's inside knowledge of the profession. But, in return, what an image of his art is offered to the playwright in the dark detestable mirror of Richard's doings! It is, one feels, because the character is so different from his maker, and so like him, that for the first time with such strength the tension inherent in dramatic creation declares itself. The paradoxical gaiety which enlivens the otherwise cruel drama bears witness to an 'alacrity of spirit' which, as much as the protagonist's, is that of the poet. For he too, engaged within himself in the deep contest of love with 'extremest hate', enjoys the exhilaration of almost incredible success.

It is not therefore because Proteus had a bad name at the time that Shakespeare would have been prevented from any sympathy with him. However briefly the figure of old may

---

[7] E. K. Chambers, *William Shakespeare* (Oxford, 1930), ii. 212.

[8] Anne Righter, *Shakespeare and the Idea of the Play* (London, 1962), p. 98.

have passed across his mind when he thought of Richard, there was that in it which was apt to retain for him an enduring significance. The fact is, at any rate, that before long he had decided to have a Proteus of his own.

From *Richard III* to *The Two Gentlemen of Verona*: I am well aware of the anti-climax. The comedy is not a well-loved play. Judicious critics have mostly written about its failure. As for the gentlemen themselves, neither of them has been favourably received. A remarkable essay has recently recalled, in a spirit of understandable feminine compassion, that George Eliot was disgusted with a work in which two girls could be treated so shamefully by their lovers. For the author of this essay, inadequate representation in dramatic terms of the evils of inconstancy accounts for the lack of consistency which she finds in the comedy.[9]

It is not my intention to plead that the play is better than one usually admits, nor that Proteus, who has the main role, is an extremely interesting person. A considerable, and possibly harmful, element of derision has, I am persuaded, found its way into the composition. For it was partly written, I think, in a spirit of retaliation for the treatment inflicted upon *The Comedy of Errors* during the Gray's Inn festivities of Christmas 1594. And the ostentatious devotion rendered to the Goddess of Amity together with the masque of 'Proteus and the Adamantine Rock', as they are complacently reported in the text of *Gesta Grayorum*, may well have inspired the main theme and the main character of the play.[10] The smugness of the gentlemen of Verona glances at the conceit of the little gentlemen of Gray's Inn.

But this is precisely where we perceive the subtle involvement of Shakespeare with his character. There is of course less that is repulsive for him in vain overweening youth than in ruthless tyranny. But with what Hamlet will call 'the proud man's contumely . . . and the spurns / That patient merit of th' unworthy takes' he is bound perhaps to be more immediately concerned. And the antagonism thus exper-

---

[9] Inga-Stina Ewbank, ' "Were man but constant, he were perfect": Constancy and Consistency in *The Two Gentlemen of Verona*', *Shakespearian Comedy* (Stratford-upon-Avon Studies, 14, London, 1922), pp 31–57.

[10] *Gesta Grayorum 1688* (Malone Society Reprints, Oxford 1915).

ienced provides another if not better occasion for dramatic consciousness to invest itself in a creature of fiction.

For this Proteus deserves his name not only because he changes from Julia to Silvia, and from friendship to treachery, but also because, in the eagerness of his wayward desire, he stages a full show of deceptive shapes. Richard is above all a consummate actor, occasionally willing to play his part in a scenario of devotion devised by Buckingham to fool the Mayor and Aldermen, but he relies mostly on his own histrionic powers. Proteus works out a mystification in which Valentine and Thurio and the Duke, as well as himself, are each assigned a role. As he says, once he has launched the action:

> Love, lend me wings to make my purpose swift
> As thou hast lent me wit to plot this drift,[11]

and the name which Thurio gives him later, 'sweet Proteus, my direction-giver', might suggest that we have indeed to do with the performance of a play.

Young Proteus as a man of the theatre, the fleeting vision is one in which Shakespeare was no doubt amused to see a reflection of himself. Amused, and, at the same time, rather serious about it. For the chameleon lover, changing and irresponsible as he may seem, is conscientious and even thoughtful. The importance of being constant is a major preoccupation with him. He swears his 'true constancy' to Julia before leaving her. If he uses treachery to Valentine, it is, as he says, to 'prove constant to myself'. And it is left to him in the end to draw the penitent conclusion:

> O heaven, were man
> But constant, he were perfect.

Even true love is resented by him at first as a regrettable alteration:

> Thou, Julia, thou hast metamorphos'd me;
> Made me neglect my studies, lose my time,
> War with good counsel, set the world at nought;
> Made wit with musing weak, heart sick with thought.[12]

---

[11] *The Two Gentlemen of Verona*, II. vi. 42–3.
[12] *The Two Gentlemen of Verona*, II. ii. 8; II. vi. 31; V. iv. 109–10; I. i. 66–9.

So he says in the first of his five monologues. And the very number of these is in itself a remarkable indication. Of all the early characters of the dramatist he is the most addicted to soliloquizing. This is admittedly not enough to make a Hamlet of him, but that the point of view and style of introspection should have been used so freely for the first time, and as it were initiated under the auspices of Proteus, this, I believe, is well worth our attention.

*The Two Gentlemen of Verona* inaugurates another feature of Shakespeare's dramatic writing which must also be considered here. Julia is the first of the girls of disguise to succeed in getting her man, a theme so dear to the author that henceforth there will be few of his comedies without at least some trace of it. Portia, Rosalind, and Viola come to mind. But even the Mariana of *Measure for Measure* and Helena, in *All's Well*, offer a variation in the more daring subterfuge of the bed-trick.

In most of these cases we are clearly dealing with a further reflection upon the idea of play-acting. Julia, for instance, does not only from the start prove highly skilled in the arts of maiden coquetry, but later in the play, disguised as Sebastian, she boasts to Silvia of successes won in 'the woman's part' in the Pentecost 'pageants of delight'. Imagination mixes here in a perplexing manner with reality, since it is a pseudo-Sebastian who claims that 'trimm'd in Madam Julia's gown', he 'made her weep agood'. For, says he (or she):

> I did play a lamentable part.
> Madam, 'twas Ariadne, passioning
> For Theseus' perjury, and unjust flight.[13]

The real Julia, however, will not know the fate of Ariadne. It is not for her to be mourned as the forlorn heroine is mourned, in Racine, by a compassionate sister:

> Ariane, ma Sœur! De quel amour blessée,
> Vous mourûtes aux bords où vous fûtes laissée![14]

No, Julia will see to it that Proteus does not finally escape her. We are told, in an article on 'Proteus in Spenser and

---

[13] Ibid. IV. iv. 156–66.
[14] *Phèdre*, I. iii. 253–4.

Shakespeare: the Lover's Identity', by William O. Scott, that 'the redeeming heroine who brings her man to a true concept of himself' is a significant part of 'the serious subject of *The Two Gentlemen of Verona* implied in the myth of Proteus'[15] —an assertion with which I am quite ready to find myself in agreement. But in that case it is hardly possible to avoid the conclusion that Shakespeare had a better knowledge of the mythical story than I have assumed so far. He must have been acquainted, even if indirectly, with more primary sources than the derivative accounts or allusions which are to be found here and there in Ovid, and perhaps Pliny. With the episode of the bees of Aristaeus in Virgil's *Georgics*, Book iv, he was no doubt familiar. And although the extent and nature of his acquaintance with Homer remains problematical, there is, I believe, good reason to accept the claim that he was not ignorant of *The Odyssey*.[16]

He would then, in the story which extends over more than two hundred lines of the poem, have learnt how Menelaus, held back by a dead calm on the shore of the Egyptian isle of Pharos, was pitied by Eidothea, daughter of mighty Proteus, the Old Man of the Sea; how she told him that the immortal seer, her father, 'who knows the depth of every sea and is the servant of Poseidon', would, though reluctantly, let him know the means of pursuing his journey; how she instructed Menelaus to lay in wait for the Old Man, as he came, according to his custom, to rest at noonday among his herd of seals; how she warned the Greek hero that Proteus would strive and struggle to escape, 'assuming all manner of shapes of all things that move upon the earth, and of water, and of wondrous blazing fire'; how she encouraged him nevertheless to hold on and said: 'only when he speaks at last and asks you questions in his natural shape, just as he was when you saw him lie down to rest, then stay thy might, and set the old man free, and ask him who of the gods is wroth with thee'. Shakespeare would have learnt further how Menelaus with three of his comrades were provided each with a skin of seal newly flayed to conceal themselves, together with some

---

[15] *Shakespeare Studies*, i (1965), 283–93.

[16] J. W. Velz, *Shakespeare and the Classical Tradition* (Minneapolis, 1968).

ambrosia of sweet fragrance against the deadly stench of the beasts; how, when the time came, they leapt upon the old man and flung their arms round his back; how he, undaunted, used his wizard arts, turning into a bearded lion, and then into a serpent, and a leopard, and a huge boar, and then into flowing water, and into a tree, high and leafy; how, for all his wiles they held on unflinchingly with steadfast heart, until, tiring of his magic, he at last offered to speak.[17]

If such is the original of Proteus, what irony there is in the name given to the pretty gentleman of Verona! How frivolous the vain youth in comparison with the athletic keeper of Poseidon's herd of seals—though like him changeful and, in the end, caught! But the dubious hero of this early comedy is only a beginning. Under different names, he will reappear and grow into something more impressive. He will be seen again, for instance, in the obstinate Duke of Illyria whose devotion to the countess Olivia is but fancy—fancy 'so full of shapes . . . / That it alone is high fantastical'. Such a man, according to Feste, ought to have a 'doublet of changeable taffeta' for his mind 'is a very opal'. He should be 'put to sea', the sea from which Viola has seemed to emerge miraculously. Even though he is to be tamed in the end by the lamb he had threatened to kill in his rage, there is in this Orsino a suggestion of savagery. Moreover the time comes when Shakespeare will devise his truly fierce and dangerous men of passion and with them he will go on pursuing his protean image among bewildering shapes of illusion.

But it is essential that this image should be seen for what it is: a myth of change confronted with the claims of identity and truth. And here we must pause to observe that, as such, it does not countenance the interpretation which the Romantics have put upon it.

The Romantics have used Proteus as a symbol of activity not only blameless but also wonderfully facile. 'He enters *easily* into every condition of human nature,' says William Richardson. Coleridge speaks of a poet who '*darts himself*

---

[17] Homer, *The Odyssey*, Bk IV, translation by A. T. Murry (The Loeb Classical Library, London, 1953).

*forth* and passes into all forms of human character and passion' and he adds in the most off-hand manner, as if the thing was simply too obvious: 'Shakespeare becomes all things yet for ever remaining himself.' This is, however, too quickly said to be convincing. The fact is that to conceive protean change as smooth and careless cannot but lead to the easy assumption of a personal identity invariably preserved among infinite variations, and ultimately to the denial of this identity. Before long the fiction of the 'chameleon' artist, traditionally associated with that of Proteus but more appropriate to the idea of instinctive effortless transformation, will serve to express a longing for the impersonal. And behind it all what is at work is the deep romantic desire to be relieved from the anguish of individual existence. A case in point is that of John Keats when he writes:

As to the poetical character itself . . . it is not itself—it has no self—it is everything and nothing.—It has no character—it enjoys light and shade; it lives in gusto, be it foul or fair, high or low, rich or poor, mean or elevated.—It has as much delight in conceiving an Iago as an Imogen. What shocks the virtuous Philosopher, delights the camelion Poet.[18]

This is no doubt admirable, and true—to a certain extent. It nevertheless remains that Keats voices here aspirations of his own, aspirations moreover that lyrical poetry cannot so ideally fulfil. For, if, listening to the nightingale, the poet almost forgets 'the weariness, the fever and the fret' of this everyday world, the moment comes for him to return from elusive ecstasy to his 'sole self', and to confess that 'the fancy cannot cheat so well / As she is famed to do, deceiving elf . . . ' Whereas this can be claimed for dramatic poetry that, as an experience which is impartially and entirely distributed among several roles, it leaves nothing to the self. As Stephen Dedalus explains when he argues that the dramatic form is, higher than the lyrical and the epical, the supreme form of art:

The dramatic form is reached when the vitality which has flowed and eddied round each person fills every person with such vital force that he or she assumes a proper and intangible esthetic life.

---

[18] *The Letters*, ed. H. E. Rollins (Cambridge, Mass., 1955), i. 387.

The personality of the artist, at first a cry or a cadence or a mood and then a fluid and lambent narrative, finally refines itself out of existence, impersonalizes itself, so to speak. The esthetic image in the dramatic form is life purified in and reprojected from the human imagination. The mystery of esthetic like that of material creation is accomplished. The artist, like the God of the creation, remains within or behind or beyond or above his handiwork, invisible, refined out of existence, indifferent, paring his fingernails.[19]

The irony of literary history is that Shakespeare, who had claimed no such apotheosis for himself, was nevertheless regarded by non-dramatic writers as the living proof that the dream is desirable and true, that it is possible through the ever renewed metamorphosis of art to be redeemed from the burden of ordinary humanity and to reach in indifference the supreme achievement and the supreme reward of a poet.

The consequences of the paradox are still with us. In the description of the dramatic artist by James Joyce, we have, I think, a still valid indication of the kind of fame which Shakespeare enjoys among our contemporaries. He had once been granted a godlike power but he is now a dispossessed god who must remain for ever absent from the world he has created. His plays are a universe which it is perfectly safe for us to go on exploring provided we do not forget that his own relation to it has ceased to be relevant. It is by no means uncharacteristic nowadays to read what Northrop Frye, for instance, writes in his book, *A Natural Perspective*:

Shakespeare seems to have had less of an ego center than any major poet of our culture, and is consequently the most decent of writers. It is an offense against his privacy much deeper than any digging up of his bones to reduce him from a poet writing plays to an ego with something to 'say'.[20]

Neither shall we be surprised to be told, as we are in the same book, that 'Shakespeare had no opinions, no values, no philosophy, nor principles of anything except dramatic structure.'[21] We may note that this is entirely in keeping with

[19] James Joyce, *A portrait of the artist as a Young Man*, ed. C. G. Anderson (New York, 1974), p. 215.
[20] *A Natural Perspective* (New York, 1965), p. 43.
[21] Ibid., p. 39.

the common attitude of our times towards what we call—significantly—works of art. André Malraux makes the remark that statues of saints, which were originally meant for worship, are now valued as sculpture, sacred only to the mystery of aesthetics. He sees in this the mark of a civilization which, seeking in art a substitute for religion, proves incapable either of welcoming or of rejecting the unknowable.[22]

To adapt the idea to our subject, I would say that exclusive concern for artistry and especially for dramatic structure in Shakespeare shows our growing incapacity either to welcome or to reject the meaning he ought to have for us. For it must be admitted that we are increasingly critical of the attempts which have been made to recognize the voice of the dramatist and to record what it is supposed to tell us. Of course, we would no longer make the mistake of believing that memorable sayings in his plays must be considered his own simply because they are memorable. We would not therefore maintain, as some have done, that Shakespeare's own philosophy consists in saying that life:

> is a tale
> Told by an idiot, full of sound and fury,
> Signifying nothing.[23]

Nor would we, in smaller matters, ascribe to him the persuasion that:

> Small have continual plodders ever won
> Save base authority from others' books[24]

or that:

> The chariest maid is prodigal enough
> If she unmask her beauty to the moon[25]

an opinion in which he would distinctly *not* be our contemporary.

No one will deny that we are now in a much better position than, say, fifty years ago, to understand what were the mental habits of the Elizabethans, their beliefs, their world-picture.

[22] André Malraux, *La Tête d'Obsidienne* (Paris, 1974), p. 237.
[23] *Macbeth*, v. v. 26–8.
[24] *Love's Labour's Lost*, I. i. 86–7.
[25] *Hamlet*, I. iii. 36–7.

Background studies of great value have made it possible for us to approach the art and literature of the period with a far more appropriate knowledge of their basic assumptions. So that, being acquainted with the views commonly shared by the people of his time, it does not seem unreasonable to claim that we have an idea of what Shakespeare might have thought. But even then there is room for doubt and controversy. To maintain, as it is tempting to do on the evidence of many eloquent passages in the plays, that he was an exponent of sound Tudor doctrine, a strong supporter of hierarchy, order, and degree, is at least a simplification. It is also a simplification to say that he was the spokesman of the rising bourgeoisie and of its class-conscious anti-feudal spirit. For not only had the Renaissance its own inner conflicts, so that in any case it would be rash to conclude that authoritative doctrine necessarily represents the personal conviction of any man, but moreover it was then as always the proper business of drama to explore and stage such perplexing contradictions. Ulysses is a most suspicious spokesman. Admirable as his speech in *Troilus and Cressida* may be, it must for us remain ambiguous.

But to disown any interest in Shakespeare's values or opinions and to profess exclusive care for dramatic structure does not really make things easier. Aesthetic pleasure cannot be enjoyed without a sense of meaning. As a matter of fact the fashionable attitude which consists in regarding a play as an artefact, an object to be treated objectively, leads to criticism that is increasingly more, not less, dogmatic. We are invited to approach the poem as something that can be thoroughly analysed, weighed, measured, computerized, envisaged as a system of lexical data, stylistic devices, image clusters, patterns, and themes, reiteration in general, especially if it tends to be obsessive. It would be nonsense to say that such methods are of no use. But they encourage the dangerous confidence that the overall indisputable meaning of the work can be rationally determined. As if its life and soul could be seized and fixed for ever.

'Shakespeare criticism is in trouble.' With these alarming words, Professor Norman Rabkin begins a paper presented in 1971 at the World Shakespeare Congress in Vancouver. His point is that 'the better our criticism becomes, and the more sharply it is focussed on explaining what plays are about, the farther it gets from the actuality of our experience in responding to them'. For, in his view, 'we have been betrayed by a bias toward what can be set out in rational argument'. *The Merchant of Venice*, which he chooses as an example, serves him to show that, while 'in recent years many of the critics have reached a consensus' which integrates 'the techniques developed in the last half-century for literary study', yet each of them is aware in his own way of an uneasy tension between the explanation and his actual experience of the play. Shylock remains particularly intractable. His large place in our consciousness fails to fit even the most subtle schematization. Professor Rabkin therefore concludes that 'we need to embark on a large-scale reconsideration of the phenomena that our technology has enabled us to explore, to consider the play as a dynamic interaction between artist and audience, to learn to talk about the process of our involvement rather than our considered view after the aesthetic event'.[26]

I could not agree more than I do with this idea of a 'dynamic interaction between artist and audience'. Only I would prefer to call it 'fighting with Proteus', for this brings me back to what the classical allegory truly means.

In the wealth of symbols which the story in Book IV of *The Odyssey* contains, it is hardly possible to ignore that of the furious fight on the sea-shore. A little imagination helps us to picture the mad wrestling, in splashing water, among the sleek nimble crowd of seals. And if Shakespeare is to be thought of as another Proteus, wrestle we must, in the like manner, with this Old Man of the Sea. No less than Menelaus, we are required to stay undaunted by changing shapes, either threatening or seductive, and to hold on unflinchingly, until at last the elusive being is seen and heard, speaking 'in his natural shape'.

The significance which I read in this is that, far from

[26] 'Meaning and Shakespeare', *Shakespeare 1971*, Proceedings of the World Shakespeare Congress, Vancouver, August 1971, eds. Clifford Leech and J. M. Margeson (Toronto, 1972), 89–106.

inviting unconcern for the person of the author, the protean image enjoins us on the contrary to do our utmost to know him. And the only way to do so is to struggle with the many changing illusions that both conceal and reveal him. Among them none are more misleading and none more instructive than the dramatic roles which he takes on under our eyes. This is why it is a good thing to be reminded—as we have been, with great authority—that the characters in his plays are not people. But on the other hand they cannot be reduced to mere elements of structure in a poem. Even Lady Macbeth (however problematic the number of her children) must have the kind of reality which Flaubert asserts in his own case when he says: 'Madame Bovary, c'est moi.' Professor L. C. Knights seems to admit as much when, returning to the question of character he sees Shakespeare 'as much more immediately engaged in the action he puts before us' and says, quoting T. S. Eliot, that the plays, which dramatize 'an action or struggle for harmony in the soul of the poet' are 'united by one significant, consistent, and developing personality'.[27] To seek acquaintance with this personality is therefore not only legitimate but necessary. It is not so much, of course, a matter of knowing the man who was Shakespeare in his day, though this cannot be irrelevant, as of searching for him in his work.

Such was in fact the purpose of a book published exactly one hundred years ago and by no means unworthy of a special tribute on its hundredth anniversary, Edward Dowden's *Shakespeare: A Critical Study of his Mind and Art*. As Dowden declares in his introduction, 'To come into close and living relation with the individuality of a poet must be the chief end of our study.' To this I would readily subscribe. And if the book, highly praised and widely influential at first, has been since severely criticized, if indeed it is largely obsolete, it is because an attempt of this kind must of necessity be constantly renewed to take into account what changing outlooks and the progress of scholarship bring to it in the course of time.

It is also because the aim is difficult to achieve, the undertaking as paradoxical as the idea of the 'natural shape' of

---

[27] *Further Explorations* (London, 1965), p. 192.

Proteus. Being so full of shapes, so changing, how can he be said to have a nature? There is only one answer to this and it lies in the true sense of our human condition. Proteus can be used as an allegory of Shakespeare because he is more fundamentally an allegory of the dignity of man. In his famous 'oration' on the subject, that great though much maligned Renaissance thinker, Pico della Mirandola, makes God speak to Adam in the following terms:

The nature of all other beings is limited and constrained within the bounds of laws prescribed by Us. Thou, constrained by no limits, in accordance with thine own free will, in whose hands We have placed thee, shalt ordain for thyself the limits of thy nature . . . We have made thee neither of heaven nor of earth, neither mortal nor immortal, so that with freedom of choice and with honor, as though the maker and molder of thyself, thou mayest fashion thyself in whatever shape thou shalt prefer.

Giovanni Pico explains further that:

On man when he came into life the Father conferred the seeds of all kinds and the germs of every way of life. Whatever seeds each man cultivates will grow to maturity and bear in him their own fruit. If they be vegetative, he will be like a plant. If sensitive, he will become brutish. If rational, he will grow into a heavenly being . . .

And thus the description of man's extraordinary privilege goes on until it is concluded with the fervent words:

Who would not admire this our chameleon? or who could more greatly admire aught else whatever? It is man who Asclepius of Athens, arguing from his mutability of character and from his self-transforming nature, on just grounds says was symbolized by Proteus in the mysteries.[28]

This no doubt is an audacious view. In a time which has some reason to fear the extremes to which mankind may be finally tempted to go in the assertion of its power over the universe and over itself, we are, as no one before, in a position to see what great risks are involved in this gift of freedom. The nature of man consists in being so free that he can deny his own nature, and there are those among us today who

[28] Translated by E. L. Forbes in *The Renaissance Philosophy of Man*, eds. E. Cassirer, P. O. Kristeller, and J. H. Randall Jr. (Chicago, 1948).

think that—after 'god'—'man' is a word which has lost its meaning. But however great the risks this freedom involves, they must be faced. And I would venture to suggest that, in the same way, the artistry of Shakespeare takes its bewildering power from being rooted in a fearless humanity.

He was, says Ben Jonson, who could claim to have loved and honoured the man, 'of an open and free nature'.[29] To my mind, this is no less true of his genius than of his person. Moralizing tendencies inspired most people in his time with a distrust of change. This is fairly clear in the case of Ben Jonson himself who cannot show enough contempt for whatever seems to flow with the flux of things. Nano, Androgyno, the monsters in *Volpone* are embodiments of the most hateful idea of metempsychosis. His own Proteus, the Magnifico of Venice, changes only for the worse. He debases himself to the indignity of animal life, and, becoming the beast he is fabled to be, finally endures 'the mortifying of a fox'.

But Shakespeare, though not unaware of the dangers of bestial degradation, is more capable of smiling upon the vagaries of man, less prepared to be systematically censorious of them. True, his young gentleman of Verona is not seen without the stigma of his own debasement. At first a courtly lover, an admirer of Orpheus who could tame tigers and 'huge leviathans', he nearly ends as a 'ruffian', a brute beast ready to rape the unyielding Silvia. Animal imagery runs significantly throughout the play, as Harold Brooks observes, in an essay pleasantly concluded on a comparison of Proteus with Crab. A real cur in his lack of feeling, treacherous to Valentine and Julia, unfit for Silvia whom he persecutes with most objectionable attentions, Proteus in his dissipation is perhaps not unfairly portrayed as a young dog.[30] Similarly Orsino can be stupid and dangerous as a bear, within the limits of comic ferociousness which his name suggests. Obviously Shakespeare finds more cause for amusement than for alarm in the wild propensities of his early protean characters.

---

[29] *Timber: or Discoveries*, eds. C. H. Herford, Percy and Evelyn Simpson (Oxford, 1947), iii. 283–4.

[30] H. F. Brooks, 'Two Clowns in a Comedy (to say nothing of the Dog): Speed, Launce (and Crab) in "The Two Gentlemen of Verona" ', *Essays and Studies* (1963), 91–100.

It is, however, the same open-minded generosity which makes it inevitable for him to face the trial of the great tragedies, and to face it, as he does, with merciless daring. The 'struggle in the soul of the poet' which those plays dramatize is so fierce that we may doubt whether it can result in harmony. His tragic figures are such strange shapes of almost inhuman terror and pity that, in them, he seems to test and challenge himself beyond all possible recovery. No easy answer is yielded to the question which Shakespeare asks himself in his great plays. Can it be that the question at last dissolves itself and that Coleridge's 'one Proteus of the fire and the flood' chooses in the end to be released with his own Ariel into the air? How admirably, at any rate, does the genius of the poet in his last works incline towards the fluidity of those elements? It is as if what Blake calls 'the human form divine' was losing its urgency for him. As, for instance, when Antony, yearning for death, muses on the undoing of his visible shape and says:

> Sometime we see a cloud that's dragonish,
> A vapour sometime, like a bear, or lion,
> A tower'd citadel, a pendent rock,
> A forked mountain, or blue promontory
> With trees upon't that nod unto the world,
> And mock our eyes with air . . .

And, a moment later:

> That which is now a horse, even with a thought
> The rack dislimns, and makes it indistinct
> As water is in water.[31]

In the romances, the beauty of metamorphosis is more than a theme; it is a mood, a manner of feeling and, we may say, of espousing the world. But as the poet—coming to terms with things continually moving and flowing into one another— seems to indulge in the freedom of change, one may well wonder whether he has finally lost or found himself.

It is not, however, and this will be my conclusion, for any man to decide of this, unless he takes up the challenge that is

---

[31] *Antony and Cleopatra*, IV. xiv. 2–11.

thrown to him in the poet's work. And he will not take it up without some truly personal motive for doing so. Returning for the last time to the story in *The Odyssey*, we note that it is told in Lacedaemon, by the king, to young Telemachus, who has come to ask about his father. That Ulysses lives is one of the things that king Menelaus has learnt of the servant of Poseidon after his mad struggle with him. It was urgent for Telemachus to know, just as it was urgent for Menelaus to be given the means of pursuing his own voyage. A need for vital knowledge is thus doubly stressed in Homer's narrative as leading to the revelation of Proteus. Neither his bewildering variety nor the secrets he can be hoped to let out are accessible to the indifferent, or the idle, or even those who are but moderately concerned. In the same way, I suggest that if Shakespeare has a message, it is only for those who are moved to ask for it by some strong personal reason, those who, in their way, are pilgrims and in quest of truth.[32] I believe that poetry, and indeed all great art, is an oracle. But it speaks only to those whom the enigmatic does not discourage, prepared as they are to strive for its meaning. They must be ready for a confrontation which Edward Dowden did not hesitate to compare with Jacob's fight in the dark against the mysterious man at Peniel. It means wrestling with the adversary until daybreak, when this strange man or angel, though still unwilling to tell his secret, gives a blessing in which he is nevertheless revealed. Shakespeare, as a poet, did not write for professors or any of those who are concerned with him professionally. The best of his strength is hardly for the lecture-room. But nor is it even to be found in the theatre, unless a truly personal response can be found there.

What then, it will be asked, is the use of Shakespearian scholars? What is the business of Shakespearian criticism? It

---

[32] On truth and Proteus, see Milton: 'For who knows not that Truth is strong next to the Almighty; she needs no policies, nor stratagems, nor licensings to make her victorious, those are the shifts and defences that error uses against her power: give her but room, & do not bind her when she sleeps, for then she speaks not true, as the old *Proteus* did, who spake oracles only when he was caught and bound, but then rather she turns herself into all shapes, except her own, and perhaps tunes her voice according to the time, as *Micaiah* did before *Ahab*, untill she be adjur'd into her own likeness. Yet it is not impossible that she may have more shapes than one.' *Areopagitica*, in *Complete Prose Works*, ii (New Haven, 1959), pp. 562–3.

serves—I would say—the same purpose as the fair goddess Eidothea, the daughter of the Old Man of the Sea. She instructs those who deserve to know. She tells them about her father, says what is to be expected of him, explains how they must proceed with him. She provides them with the necessary equipment, warns them against the risks they run, and lets them shift for themselves. And we, 'abstracted' academics, who are but her journeymen, the only thing we can do is to help her in her task by contributing something to the indication she gives; we can, by throwing some light on this or that detail, by adding a touch here or there, perform our part of the needful work, of the work that is always in progress and always incomplete, always necessary and, in itself, never sufficient: the portrait of the artist as Proteus.

# 3. SHAKESPEARE'S PRIMITIVE ART

## By M. C. Bradbrook

Spectacle is that part of tragedy which has least connection with the Art of Poetry, as Aristotle believed: but, when the text of plays—even of Shakespeare's plays—provides only raw material for John Barton and other theatre directors, it might be thought 'So much the worse for poetry.'

Today Bali rather than Athens supplies dramatic models, and the cult of primitive theatre is so strong, that it may have been suspected I come to praise Shakespeare as a barbaric contemporary, after the fashion of Jan Kott—to enrol him in the Theatre of Cruelty. On the contrary, taking a conventionally historic view, I shall try to recover traces of the archaic spectacular tradition from which Shakespeare first started and to which, in the richly transmuted form of his final plays, he returned. I hope to identify the scenic proverb, the elements of that unspoken language which derives from the primal stage arts of gesture, costume, grouping, pantomime; to reveal the influence of those inexplicable dumb shows, which, although he rejected them, Shakespeare never forgot.

In doing this, it may be possible to uncover also something of his creative process. As his poetic imagination subdued itself to what it worked in, the visual and scenic basis of his art became absorbed into his poetry. An actor before he was playwright, Shakespeare carried always with him the memories of his repertory. It has been convincingly shown by Dr Edward Armstrong that Shakespeare's memories, as they sank below the level of consciousness, formed themselves into 'image clusters' or associative groups. Image clusters would have had visual and scenic counterparts, but since 'memory is an *imaginative* reconstruction',[1] what Shakespeare recalled from the stage, more especially when it need not have been

---

[1] E. A. Armstrong, *Shakespeare's Imagination*, 2nd Edition (Lincoln, Nebr., 1963), p. 122, quoting Sir Frederick Bartlett.

conscious recall, was converted by that act 'into something rich and strange'.

I would begin by distinguishing two traditions of spectacle in his inheritance, which might be termed the high road and the low road to drama proper. There are the lofty Icons or tableaux of coronation, triumph, great marriages or funerals; and, at the other extreme, tumblers and jesters, comic quick-change artists, such as the poor tatterdemalion dwarf that William Dunbar introduced running through his parts at the Market Cross of Edinburgh (in *The Manere of Crying of Ane Playe*). Both extremes met in the ring of Burbage's Theatre, London's 'game place' or 'playing place'; but Marlowe and Shakespeare began by taking the high road and rejecting 'such conceits as clownage keeps in pay'. Marlowe's lofty first creation, Tamburlaine, is descended from the King of the Moors, who rode in many civic processions, followed by his train, and gorgeously attired in red satin and silver paper; the spectacle is transmuted into heroic poetry,[2] by which it has been preserved for posterity. The originals are long forgotten.

Marlowe's doctrine of power and glory was very largely a doctrine of sovereignty and he made use of another image by which it was forcibly brought home to the simple. Every parish church in the land contained a copy of Foxe's *Book of Martyrs* and the edition of 1580 has for frontispiece a crowned king mounting to his throne by trampling on a prostrate foe, whose triple crown is falling from him. The king is Henry VIII. The footstool is the Pope. Tamburlaine trampling on Bajazet repeats the image.

For many people the royal image assuaged a deep privation they felt in the loss of those older images that had been familiar for so long, whose simple wonder-working mechanisms the Reformers had triumphantly torn out. Opponents of the stage were apt to charge the common players with what seems to us the very incongruous sin of Idolatry, because they perceived a line of descent from the older Icons to the new. One such sour cleric, writing in 1587 *A Mirror of Monsters*,[3]

---

[2] See J. P. Brockbank, *Dr Faustus* (London, 1962), pp. 23–4. The following paragraphs develop from Chapter III of my book *English Dramatic Form* (London, 1965).

[3] William Rankins, *A Mirrour of Monsters* (1587), sigs. C1–C2. The image of Cupid

describes a marriage procession of Pride, Lord of the Theatre, and Lechery, Lady of Worldlings, which passed through the streets to the Chapel of Adultery at Hollow-well (that is, Burbage's Theatre in Holywell Street in the old grounds of a Benedictine nunnery). It was presided over by a magic winged image of a Holy Child, made of alabaster and painted in lifelike colours. The Child Cupid carried emblems of torch and dart, and could nod the head in a magic fashion, which excited wonder as he was set up in a niche in the Parlour of Payne, where the North Wind assisted the miracle. The cleric adds to this infernal revelry a troop of monsters sent from Satan.

A grand wedding tableau also concludes *Tamburlaine*, Part I, where the royal virgin Zenocrate is crowned by a trinity of kings. This, though doubtless without overt intent, recalls the sacred Icon of a humbler Virgin crowned by a loftier Trinity; and the depth of conflict resolved in this play is suggested by its unconscious combination of Catholic and Reformed Iconography.

In Marlovian style, Shakespeare develops *Titus Adronicus* as a series of tableaux. The well-known contemporary illustration of the opening scene, by Henry Peacham, shows the Blackamoor flourishing a drawn sword over Tamora's doomed sons. In spite of the fact that he is himself a captive at this point, I think Aaron might have momentarily assumed the pose of a black-visaged headsman, to produce a tableau that must have been common enough in martyrology. The Magician, the King, the Blackamoor, the Weeping Queen, had long been familiar, so that imaginative roles of Shakespeare and of Marlowe are but half-emerged from a penumbra which surrounds and enlarges them beyond the dimensions of individual parts, to the sacred and archaic originals from which they derive.

The most powerful Icon of *Titus Andronicus* is the silent figure of Lavinia mutilated. The first of her family to meet her unconsciously evokes the image of the green and the withered tree, one commonly used in festive procession to symbolize a

---

and the presence of Venus seem to point to the infernal Venus of Robert Wilson's play, *The Cobbler's Prophecy*, and her adultery with 'Contempt', which is celebrated by a masque of animal forms led by Folly.

flourishing and fading commonwealth; when she is next
compared with a conduit running red wine, the shock of the
conflicting festive image inflates the horror. She becomes
herself, in metamorphosis, a stony silent image of violence
and outrage:

> What stern ungentle hands
> Hath lopped and hewed and made thy body bare
> Of her two branches—those sweet ornaments
> Whose circling shadows kings have sought to sleep in? . . .
> Alas, a crimson river of warm blood,
> Like to a bubbling fountain stirr'd with wind,
> Doth rise and fall between thy rosed lips . . .
> And notwithstanding all this loss of blood,
> As from a conduit with three issuing spouts,
> Yet do thy cheeks look red as Titan's face,
> Blushing to be encounter'd with a cloud.

(II. iv. 16–32)

The heraldic conventions of its images and the extreme
violence of its plot[4] make *Titus Andronicus* unique among
Shakespeare's works. In his English histories, I would like to
think that he borrowed a tableau from that Coventry play
given by the townsmen before Queen Elizabeth at Kenilworth
in July 1575, when Shakespeare, a boy of eleven, was living
not far away. An old Hocktide contest between men and
women had become associated with the memory of a battle
between English and Danes, in which, after initial victories,
the Danes were led captive by English women; this was
combined with a drill display by the town's muster men. The
image of this play may have been revived in *King Henry VI*
when Joan la Pucelle or Margaret of Anjou triumphed over
English warriors; but since 'remembering is an imaginative
reconstruction', the image has been reversed, and the foreign
women triumph over Englishmen.

Londoners would not have recognized this image, since
they did not know the original, but by the time he wrote the
second part of *King Henry IV*, Shakespeare felt sufficiently a
Londoner to mock their local show. The London archery

---

[4] See Eugene Waith, 'The Metamorphosis of Violence in *Titus Andronicus*',
*Shakespeare Survey*, x. (1957), 39–49.

band was led by a small group of the élite known as Prince
Arthur's Knights, who marched annually in procession, each
with his name from Arthurian story, and bearing his arms
emblazoned. Justice Shallow, in recalling the exploits of his
youth, claims to have played the part of the jester, Dagonet;
but his memory prompts him rather to enact another part,
that of a craftsmaster whom he had admired.

I remember, at Mile End Green, when I lay at Clement's Inn—I
was then Sir Dagonet in Arthur's shew—there was a little quiver
fellow, and 'a would manage you his piece thus; and 'a would about
and about, and come you in, and come you in; 'rah, tah, tah', would
'a say; 'bounce', would 'a say; and away again would 'a go, and
again would 'a come; I shall never see such a fellow.

(2 *Henry IV*, III. ii. 297–306)

This is not very far from the open parody of Beaumont's *The
Knight of the Burning Pestle*, when Ralph the bold Grocer-
Errant reaches the culmination of his glory by playing the
May Lord on a conduit head, and then leads out the musters
to Mile End Green.

The high tradition of early tragedy had been established by
Marlowe and mediated through the majestic presence of
Edward Alleyn the tragedian. Alleyn was, however, a master
of more than one style—of all the 'activities of youth,
activities of age' that were found among strolling players,
where he had learnt his trade. One of his star performances,
the title role in Greene's *Orlando Furioso*, offers a display of
virtuosity such as Dunbar's dwarf suggests. His own copy of
the part, preserved at Dulwich, shows how gaily Alleyn could
point it up. As he turned from lover to madman and back to
warrior, Orlando must have raised both a shudder and
guffaw. He tears a shepherd limb from limb (offstage) and
enters bearing a leg on his shoulder; he fights a battle with
spits and dripping pans (a familiar comic turn); his action and
speech are constantly changing, and different rhetorical styles
must have been put into play, as Alleyn, like a practised
juggler whirling a set of clubs, spun up one after another his
brightly coloured lines.

A single actor could hold an audience with such rapid

transitions (the Admiral's men later developed a group of plays for the quick-change artist) and the greatest actors prided themselves on 'Protean' mutability. 'Medley' plays rose from the mixed activities of the theatre. Burbage's playhouse could accommodate a monster, an antic, a grotesque dragon made of brown paper that 'would fright the ladies that they would shriek'. In medieval times such an irruption would have been termed a Marvel; today, it would be a Happening. The 'Medley' evoked a mingled feeling of fright and triumph, gasps and laughter; but it was a professional show, as the older romantic adventures were not. There is much more professional distinction than at first appears between a shambling Romance like *Sir Clyamon and Sir Clamydes*, which is older than the Theatre, and a Medley like *The Cobbler's Prophecy*, written by Wilson in the late eighties. In his *Apology for Poetry*, Sidney's description of a romance implies that the stage was set out with a group of symbolic objects, which, protected by the heavens, attracted the players into a variety of settings. The Garden, the Shipwreck, the Cave with its fire-breathing monster, and the Battle Field, must have made up a most elaborate play. Thanks to modern studies, we are now familiar with the visual aspects of the City Gates, the Tree, the Cave, the Ship, the Arbour of the medieval and Tudor stages; these provided a gift for the artist's imagination to which only a Melanie Klein could hope to do justice.

Such symbolic objects were used also by Wilson and others in the Medley plays, and in Shakespeare's early theatre. Studied coldly on the page, the Medleys may appear to offer sheer nonsense, for their effect depends on what a modern French writer has termed 'the theatre's magic relation to reality and danger'. The magician with his wonderful shows (a type of the playwright) was a central figure, together with a pair of lovers, a clown, a speaker of riddles and prophecies, one or more of the classical gods and goddesses, and some fireworks. In Wilson's play, one of the 'pavilions' was set on fire; in another, a juggler appeared to whisk away the serious title board 'Speculum' and to substitute 'Wily Beguiled'.

Medleys evolved their own set of sequences when they were the property of a famous troupe like the Queen's Men, and eventually must have delighted the audience only by an unpredictable mixture of predictable items, that belong together because they have been seen together before.[5]

In *The Old Wives' Tale*, George Peele raised the Romance to a similar professional level by setting it in the framework of a story about three actors who have lost their way in a wood. Antic, Frolic, Fantastic, the servants of a lord, whose names proclaim their quality, take refuge in a cottage, where the old wife's tale comes to life; but the audience are released from the confines of time and space and move freely between a magician's study, a well, a hillock with magic flames upon it, and crossroads in a wood. There is no need for a plot; the princess 'white as snow and red as blood', her two brothers, the wicked enchanter, the wandering knight, are as familiar as the set of emblematic objects among which they move. Gaps in the action are taken for granted. There are twenty-four parts (many silent) in this brief play, designed for a company of about ten.

Shakespeare began by turning his back upon Medley and Romance, to write classical plays like *Titus Andronicus* and *The Comedy of Errors*. The fecundity of the early staging was transferred to his vocabulary, where he poured out crowded images, mingled, as Dr Johnson was to observe, with endless variety of proportion and innumerable varieties of combination. The conflict of incompatible and paradoxical images which surges through his comedy derives indirectly from the physical crowding of the old stages, and therefore was readily acceptable to his audience. Ben Jonson thought that Shakespeare was carried away by his own facility—'His wit was in his power; would the rule of it had been so too.' Charles Lamb noted that 'Before one idea has burst its shell, another has hatched and clamours for disclosure'. Primitive art, repudiated as spectacle, is transformed by Shakespeare into a characteristic mode of imaginative working, where the dumb language of shows combines with higher, more articulate, forms. Greene, railing on Shakespeare as an 'upstart Crow', was putting him in the shape of an Antic, the lowest and most

[5] Among such plays are *The Cobbler's Prophecy, The Rare Triumphs of Love and Fortune, John a Kent and John a Cumber*; perhaps *Friar Bacon and Friar Bungay* and *The Woman in the Moon* might be considered variants on this form.

scurrilous type of dumb player; but as author ('Johannes Factotum') Greene suggests he has turned the actor's versatility into writing, with the 'ease' and 'facility' that his friends were later to praise. He sees the connection between Shakespeare's two activities, the second an extension of the first.

Shakespeare has left at least three accounts of this process: Richard II's soliloquy in Pomfret Castle, Duke Theseus on the poet's eye, and the fifty-third Sonnet, all (as I would think) written somewhere about his thirtieth year, in 1594.

Alone in a prison cell, the uncrowned Richard peoples his little world with a teeming succession of diversified forms, which come nearer to the comic actor's multiple roles than to the playwright's art. [And Burbage, it should be remembered, was an even more Protean actor than Alleyn.]

> Thus play I in one person many people,
> And none contented. Sometimes am I king
> Then treasons make me wish myself a beggar,
> And so I am. Then crushing penury
> Persuades me I was better when a king,
> Then am I king'd again; and by and by
> Think that I am unking'd by Bolingbroke,
> And straight am nothing.
>
> (v. v. 30–7)

Richard tries to hammer out his inner conflict to a set pattern; but a charm of music hushes his restless activity of mind and returns him to the hard immures of his prison. This suddenly begets an image or Icon of the tragic mode.

> I wasted Time, and now doth Time waste me,
> For time hath made me now his numbering clock.
>
> (v. v. 49–50)

The prisoner develops the image of a clock at length, his finger becoming the hand, his face the dial (from which he is wiping the tears), and his groans the bell; while the gay motion of organic life is transferred in his imagination to the coronation of his supplanter. He sees himself as a wooden 'Jack o' the clock' such as provided a simple foolery for onlookers by its movement.[6]

---

[6] The famous figures of the pageant in the clock of St Mark's Venice are the best-

Recalled again to his surroundings, he hears from a poor groom of the stable of the usurper's triumph, and 'in the quick forge and working house of thought' transforms himself in his degradation as Bottom was transformed, by the ass's head.

> I was not made a horse;
> And yet I bear a burden like an ass,
> Spurr'd, gall'd and tir'd by jauncing Bolingbroke,
>
> (v. v. 92–4)

A popular game with the Coventry men and others—mounted men on one another's shoulders for comic mock-tournaments.

The nature of our general perception of the world, and of our own body, is so primitive and deep-seated a foundation of our identity that we cannot imagine how these basic levels of perception may change from age to age. But from Shakespeare's work it may be gathered how the Icon's immobility and the Medley's ever-changing succession of 'streamy associations'[7] became integrated in full poetic drama, the fusion of poetry and spectacle, of inner and outer worlds. This remains primitive art only in the sense that our perception of the world is itself analogous to a work of art—'a complex ordering of attitude and belief achieved a stage earlier than discursive statement'.[8] It utilizes but is emphatically not the same as that mental process (conducted largely through visual symbols) which we meet in dreams—primitive thinking, as one psychologist terms it.[9] Plays are 'such stuff as dreams are made on'—they are not dreams.

The capacity for pre-conscious and intuitive ordering found in both Marlowe and Shakespeare is characteristic of drama, where pre-verbal and verbal language combine in one total statement. As Duke Theseus observes, the 'seething brain' of the poet apprehends more than cool reason ever

known examples; but a crowd will gather today to watch the figures in Fortnum and Mason's clock in Piccadilly. It is interesting to compare Marvell's satire on kings:
> Image like, an useless time they tell
> And with vain sceptre, strike the hourly bell.
>
> (*The First Anniversary*, ll. 41–2)

[7] The term is Edward Armstrong's; *Shakespeare's Imagination*, chapter xiii.
[8] D. W. Harding, *Experience into Words* (London, 1963), p. 182.
[9] J. A. Hadfield, *Dreams and Nightmares* (London, 1954), chapter 6.

comprehends, giving to things unknown, to airy nothing a *shape* (which was the technical name for an actor's costume) a *habitation* (or 'locus' on the stage) and a *name* (which the early actors wore pinned to their chests on a scroll). *A Midsummer Night's Dream* is full of the magic of the early stage; Professor Coghill has recently pointed out some links with the play of magic and quick changes of identity, *John a Kent and John a Cumber*.

The Sonnets, which I take to have been written about the same time, open with a strong and familiar Icon. A beautiful youth, embodiment of spring, is urged to marry and produce an heir. The choice of topic has caused some surprise, and C. S. Lewis went so far as to inquire: 'What man in the whole world, except a father in law or potential father in law cares whether any other man gets married?'[10]

But *was* the theme so very unusual? Was there not at least one great person, in whose excellence the red and white rose united, who for some thirty-five years had been constantly exhorted not to let beauty's flower fade unpropagated? Any poet approaching a new patron would find the royal model readily adaptable, since every noble household reproduced in minature the patterns of royal service. Beginning to learn his courtier's alphabet, Shakespeare naturally fell to his copy book. That great Icon of springtime beauty which Spenser had once delineated in his April Eclogue remained the fixed form for praises of the Queen, in her public capacity, though she was now sixty years old: Sir John Davies produced in 1596 *Astraea*, his enamelled acrostics, in which she magically controls the seasons, like Titania and Oberon.

> Earth now is green and heaven is blue,
> Lively spring, that makes all new,
> Jolly spring, doth enter;
> Sweet young sunbeams do subdue
> Angry, aged winter.
>
> Blasts are mild and seas are calm,
> Every meadow flows with balm,
> The earth wears all her riches.
> Harmonious birds sing such a charm,
> As ear and heart bewitches.

[10] C. S. Lewis, *English Literature in the Sixteenth Century* (Oxford, 1954), p. 503.

> Reserve, sweet spring, this nymph of ours,
> Eternal garlands of thy flowers,
> Green garlands never wasting;
> In her shall last our youth's fair spring,
> Now and for ever flourishing,
> As long as heaven is lasting.

In her private person Elizabeth might typify 'angry, aged Winter': but not as Astraea. Shakespeare's youth is more vulnerable than this changeless image; 'the world's fair ornament', he dwells where 'men as plants increase' and beauties must 'die as fast as they see others grow'. His beauty must therefore be transmitted to his heir (and this was also his duty as heir of a great family); yet the poet too, as father-creator, can dream that in his verse 'I engraft you new'. The play of fancy deepens, the royal Icon gives way to a multitude of images, as the beloved is seen to sum up 'all those friends which I thought buried'. Now 'their images I loved, I view in thee', till ultimately the whole world becomes reflected in this one being and so integrated in the poet's mind. The beauty of the beloved, like that of God, is seen everywhere, and he sums up the loveliness of past and present, of both the sexes, of all the seasons, of history and poetry. In the fifty-third sonnet, Shakespeare's Adonis and Marlowe's Helen attend on the beloved, who combines the loftiness of a Platonic ideal with the Protean 'shadows' and 'shapes' of the actors' art.[11] Here is the swarming profusion of the medley—gods, shepherds, lovers, magicians with their attendant spirits—completely harmonized and introjected by a complex poetic image.

> What is your substance, whereof are you made,
> That millions of strange shadows on you tend?
> Since every one hath, every one, one shade,
> And you, but one, can every shadow lend.
> Describe Adonis and the counterfeit
> Is poorly imitated after you;
> On Helen's cheek all art of beauty set,
> And you in Grecian tires are painted new.
> Speak of the spring and foison of the year,
> The one doth shadow of your beauty shew,
> The other as your bounty doth appear,

---

[11] According to Stephen Gosson, a 'shadow' is a minor actor; compare Macbeth's 'Life's but a walking shadow', and Puck's 'If we shadows have offended'.

And you in every blessed shape we know.
In all external grace you have some part,
But you like none, none you, for constant heart.

Eventually, in Sonnet 104, Shakespeare denies that Time moves for his beloved, and in the last poem of all, the lovely boy, an emblem of eternal youth, stands charming the glass of old Father Time, stilling in its clockwise motion the onward sweep of Chronos' 'sickle hour'.

It is no part of my present argument to trace the development of Shakespeare's art after the stage of full integration represented by *Richard II*. From 1594, his career was bound up with the Lord Chamberlain's Men; stability and cohesion came to his theatre. It was true of the whole age, but especially of Shakespeare, that he united the cosmic with the human image, most powerfully in his great tragedies.

If I may quote a poet of our own day:

Sorrow is deep and vast—we travel on
As far as pain can penetrate, to the end
Of power and possibility; to find
The contours of the world, with heaven align'd
Upon infinity; the shape of man!

Kathleen Raine, 'Sorrow'
(from *Living in Time*)

In *Hamlet* Shakespeare refashioned an old tragedy, where the original Hamlet may have offered the same kind of protean jesting as Orlando Furioso, the comic madman. By transforming and incorporating such a role, Shakespeare regained imaginative access to a great fund of energy, and the character is his most complex creation. Yet there is a void at the centre of Hamlet the man—the unfocused, unplumbed grief, the 'pang without a name, void, dark and drear' which all his complex introspection leaves a mystery, an eloquent silence. And there is a ghost at the centre of *Hamlet* the play; the chthonic King is the only true ruler. Echoes of Marlowe cling to the part of the Ghost; for example, the story of his murder recalls a trick of the devilish Lightborn, murderer of Edward II:

Whilst one is asleep to take a quill
And blow a little powder in his ears,
Or open his mouth and pour quicksilver down.

(ll. 2366–8)

The great Icon which unites the two Hamlets, father and son, is also Marlovian in style; it emerges with the arrival of the actors at Elsinore, in the First Player's speech of the death of Priam. The apparition of Pyrrhus, avenger of his father Achilles, upon Priam (with whom, as the murderer of Hector, Priam has pleaded for his son) is a figure of strange but arrested power. As he finishes the description of Pyrrhus, Hamlet hands over to the first Player, who recounts how the very wind of Pyrrhus' sword felled Priam, but at that moment the crash of the falling towers amid 'the nightmare of smoke and screams and ruin'[12] arrested his action. Pyrrhus stands in tableau, flourishing his sword, a mechanical figure of destruction in his black armour smeared with blood, a kind of Iron Man.

Like Tamburlaine, or like Aaron in *Titus Andronicus*, he remains larger than life:

> So as a painted tyrant, Pyrrhus stood,
> Like a neutral to his will and matter,
> Did nothing.

(II. ii. 474–6)

and there was silence for a space, till the burning towers crashed thunderously again, and the blade fell.

After meeting this Icon, Hamlet in a great burst of self-directed rage recognizes the embodiment of what he had before encountered in the Ghost, issuing its archaic but absolute command, 'Revenge!' It is a compulsion, it is a *must*, laid upon a man by an archaic part of himself, a decayed part reactivated by his father's death. The compelling power of that part of ourselves which we do not desire to meet can return only in such images. Yet the tempest of Hamlet's passion evokes in him the notion of the play-within-the-play, by which he catches the conscience of King Claudius, even as he

---

[12] The phrase is Harry Levin's.

himself has been caught. All this depends on the 'theatre's magic relation to reality and danger'; for Hamlet remembers how guilty creatures sitting at a play have been forced by what they saw to recount their crimes. After the play has indeed caught its victim, we see Hamlet stand with drawn sword flourishing over the kneeling figure of the praying Claudius, in exactly the same posture as that of Pyrrhus over Priam. The Icon is re-enacted in the prayer scene; but Hamlet does not let his sword fall. He puts it up with the thought of yet more horrid and complete revenge, which shall damn Claudius both body and soul.

Shakespeare here appeals to the most primitive and terrifying aspects of theatrical participation; the sequel to this act is the second and final appearance of the Ghost.

When Shakespeare came to the writing of his final plays, popular art was dying in the countryside. Robin Hood and the hobby horse were everywhere put down; the court was evolving a new Italianate form of masque, and a new theatre. Shakespeare reactivated his own early memories and transformed into scenic terms for the new stage the medleys of twenty-five years before—'tales, tempests and such drolleries', as Ben Jonson scornfully termed them. The utmost reaches of his imagination evoked the scenic emblems of Shakespeare's youth—the Cave, the Living Statue, the Ship—and some of the ancient roles—the May Queen, the Monster, and the Magician —using them to explore an interior world where fine and delicate sensibilities alternated with 'imaginations foul as Vulcan's stithy'.

*Pericles*, the first of these plays, is presented by the ancient poet Gower, who here performs the kind of Induction that old Madge, Frolic, and Fantastic had given in *The Old Wives' Tale*. But he is a Ghost.

> To sing a song that old was sung
> From ashes ancient Gower is come . . . .
> It hath been sung at festivals,
> On ember eves and holy ales,
> And lords and ladies in their lives
> Have read it for restoratives.
>
> (Prologue, 1–8)

Much of the moral action is in dumb show, and much of the writing is absurd. Like the hero of the old romance, Sir Clamydes, the wandering knight Pericles is shipwrecked on a foreign coast and wins its princess for bride in spectacular tournament. His father-in-law plays fast and loose with the unknown prince and his own daughter in a style which burlesques the old quick changes:

> Will you, not having my consent,
> Bestow your love and your affections
> Upon a stranger, who, for aught I know
> May be, nor can I think the contrary,
> As great in blood as I myself?
> Therefore hear you, mistress; either frame
> Your will to mine—and you, sir, hear you—
> Either be ruled by me, or I will make you—
> Man and wife.

(II. v. 75–83)

This clownish jocularity is exercised in a play which seems to exist only as matrix for the great tableau and Icon, the discovery scene of the last act. When Marina's sacred charm of music has reanimated the frozen image of Grief that is Pericles, then a figure no longer of cosmic dimensions, but subject to cosmic influences, has been recalled from dereliction so extreme that it could have been embodied only in traditional forms, not originally carrying the personal stamp that Shakespeare here bestows upon them. In returning to these archaic forms Shakespeare breathed new life into them and recovered a 'radical innocence'.[13] The basis is so simple and the shaping spirit of imagination so concentrated that there is in *Pericles*, so to speak, more gap than play. This is no longer, as in the original old wives' tale, a gap in narrative, but a gap in realization. Shakespeare has gone so deep that he has momentarily lost his unifying power, so splendidly displayed in the Roman plays. The single Icon emerges, surrounded by old-fashioned Romance in debris, and by the macabre comedy of the brothel scenes. Shakespeare even needed to lean on the work of an inferior collaborator.

---

[13] 'All hatred driven thence, | The soul recovers radical innocence | And learns at last that it is self-delighting | Self-appeasing, self-affrighting.' Yeats, 'A Prayer for my Daughter', from *Michael Robartes and the Dancer*.

*Cymberline* carries echoes of several medley plays, in particular of *Sir Clyamon and Sir Clamydes* and *The Rare Triumphs of Love and Fortune*.[14] From Jupiter to Cloten, the roles repeat earlier counterparts; Imogen's later adventures as Fidele have their counterpart in those of Fidelia and Neronis. In 1957, at Stratford, the stage was arranged in a simultaneous setting, Tudor-fashion, so that the emblems of castle, bedchamber, cave, and wood in surrealist fantasy appeared together, 'throwing over the whole production a sinister veil of faery, so that it resembled a Grimm fable transmuted by the Cocteau of *La Belle et la Bête*'.[15]

The costumes, disguises, tokens, tricks of this play, the medley of Roman, British, and medieval themes, turn all to dream and fairy-tale; by this means the sensitive core of tenderness, anguish, and vital playfulness that Imogen embodies can come into being. Imogen is a heroine who would be at home in the high romance of Sidney's *Arcadia*, with Philoclea, her sister in affliction. She is one who makes an art of living, from cookery to leave-taking of her banished husband, devising 'pretty things to say' even for that moment of separation, after which, as she tells her father,

> I am senseless of your wrath; a touch more rare
> Subdues all pangs, all fears.
>
> (I. i. 136–7)

When she reads Posthumus' accusation, Pisanio comments:

> What shall I need to draw my sword? The paper
> Hath cut her throat already.
>
> (III. iv. 30–1)

These are wedded lovers, and the poisoned imagination of Posthumus sinks far below Sidney's world of romance, to the level of Iago and of the brothel scenes in *Pericles*. Yet in spite of his words, Posthumus' actions suggest that he believed in Imogen's innocence all the time; the letter which summons her to Milford on the dangerous journey from her home would have had no effect on one who had really forgotten

---

[14] See *The New Shakespeare*, ed. J. C. Maxwell, (Cambridge, 1960), pp. xxii–xxvii.
[15] Ibid., p. xl (quoting Kenneth Tynan).

him completely, and given away 'the manacle of love', the bracelet which was his last token. When he himself appears in real gyves, Posthumus has spontaneously repented; and a vision of his dead father and two brothers mysteriously links with the next scene, in which Imogen also meets again her father and her two long-lost brothers. Thus the union of the wedded lovers is shown to exist at a level beyond that of overt statement.

The fairy-tale gives underlying support to the impossibilities of this play. To reach the totally unfamiliar, it is necessary to cling to the familiar; from moment to moment this new kind of medley convinces, although the princess so wounded by the accusation of Posthumus could not have assumed the role of Fidele, and lived to be struck down once again. It is a kind of posthumous life for *her*, she is playing a part; the grotesque symbolism of Cloten's dead figure in her husband's garments is impossible and hideous, but perhaps also a kind of black comedy of actors' 'shapes'. The magic drinks, changes of identity, and visionary spectacles of the last part of the play no longer carry any relation to reality and danger; they are the means by which Shakespeare can leave gaps in his work. They also seem to function by some associative process in the release of energy from below; the primitive art assists or accompanies or is a necessary concomitant of new, difficult poetry for which the play reaches out.

The original of the next play, *A Winter's Tale*, belongs to the same period as the medleys and was a narrative of Shakespeare's old enemy and detractor, Robert Greene. The old tale ended tragically and was named *Pandosto or the Triumph of Time*. Construction through gaps in the story is emphasized by the appearance of Time as Chorus, who separates the two halves of Shakespeare's play: but the action is clearer, and firmer, the poet has regained his mastery of plot. In the first half, Leontes is overwhelmed by that poisoned level of the imagination which Posthumus had shown, and which had been displayed in the brothel scenes of *Pericles*. Leontes' jealousy invades him suddenly and spontaneously at the moment when he *sees* his wife and his friend in playful familiar talk together. The image speaks to him of what might be. All this is imaginatively realized, but then the

marvels begin. They are the work of Apollo, a much more
effective deity than Diana in *Pericles* or Jupiter in *Cymbeline*.
First comes an oracular message, then the death of Mamilius,
and finally the Icon of Hermione as she appears in Antigonus'
dream. The significance of this dream was pointed out by
Anne Righter in a paper read last year at the International
Conference at Stratford. As the instrument of Leontes'
vengeance, Antigonus is accursed, and the vision of the
Queen comes to warn him of this fate. Although she appears
'in pure white robes, Like very sanctity', her eyes 'become
two spouts'; she is portentously like Lavinia. Antigonus
falsely accepts this as an omen that the babe is indeed a
bastard; no sooner has he laid it on the earth than thunder is
heard, and the sounds of a hunt. It is the god Apollo,
descending in storm, Apollo the Hunter, who chases the
guilty man as Prospero and Ariel hunt the guilty with dogs in
*The Tempest*. Antigonus himself becomes the quarry, and the
'Marvel' of the bear, at once grotesque and horrifying, would
raise the old mixture of fright and laughter in the audience—
especially if a real bear were let loose among them.

By contrast, in the last scene, the high magic of the holy
statue that comes to life is Christian in its forms. The Icon of
Hermione is kept in a chapel 'holy, apart' as Paulina tells the
penitent king. Perdita kneels before it with the pretty proviso:

> Give me leave,
> And do not say 'tis superstition, that
> I kneel, and then implore her blessing. Lady,
> Dear Queen, that ended when I but began,
> Give me that hand of yours to kiss.

> > (v. iii. 42–6)

The coldness of the stone has chid his own coldness in
Leontes, but Paulina tells him

> It is required
> You do awake your faith.

> > (v. iii. 94–5)

The magic is powerful, the charm is musical; the figure is
transubstantiated back to flesh and blood, and Leontes puts
all in three words: 'Oh, she's warm.'

Although a statue which comes to life is not unknown to earlier plays, or to later ones for that matter,[16] this single scene offers the deepest integration of spectacle and poetry in the last plays; and for the audience, who have been given no more than hints and guesses that Hermione may be living, the final descent is a most powerful *coup de théâtre*, made eloquent by silence and music wedded to poetry.

In this, it is a wonderful advance on the descent of Jupiter, spectacularly the highlight of the whole play *Cymbeline* but poetically a gap and a void. Hermione has replaced the gods in this scene; the triumph is that of a divine humanity. Was there here some unconscious recall of a Catholic image of the Mother, mingled with the semi-divine Elizabeth, Virgin Queen but nursing mother of her people (as she termed herself to Parliament), wedded to her kingdom, whose reign was already assuming legendary greatness as the weakness of her successor appeared?

In its spontaneous-seeming, yet perfectly disciplined, form, *The Tempest* represents the final triumph of art, an art based on imagination perfectly attuned to the stage. Spectacular but not naïve, classical in form, poetic but no longer with the poetry of the gaps, it presents a close, delicate wholeness:

> A condition of complete simplicity
> Costing not less than everything.

*The Tempest* is a play of high magic throughout, although its ruling intelligence is human and fallible. Prospero's magic is Pythagorean, based on that 'monstrous imagination' that Bacon was to reject:

that the world was one entire perfect living creature; insomuch as Apollonius of Tyana, a Pythagorean prophet, affirmed that the ebbing and flowing of the sea was the respiration of the world, drawing in water as breath and putting it forth again . . . . They went on, and inferred that if the world was a living creature, it had a soul, and spirit, calling it spiritus mundi.

> (*Sylva Sylvarum*, century x)

---

[16] A statue on a grave comes to life in *The Trial of Chivalry*; and pictures in Massinger's *The City Madam*. There is a portentous set of statues in Middleton's *A Game at Chess*, but these are idols of the Black, i.e. Spanish, party.

White magic, by 'giving a fit touch to the spirit of the world', can make it respond. Prospero is at first subject to the stars and courts an auspicious influence; whereas the monstrous Sycorax had worked black magic by the manipulation of physical charms on the sublunary level. She was able to exert physical compulsion on the higher spheres, even those beyond the moon—for so I read the crux

> That could control the Moon, . . .
> And deal in her command, without her power.
>
> (v. i. 270–1)

To the guilty Alonzo the whole world speaks with one voice:

> O, 'tis monstrous, monstrous.
> Methought the bellows spoke and told me of it.
> The winds did sing it to me; and the thunder,
> That deep and dreadful organ pipe, pronounced
> The name of Prosper.
>
> (iii. iii. 95–9)

It is from the spirit Ariel that Prospero himself learns to feel sympathy with Alonzo, returning from his stony remoteness to that quick freshness of feeling with which his own child responds.

> Oh, the cry did knock
> Against my very heart.
>
> (i. ii. 8–9)

Ariel's strange shapes, which include that very old-fashioned one of a coat of invisibility, sometimes reflect the inner states of those he works on. Dozens of strange shadows attend on him, and not every one of them is a blessed shape; for the men of sin he plays the Harpy, for the lovers a bounteous Ceres; when he comes to the clowns 'like the picture of Nobody', he plays old tricks from the repertory of earlier spirits,[17] and piping a merry catch, leads them into a horse-pond. His imprisonment, told by Prospero, recalls a potent device of the early stage; in *The Fairy Pastoral*, William Percy described

---

[17] For instance, Shrimp of *John a Kent* and Robin Goodfellow of *Wily Beguiled*.

exactly how the Hollow Tree was constructed. The clowns are clowns of the old type, and to them Caliban is but a fairground monster, to be shown to gaping crowds. He is confined by Prospero in a Rock, another familiar scenic device. The old emblems of the Ship and the Cave are used, and a special 'quaint device' for the banquet that vanishes, leaving a bare table, which is carried out by spirits.[18] Pure shows, like the dance of harvesters, unite the Jacobean masque with the revels of *The Old Wives' Tale*, where there is also a harvesters' dance.

Prospero's physical needs are served by Sycorax's son till, by way of ordeal, Prince Ferdinand takes his place as logman. Caliban accuses Prospero of usurping his island, and Prospero later accuses Ferdinand of this design, thus visiting the sin of the father upon his child. The murderous conspiracy of the false princes and the grosser rebellion of the clowns are alike frustrated by Prospero (whose art of government had certainly improved in exile) and the theme of usurpation dissolves in a lovers' jest, in the final tableau where Miranda and Ferdinand are revealed playing with ivory kings and queens at chess.

> *Miranda.* Sweet lord, you play me false.
> *Ferdinand.* No, my dearest love,
>   I would not for the world.
> *Miranda.* Yes, for a score of kingdoms you should wrangle,
>   And I would call't fair play.

(v. i. 171–5)

Alonzo greets this restoration of the son he had lost as 'a most high miracle', but the disclosure has not the startling quality of that in *The Winter's Tale*, and Gonzalo's quiet comment points the distinction:

I have inly wept.          (v. 200)

Finally, the whole dramatic action is dissolved by a series of transformations. For what is the magician but, as always in the old plays, a stage manager of shows, with his wand and his

---

[18] A. M. Nagler, *Shakespeare's Stage* (New Haven, 1958), p. 100, discusses this trick; in medieval terms a 'secret'.

magic inscribed 'book'—what is this but a sublimated Master of the Revels? What the fellowship of the bottle with their stolen frippery and their game of kings and subjects, but a reductive mockery of the poorest players in the service? Pointing to the royal badge of Naples on the sleeves of Trinculo the fool and 'King Stephano', Prospero asks,

> Mark but the badges of these men, my lord,
> Then say if they be true.
>
> (v. i. 267–8)

A man wearing King James's badge spoke the lines.

Finally, with no more dignity than a fashionable hat and rapier will confer, yet as one who dares more than Dr Faustus did—to make every third thought his grave—the old man appeals in his epilogue to the theatre's magic relation of reality and danger in a prayer of primal simplicity:

> As you from crimes would pardon'd be,
> Let your indulgence set me free.
>
> (Epilogue, 19–20)

The final plays represent an interior conflict, resolved in association with revived memories of a more primitive stage, and asserted with ever clarifying force.[19] It would be dangerous to speculate further than this. We may note the prevalent themes of death and rebirth, petrifaction and release; the common element of false accusation, banishment, and usurpation; the relations of fathers and children; the combination of extreme purity and scurrility. Do these suggest some possible conflicts of an ageing man? Prospero's farewell to Art, though not actually Shakespeare's last word (things do not work out quite so tidily as that) may represent an inner acceptance, that only at great price could be put into speech, and after many attempts; but here, as always, the Actor-Poet found, for his familiar ritual, the fitting words.

---

[19] That there was perhaps a general movement in this direction does not modify the nature of Shakespeare's achievement, for he was the only actor-playwright with personal knowledge of the earlier stage. For a useful summary of the common stage practice, see Dieter Mehl, *The Elizabethan Dumb Show* (London, 1965), chapter 2.

# 4. UNBLOTTED LINES: SHAKESPEARE AT WORK

## By M. M. MAHOOD

### I

It may seem a poor return for the honour of being invited to give this British Academy lecture on Shakespeare that I should, apparently, have chosen to talk about that aspect of Shakespeare's work which has, in the past, caused Shakespeareans most embarrassment. Shakespeare's own friends recognized that his pen ran away with him. For Heminge and Condell this fluency was a marvellous gift; Ben Jonson saw it rather as a dangerous facility: 'I remember, the players have often mentioned it as an honour to Shakespeare that in his writings, whatsoever he penned, he never blotted out line. My answer hath been, would he had blotted a thousand. Which they thought a malevolent speech.' Jonson, we know, was thinking of such lines as 'Caesar did never wrong, but with just cause'—which, if Shakespeare wrote it at all, was blotted into better sense before ever *Julius Caesar* was printed. But Shakespeare's headlong method of composition has wider consequences for his art than the odd solecism or syntactical tangle.

Shakespeare's plays abound in loose ends, false starts, confusions, and anomalies of every kind. They can all perhaps be typified in the Duke in *Two Gentlemen of Verona*, who is on occasion called an emperor but in fact behaves very much as a private individual, and who simply does not know from one scene to another whether he is ruling over Verona or over Milan. At one time, editors and critics felt Shakespeare must be exonerated from all such absurdities, and there resulted that disintegration of Shakespeare that Sir Edmund Chambers challenged in the British Academy lecture for 1924 and in his subsequent writings. Chambers's cool declaration that Shakespeare was 'often careless and often perfunctory' did much to check the dismemberment of Shakespeare's text into revisions and collaborations, and for this we must be lastingly grateful. But the admission of slovenliness remained; in a decade dominated by William Archer and Bernard Shaw it could not be other than an admission. I would like today to take advantage of the very different aesthetic climate in which we now live to suggest that Shakespeare's spontaneity is not a reproach but—as Heminge and Condell maintained—an honour to him; and that the plays' contradictions are evidence, not so much of Shakespeare's absent-mindedness, as of the presence of an exploring and adventurous mind, deeply involved in all the issues bodied forth through the actions of his characters. A birthday lecture should surely be a celebration, and this is to be, if you like, a celebration of Shakespeare's inspired carelessness, a justification of that indeterminacy which reveals to us, in Wallace Stevens's phrase, 'the process of the personality of the poet'.

Shakespeare's changes of mind sometimes take the simple form of an immediate dissatisfaction with a word, a speech, or even a whole scene. Because it is not his habit to go back and tidy up, to sweep up the chippings, duplications survive in his text and alert us to the fact that here are places where we can actually watch Shakespeare at work. Juliet is told that Romeo has killed her cousin Tybalt, and the playwright is soon busy expending all his eloquence on her rhetorical outcry:

> O serpent heart, hid with a flow'ring face!
> Did ever dragon keep so fair a cave?
> Beautiful tyrant! fiend angelical!

> (III. ii. 73–5)

Shakespeare is at this time still in love with the formal lament, so the highly-wrought oxymora of this line seem to him just right: two stresses balanced neatly each side of a central caesura to emphasize the patterning of the thought into the antitheses of good–bad, bad–good. He tries to repeat the effect. 'Ravenous dove'. No, that won't do. He has started, literally, on the wrong foot; here are only four syllables where he needs five, and bad–good where he wants good–bad. Better to start with 'dove'. 'Dove-feather'd raven'—that's it—

> Dove-feather'd raven! wolfish-ravening lamb!
> Despised substance of divinest show!
> Just opposite to what thou justly seem'st,
> A damned saint, an honourable villain!
>
> (III. ii. 76–9)

By now he is well away, and has forgotten all about the discarded 'Ravenous', which remained to baffle the compositor with an extra-long line, 'Ravenous dove feather'd raven, wolfish ravening lamb', which he split into two, wrecking the forceful symmetry of the speech.

Modern editors of course blot out 'Ravenous' on Shakespeare's behalf, but they leave intact longer instances of Shakespeare's rewritings. There is for example the moment in *Love's Labour's Lost* when the four men who have foresworn women's company in order to concentrate on their studies are all found to be hopelessly in love. Berowne, as the leading wit among them, is asked to justify their volte-face, and he starts with a fine, challenging line: 'Have at you then, affection's men at arms!' But Shakespeare has, in this scene alone, penned some three hundred lines of verse, including a lyric and a couple of sonnets; although we do not know at which point his day's stint began, it is soon evident in this speech that he just cannot keep up the vigour of his opening. The rhythm flags, the diction begins to creep, the logical distinctions of the speech grow blurred. Lecturers on Shakespeare know as well as Shakespeare himself that there is only one sensible thing to do in such a situation and that is to sleep on it. And when Shakespeare returned, refreshed, to the speech, he must have felt an intolerable flatness as he read over such lines as:

> For when would you, my lord, or you, or you,
> Have found the grounds of study's excellence
> Without the beauty of a woman's face?
>
> (IV. iii. 295–7)

Now he piles up fresh epithets, carries the sense impetuously forward from line to line, and relates the thought closely to the scene's action—all the courtiers have been writing poems—

> For when would you, my liege, or you, or you

In leaden contemplation have found out
Such fiery numbers as the prompting eyes
Of beauty's tutors have enriched you with?

(IV. iii. 316–19)

And so on through the whole speech till Shakespeare finds himself carried away in Berowne's poetic cavalry charge—'Saint Cupid then! and soldiers, to the field!'—so that there is no time to go back and blot out the twenty-eight lines of false start. The two versions are left standing, one after the other, much as in *Julius Caesar*—if I may finally instance a whole duplicated passage of dialogue—there are two versions of the scene in which the audience learns of Portia's death.

The first of these, it will be recalled, occurs at the end of the quarrel between Brutus and Cassius, when Brutus reveals that throughout the scene he has been keeping to himself the news that Portia has 'swallowed fire'. There follows a council of war during which Messala tells Brutus that Portia is dead and Brutus receives the news as if he were hearing it for the first time. The scene as it stands has had its defenders, but most readers recoil from the suggestion that Shakespeare meant Brutus to put on a display of equanimity in order to impress Messala and Titinius. We assume Shakespeare was dissatisfied with the scene and changed it. Because the passage between Brutus and Cassius is by far the more moving, it has been suggested that it is an inserted revision, meant to replace the dialogue with Messala; and certainly the rough edges fit so neatly together that I almost hesitate to pose the question; ought we to assume that Shakespeare's second thoughts are always improvements on his first?

I would like, very tentatively, to suggest that we may have here two successive attempts to force back Brutus and Cassius into the roles and relationship they have in Plutarch. Throughout the play, Shakespeare has found it very hard to follow Plutarch in exalting the stoical self-command of Brutus and denigrating the impulsiveness of Cassius; in the relationship of the man who is unmoved, cold and to temptation slow with the man who is passion's slave, which runs as a steady theme through the plays and sonnets that Shakespeare wrote towards the end of Elizabeth's reign, his sympathies repeatedly veer towards the warmer and more passionate nature. The quarrel scene in particular has an authenticity which, we know, thrilled the Elizabethan audience. But Brutus' anger here is that of an insufferable self-complacency, whereas Cassius' is the anger of wounded love. Shakespeare seems to recognize that he has distorted his source, and fastens on the death of Portia as a way of rehabilitating Brutus. He makes two attempts to use it, and they may stand in the order in which he wrote them. The first fails to restore Plutarch's characters; the Cassius who cries 'How 'scaped I killing when I cross'd you so? / Oh insupportable and touching loss!' is still Shakespeare's Cassius. Shakespeare passes on to the war council, and there perhaps discovers another way of informing us of Brutus' loss. This time he calls to his help a piece of stage business, a single candle lighting a face that is trying to maintain a stoical calm (he will use the same device at the end of *Othello*). And he gives Cassius a reaction to the news which makes him once again the envious, self-centred Cassius of Plutarch: 'I have as much in this in art as you / But yet my nature could not bear it so.' If the episode seems crude and clumsy by comparison with the earlier dialogue, it can be because Shakespeare is doing deliberate violence to his own dramatic instincts in order to defer to Plutarch, who was an ancient and an authority.

II

I have dealt at some length on this duplication in *Julius Caesar* because it serves as a reminder that whereas most false starts in Shakespeare are followed by scenes or passages in which he seems imaginatively liberated at finding himself on the right track, there are also false starts and anomalies that show the exploratory freedom of Shakespeare's mind being curbed by some external factor. Here the factor may well have been deference to his source. But even in the comedies, where Shakespeare's fancy might seem most free to roam, false starts occur when Shakespeare realizes he has embarked on something that is not going to be theatrically feasible. A good many of Shakespeare's ghosts can be explained in this way; I do not mean the solid, communicative ghosts of tragedy, but textual ghosts, characters named in scene headings who never speak, or who are named in speeches but never appear. The Dutchman and the Spaniard who are given entries at the beginning of the wager scene in *Cymbeline* could conceivably be mutes; but the Elizabethan audience would have felt cheated by the failure of two funny-looking foreigners to say anything ridiculous, and the likelihood is that Shakespeare remembered, after he had begun the scene, that he had not enough actors for these supernumerary roles.

The same explanation may serve for the disappearance of a character such as Innogen, Hero's mother in *Much Ado*; only a small group of boy actors was available for female parts. But the cast of *The Tempest* is not very large, and an actor could presumably have been found to play the Duke of Milan's 'brave son', whom Ferdinand speaks of as having been involved in the shipwreck. Once Shakespeare's imagination is fully engaged on the island's enchantments, however, there is no place for a character who would draw aside interest from Ferdinand and who would be left unpartnered at the stage when Jack should have Jill. Above all, Antonio as a father was unthinkable. The fallen chracters of the romances— Cymbeline, Leontes, Alonso—are all threatened with childlessness, and in earlier plays of Shakespeare the bad are almost always barren; he found he had to take Iago's little daughter out of his source story when he wrote *Othello* even though this landed him in some difficulties with the plot. So he must leave the brave son of the Duke of Milan to be picked up by another vessel of the Neapolitan fleet before it vanishes over the horizon, for he can have no real part in the imaginative fabric of the play.

When we turn to bigger anomalies than these odd ghost-characters we again find that theatrical exigency can account for only some of them. It may explain the disappearance of Sly and the Hostess at the end of *The Taming of the Shrew*. If we subscribe to the older view that Shakespeare's play is a rewriting of *The Taming of A Shrew*, where of course Sly does come back, we can watch him using up every available actor in the process of enlarging and enriching the intrigue, so that Sly has to slip off stage and reappear as one of the bearded pantaloons, and the Hostess, initially preserved by

Shakespeare's elimination of Bianca's second sister, has in the end to disappear and double as the third bride necessitated by the folk-tale climax of the story. Even if Shakespeare's play is the original, he could have found he had been more prodigal of actors' parts than he intended. The Bad Quarto, which *A Shrew* then becomes, shows that there were other men of the theatre then as now who were convinced that Sly's awakening was the proper ending of the play; and Shakespeare himself seems, with his usual economy, to have conceived it and saved it up for Bottom's unforgettable emergence from his mid-summer night's dream. Either way, the Sly scenes of *The Shrew* are a kind of false start which Shakespeare, thank goodness, left unblotted.

A practical explanation is possible too for a marked change of plan in the second act of *The Merchant of Venice*. We are led to expect a masquerade in which Jessica, disguised as a torch-bearer, will be abducted under Shylock's very nose. Now a masque in Shakespeare is always a skirmish in the sex war. But of the three boy actors who might be considered skilled in this kind of badinage, two are in distant Belmont and the third is disguised as a mere torch-bearer. There is no one available to give pert feminine back-answers to the masqueraders. The masque is called off; the wind has 'come about' and Bassanio and Gratiano must hurry abroad the ship for Belmont. Something much more fundamental than the availability of actors seems to me to be involved in this change. The writing of this second act has been noticeably slack; the sorry humour of Gobbo and Old Gobbo might almost be designed to keep the audience occupied in Shakespeare's absence, and the masquerade is planned with much the same purpose. Shakespeare's imagination lies becalmed. Then, with the suddenness of the wind that fills Bassanio's sails, he gets a grip of the play's theme of love's recklessness: Bassanio's brave venture for Portia's love, Antonio's yet braver venture for Bassanio's, the audacity of Portia's venture to save Antonio's life. Once Shakespeare knows just what the play is about the writing rises steadily to the double dramatic climax of Bassanio's choice and Portia's judgement; but the dramatist has not forgotten his half-promise of a set of wit well played, and the comedy of the rings follows at the point where it is most theatrically feasible, and most dramatically satisfying in restoring the mood of festive comedy.

Sometimes, unhappily, this moment of engagement, of 'all systems go', does not occur. In the good company of Mr John Wain I have to admit to disappointment with the intrigue of *Much Ado*, in which Shakespeare seems to me to dodge down one blind alley after another, forced in the end to rely on Dogberry, Benedick, and Beatrice between them to save the play as an evening's entertainment. The insecurity of this play contrasts strongly with the way that Shakespeare handles a change of plan early in *Twelfth Night*. Originally he intended to make Orsino employ Viola as a singer, and the fact that in the second act Feste, not Viola, sings 'Come away death' has been explained as the result of Shakespeare discovering either that his Feste could sing, or that his Viola could not. But in the process of writing himself in, of becoming involved in the fortunes of his characters, Shakespeare has surely made a much more important discovery—the intense dramatic pathos of Viola's predicament. If she were to sing to Orsino at this point her character would be effaced by the masking impersonality of a boy's voice. By making her a listener to the song, Shakepeare wins from the situation its full aural and visual effect. We cannot take our eyes off Viola as she feasts her own gaze upon Orsino, secure in the knowledge that he in turn is lost in the image of Olivia evoked by the song's artificial melancholy. And once again a poetic quickening, emphasized here by the inter-weaving of speech, song, and instrumental music, indicates Shakespeare's own excitement at finding himself on the right track.

So far, I have concentrated on comedies. Even those who feel most uneasy at the thought of Shakespeare making up his plays as he went along can tolerate a measure of improvisation here, because the inconsequential happenings of comedy are felt to have an affinity with the cheerful ad-libbing of seasonal revels. A tragedy, the imitation of a great action, demands, we might think, far more scrupulous planning. Yet we have already seen the possibility, even in the historical tragedy of *Julius Caesar*, that Shakespeare made an *ad hoc* decision to introduce Portia's death where he did. When a tragedy has a

fictional rather than a historical source, Shakespeare's approach
to his story can be just as exploratory as it is in the comedies.
The Iago of Cinthio's story—I am keeping to Shakespeare's
names for the characters—desires Desdemona, but believes
her to be in love with Cassio; his love turns to hate, so that he
seeks to destroy Cassio out of jealousy, Desdemona out of
chagrin, and Othello out of envy. We might think this
motivation enough, but Shakespeare's Iago offers us a
startling elaboration of these motives. He hates Cassio with a
professional jealousy, because he has been passed over for
promotion. He hates Othello for passing him over and
because he suspects him of an affair with Emilia. If he desires
Desdemona it is not, he tells us, out of 'absolute lust', but
because he wants to revenge himself on his cuckolder. He
even suspects Cassio with Emilia. Bewildered critics talk of
Iago's rationalizations, but it may well be Shakespeare, rather
than Iago, who is hunting for motives. Until the end of the
second act Shakespeare has not fully realized, brought to life,
Iago as a character. He knows an Iago capable of genuine
passion for Desdemona is inconceivable, yet no other
motivation that he tries out seems to work. It is almost as if he
has to watch Iago act before he knows what kind of being he
is. His difficulty is that summed up in the question: 'How do
I know what I think till I see what I say?' Or as Iago puts it at
the end of his second soliloquy—'Knavery's plain face is
never seen till used.' As Iago's knavery goes to work to get
Cassio cashiered, Shakespeare perceives that the very existence
of innocence is the bright day that brings forth the serpent;
that Iago needs no motives for his actions because he is a pure
agent, the embodiment of destructiveness. So in his soliloquy
at the end of this act, before he embarks on that undermining
of Othello's nobility which is perhaps the crowning achievement of Shakespeare's dramatic poetry, Iago makes no further
parade of his motives. He is driven only by a plain will to
harm: evil itself pitted against goodness itself.

### III

The anomalies and confusions of Shakespeare's plays, then,
although they may sometimes have causes outside of his
involvement in the play's action, arise far more frequently

from the nature of this involvement, from his habit of plunging into a play before he has fully conceived its direction and outcome. There are critics who do recognize this element of improvisation in such plays as *Othello*. The pity of it is that they are affronted by it. Perhaps the greater pity is that so many Shakespearean critics are also pedagogues. As such, our natural instinct is to scold Shakespeare for not having done his homework; for not thinking out all the play's issues before he begins to write, or for not rewriting once he has run into difficulties. These protests however only throw the sand against the wind. The prevailing temper in the arts today favours indeterminacy, spontaneity, extemporization; as we can glimpse if we momentarily raise our eyes from the minutiae of Shakespeare's text and, risking the rashest of *Zeitgeist* generalizations, survey the scene of the seventies.

As a scene, it is more a battlefield than a landscape; but one concept does seem to have gained dominance in the past twenty-five years. That is the concept of the work of art not as the Grecian urn, the creation detached from its creator and so at best a cold pastoral, but as Jacob's wrestling with the angel; art as artifact has in large measure yielded place to art as act. Even literary scholars do not escape this trend of the times; we demand more and more manuscripts in print so that we can follow every flexion of the novelist's or poet's mind in the act of composition, just as in the painting of the past critics take greater pleasure in the immediacy of the roughest sketches than in the finished painting, or call in the aid of spectroscopy to reveal every false start and change of plan on the final canvas. And when we turn to the creative artists, the makers themselves, we find the two obvious strongholds of the artifact, painting and lyric poetry, repeatedly assaulted by such movements as projective verse and action painting. Art exhibitions in particular have taken on the animation of fairgrounds. In music, a generation whose parents were guided by Tovey into an understanding of the formal perfections of the great European classics now bring an equal sensitivity and seriousness to the extemporizations of Indian *raga* and Afro-American jazz. For the quest for art as act has inevitably led away from the cultures that have promoted and preserved the artifact, to non-European concepts of art. In the

east of Nigeria, a hundred people will sometimes go into the
forest to build a shrine to the goddess of creation, and to
shape and paint for it a wealth of life-sized figures. The
completion of such a Mbari house may take a year or more.
When it is finished the people go home, leaving their work to
rapid destruction by rain and termites. Their achievement has
been the act of making, and not the object made. There could
be, as some artists have recognized, no better emblem than
this of the aesthetic which has come to dominate the third
quarter of our century.

'What gives the canvas its meaning', says Dr Harold
Rosenberg, writing of the American action painters, 'is not
psychological data but role, the way the artist organizes his
emotional and intellectual energy as if he were in a living
situation. The interest lies in the kind of act taking place in the
four-sided arena, a dramatic interest.' Contemporary arts all
aspire to the condition of drama, since this is by definition art
as act. When the dramatist is, like Shakespeare, also an actor,
his art is doubly act in that the writing of a play is for him a
performance, an improvisation in slow motion. There is
nothing startling in the notion of Shakespeare writing a
comedy in a fortnight; one leading dramatist of the present
time averages ten days on the writing of his plays, while
another has on occasion composed verse and prose alike
straight onto a stencil, so that each page could be immediately
run off and handed to the actors. And it would no more occur
to the actor-playwright Shakespeare to turn back and blot out
such false starts as Iago's motive-hunting than it would occur
to him in performance to re-enact a scene in which he had
muffed his lines. The important thing is to press on in search
of the right track, knowing that once this is found the
audience will forget any aberrations. Left to itself—which
means left to the controlling power of the play—would any
theatrical audience ever have noticed the double time in
*Othello*?

But there are no such anomalies in, say, Molière's plays,
and this is a reminder that Shakespeare's spontaneity derives
as much from the kind of artist he is as from his situation as an
actor writing at speed for his fellow actors. Because Molière
knows from the outset where he stands in relation to all that

happens in one of his plays, he is able to put himself into the play as a *raisonneur*, or spokesman character. Such a role is impossible for Shakespeare, because he is immersed in every part of the action, organizing, in Dr Rosenberg's phrase, his emotional and intellectual energy as if he were in a living situation. It follows that the Shakespearean counterpart of the spokesman in Molière or Jonson is the playwright-within-the-play, the character who tries to shape events—and a playwright is after all a shaper and not a writer of plays; shapes them, that is, to good not villainous ends, since for Shakespeare as a man of the Renaissance art betters life. And like their creator when he immerses himself in his chosen tale, these playwrights-within-the-play get more than they bargained for. The hot Verona dog-days, provoking street brawls and bringing plague to the city, frustrate Friar Lawrence's attempt to reconcile Montagues and Capulets through the marriage of Romeo and Juliet. Rosalind, as she directs the destinies of all the lovelorn in Arden towards the final wedding masque, not only has to put up with a leading man who is persistently late for rehearsal, but very nearly loses him to a lioness; it is a measure of the exploration of art's relationship to life which goes on beneath the elegant surface of *As You Like It* that 'reality' should intrude in this preposterous romance incident, and that Rosalind's real faint should be 'well counterfeited'. Bottom too, taking over-weening charge of the Pyramus and Thisbe interlude, finds himself carried far beyond that stereotype of romance into the bottomless mystery of love's choices, which are always ready to transpose things base and vile to form and dignity, to translate an ass to an angel.

Two plays in particular offer an extended metaphor of the playwright's continuous struggle with his material in the very process of composition. Duke Prospero in *The Tempest* and Duke Vincentio in *Measure for Measure* seek so absolute a control over the events of the plays in which they appear, that both have been seen as providential figures. But the experience that Shakespeare relives through them is surely a human and fallible one. If there is allegory at all in Prospero's magic, is it not an allegory of the effort and pain, accompanied by a good deal of human testiness, of the artist's struggle to order experience into a total vision? Prospero nearly fails with Trinculo, Stephano, and Caliban, whose remembered plot startles him into such agitation. Perhaps he fails also with Sebastian and Antonio, who cannot be charmed asleep by Ariel and who remain recalcitrantly silent and outside the scheme of things at the end of the play. The dramatist's vocation is a mental fight that leaves Prospero wearied at the close; yet it has its exhilarations for which flight is the only just image, and to relinquish it is to let go of the poetic spirit. Prospero is going to miss Ariel.

Duke Vincentio has fewer powers; he does not assume a magic robe, but the habit of a friar. In giving him this disguise, Shakespeare was departing from his sources, as he was also doing in making Isabella a novice and rearranging the action to preserve her virginity. He may have had no clear conscious intention in making these changes, but their effect is to plunge him into the exploration of ideas that have never troubled him before. As a disguised friar, the Duke speaks with the voice of medieval asceticism, the *de contemptu mundi* of Innocent the Third, and these great religious commonplaces come easily to Shakespeare's pen. Still, the hood does not make the monk, and the Duke's response to Claudio's profoundly disturbing cry for life is to seek every means of saving him, first by the substitution of Mariana for Isabella by night and then, when Angelo fails to keep his part of the bargain, by the substitution of a criminal's head for Claudio's. But the Duke's control of the action is squarely challenged when the criminal himself, Barnardine, reels onto the stage and declares, with drunken dignity, that he will not die 'for any man's persuasion'. The Duke has to concur, for the good friarly reason that Barnardine is unprepared for death, and another head is conveniently found.

The fascinating thing about this minute but vivid scene with Barnardine is that it is both an image and an illustration of Shakespeare's exploratory method as a dramatist. Time and again in the very course of writing a play Shakespeare finds his material resists his control as Barnardine resists the Duke's plot to make a convenience of his head. When this occurs a writer often speaks of the character taking control; but what happens is rather that the character has embodied some aspect of the writer's sensibility which he has been reluctant to recognize, even as Prospero is apt to forget Caliban, the thing of darkness that he at last acknowledges as his. In *Measure for Measure*, Shakespeare virtually stumbles upon a confrontation of asceticism and sensuality and then, in the course of writing the play, finds this antithesis drives him yet deeper into the conflict between the wish to die and the will to live in which he inevitably takes sides with those who affirm the gift of life: the side of Barnardine who will not die for any man's persuasion; of Juliet, serenely carrying Claudio's child; of the irrepressibly vital Lucio, driving Isabella back to plead for her brother or teasing the Duke as if he were the victim of a feast of fools in some medieval monastry; of the pimp Pompey, 'a poor man, who must live'. There are always those who like the Victorian novice-master 'do not see the necessity', and Shakespeare here listens to them more carefully than he has every done before; but their other-worldliness is rejected at the end, when Isabella saves Angelo's life and, all postulated vows abandoned, marries her duke.

The writing of *Measure for Measure* may well have been Shakespeare's most difficult voyage of discovery. The second part of the play bears many signs of strain from which it recovers only in the last scene. But improvisation lends dramatic immediacy to Shakespeare's very greatest plays. Two high points of Shakespeare's dramatic achievement, the death of Lear and the restoration of Hermione to Leontes, were very probably conceived in the actual process of writing the plays in which they occur. Bradley rightly complained of the inadequate motivation for the deaths of Lear and Cordelia. An audience that knew earlier versions of the tale must have been totally unprepared for Lear's entry with Cordelia dead in his arms. Preceding events stand in little or no causal relationship to these deaths; the great wheel of Lear's experience which has carried him through the nadir of despair is complete when he is restored by Cordelia to his royal robes and his right mind. None the less, the catastrophe, not to be found in any earlier treatments of the tale, surely follows as the direct experiential outcome of the playwright's share in Lear's discoveries. Lear's ripeness has placed him beyond the worst that fate can do: the death of Cordelia, which is felt by Lear in a way that evokes our pity and at the same time transcended by him in a way that commands our awe—the Aristotelian 'terror'. Like all successful turns in a dramatic action, the scene is both surprising and inevitable; it can well have taken Shakespeare himself by surprise even as he discovered that there was no other way open to him to end the play.

Just as Bradley objected to the unexpectedness of Lear's and Cordelia's death, Coleridge reproached Shakespeare for 'mere indolence' (a very Coleridgean reproach) in not having his oracle, in *The Winter's Tale*, prepare us for Hermione's survival. But in Greene's novel, which is Shakespeare's guide, the queen does not survive; and when Shakespeare has Leontes make arrangements for her burial and has Antigonus visited by her ghost, it seems certain that at the end of Act III of the play Hermione is dead to Shakespeare too. There is no way of telling when Shakespeare discoverd her to be alive, though perhaps the discovery occurred during the writing of those Whitsun scenes that take us clean out of the atmosphere of guilt and retribution and tranform the vengeful Apollo into the sun that shines on the just and unjust. It is the inevitable completion of the Leontes experience that he should get more blessing than he or any man deserves; but once again Shakespeare discovers the inevitable only in the course of writing the play, and the wonder of that discovery communicates a miraculous freshness to Paulina's revival of Hermione. Once again, too, the scene supplies both image and illustration. The statue that comes to life is art as Shakespeare understood it, not only because the playwright needed the living actors for the realization of his ideas, but because the very act of writing plunged him, however set and traditional his story, into a maze of innumerable choices. Writers from the romantic revival onwards have sought with more or less success for such an image of the artist's ability to have his cake and eat it, to get the best of both worlds: the determined world of the planned artifact and the indeterminate world of the artificer wrestling with his material. For Blake the image is that of Los, continually building, continually destroying; or there is that Los of twentieth-century London, Gulley Jimson painting the Creation on walls that are always threatened with demolition, a fate reserved too for the Elizabethan theatre:

> But I can do something to the foreground now . . . And it struck me
> all at once that what I wanted there was a pattern, not in the flat, but
> coming and going. Leaves, waves. Tufts of grass bending in the
> breeze. Flowers. I began the flowers, but they felt wrong. And all at
> once I made a thing like a white Indian club. I like it, I said, but it's
> not a flower, is it? What the hell could it be? A fish. And I felt a kick
> inside as if I was having a foal. Fish. Fish. Silver-white, green-white.
> And shapes that you could stroke with your eyebrows.[1]

This is the kick of creation that we feel repeatedly as the
prelude to the great scenes of Shakespeare, and if hesitations
and muddles often accompany such moments of engagement,
I for one welcome them as the signs that here, stepping over
the obliteration effected by four centuries, we are brought as
close as we can ever come to Shakespeare at work.

---

[1] Joyce Cary, *The Horse's Mouth* (London, 1944), p. 37.

# 5.  SHAKESPEARE'S POLITICS: WITH SOME REFLECTIONS ON THE NATURE OF TRADITION

## By L. C. Knights

As my rather cumbersome title indicates, this lecture is an attempt to bring together two interests—an interest in the nature of Shakespeare's political wisdom, and an interest in the nature of tradition. Shakespeare, as is proper, will get most of the attention, but I should like to begin by indicating the wider concern. There is no need to emphasize the importance for us in these days of an understanding of the nature of a living tradition. It is something which literary studies and studies in the background of literature should foster. But there are two dangers that—it seems to me—are insufficiently guarded against. There is the danger of allowing the 'background' metaphor to dominate our thinking. We need to think in terms of promptings and incitements to decent living and clear thought, rather than in terms of assumptions that are merely accepted and taken for granted, which is what 'background' tends to suggest. The second danger is inherent in the increased availability of information about a past age. One result of the accumulation of 'background' studies—even of necessary and valuable studies —is to suggest that what was peculiar to an age, what can only now be recovered by thinking our way into past systems of thought, is what we most need to know if we are to enter fully into the imaginative achievements of that age. Certainly we need, at times and according to our capacities, to make ourselves into Elizabethans, and to think in terms like those that Dr Tillyard, for example, has made generally available in *The Elizabethan World Picture*. But I sometimes suspect that in concentrating on what was peculiar to the age, on categories of thought that can only be reconstructed by an effort of the historical imagination, we are in danger of losing sight of something even more important. May it not be that what was most nourishing of creative achievement in the past was what, in the tradition of the time, is—or should be—most available for us now? It is towards some under-standing of one aspect of tradition in the sixteenth century— the promptings, namely, that lie behind Shakespeare's indi-vidual approach to political issues—that this inquiry is directed. I use the word 'directed' deliberately: neither the time at my disposal nor my own severely limited equipment will allow me to do much more than to lead up to the questions that I should like to see answered.

I

When we speak of Shakespeare's politics there are possibilities of misunderstanding to guard against. 'Policy', 'politic', and 'politician' are words that occur in Shakespeare, sometimes with a pejorative implication—'a scurvy politician', 'base and rotten policy'—that might tempt us to suppose a context like that of the modern political platform. The supposition would of course be wrong. 'Politics' (which Shakespeare does not use) only acquired its most frequent modern meaning— 'political affairs', 'political principles or opinions'—much later, with the rise of the parties. If you had said to Shakespeare, 'Do you take any part in politics?' or 'What are your politics?' he would probably have been puzzled. 'Politics' still implied systematic thought on the constitution of states and the art of government—a matter for philo-sophers: our 'politics', the conduct of internal affairs of state, together with the observation of 'who's in, who's out', and plans to reverse that order—these were matters for the men who did the work, of constant interest only to them, to those with special interests to press, and to a fringe of Polictic Would-be's. Shakespeare, like the great majority of his fellow countrymen, 'had no politics': he had too many other things to think about. The fact remains, however, that although he made no arbitrary separation between what is politics and what is not (and this, to anticipate, is a notable aspect of his political wisdom), he showed throughout his career a lively concern with men not only in their private and personal, but in their public and formal, relations. And this concern included questions of power and subordination, of mutual relations within a constituted society, of the ends and methods of public action, so that we may properly speak of Shakespeare's political philosophy—so long, that is, as we remember that this philosophy is not something ready formed once for all, and applied or exhibited in varying circumstances, but a part of that constant search for meanings that informs his work as a whole.

A recent writer on the history of political thought has called Shakespeare 'a superb interpreter of group psychology and an almost unrivalled observer of political behaviour'.[1] I doubt whether these phrases quite do justice to Shakespeare's political wisdom. They do, however, call attention to one element in it, namely its realism. Shakespeare's political realism is not of course Machiavellian or modern realism ('How realistic is the realist?' is a question that the plays force us to ask), but it is certainly based on a clear perception of the actualities of political situations. Consider for example the implicit comment made by the play *Richard II* on the wishful thinking of a king for whom words and dramatic postures take the place of action; the explicit comments of the Bastard on 'commodity' in *King John*, and the place his comments have within the larger political action; or the sombre demonstration in *King Henry IV* of what is involved in getting and keeping power: the recognition of inevitable consequences by the dying Bolingbroke

> —For all my reign hath been but as a scene
> Acting that argument—

(IV. v. 198–9)

enforces the same political moral as Marvell's Horatian Ode

> —The same Arts that did gain
> A Power must it maintain—

(lines 119–20)

and enforces it with a similar effort of irony. But Shakespeare's

---

[1] Christopher Morris, *Political Thought in England: Tyndale to Hooker* (London, 1953), p. 103.

realism goes further than this; fundamentally it is a refusal to allow the abstract and general to obscure the personal and specific. After the earliest plays on English history Shakespeare's political plays are not shaped by a predetermined pattern of ideas: like the rest of his work they are the result of a full exposure to experience. If they unavoidably raise moral issues it is because of the felt pressure of life itself.[2] If they clarify for us Clarendon's phrase about 'that fathomless abyss of Reason of State', it is because they insist on setting every 'political' action in the widest possible human context and so—implicitly, if not always explicitly—assessing it in relation to that context. It is of especial significance that the political action of *Henry IV* has for setting scenes in which the actions of great ones take on a quite different appearance, in which the assumptions of the dominant groups are by no means taken for granted, and which therefore act as a challenge to those assumptions.

In the two political plays that follow *Henry IV*, in *Henry V* and *Julius Caesar*, Shakespeare continues the questioning of what statesmen are likely to accept without question. It is one of the curiosities of literature that *Henry V* should have been seen so often as a simple glorification of the hero-king. I am not suggesting that we should merely reverse the conventional estimate. It is simply that, on the evidence of the play itself, Shakespeare's attitude towards the King is complex and critical. As M. Fluchère has said, 'While making the necessary concessions to patriotic feeling . . . Shakespeare lets us see . . . that the political problem, linked with the moral problem, is far from being solved by a victorious campaign and a marriage with happy consequences for the country.'[3] In other words, the political problem, purely at the level of politics and the political man, is insoluble. In *Julius Caesar*, freed from the embarrassments of a patriotic theme, and with the problem projected into a 'Roman' setting, Shakespeare examines more

[2] I have in mind the passage in Henry James's Preface to *The Portrait of a Lady*, where he speaks of 'the perfect dependence of the "moral" sense of a work of art on the amount of felt life concerned in producing it'.

[3] Henri Fluchère, *Shakespeare* (London, 1953), p. 204. I also agree with Mr D. A. Traversi that the effect of the play is 'to bring out certain contradictions, human and moral, which seem to be inherent in the notion of a successful king'. 'Henry the Fifth', *Scrutiny*, ix. 4 (1940–1), p. 363.

closely the contradictions and illusions involved in political action. The matter cannot be properly argued here, but it seems to me undeniable that the play offers a deliberate contrast between the person and the public persona, the face and the mask; that tragic illusion and error are shown to spring from the wrenching apart of the two worlds—the personal and the public; and that Brutus, in particular, is a study in what Coleridge was to describe as the politics of pure—or abstract—reason, with the resulting sophistries and inevitable disappointments.[4]

I hope that even from so cursory a survey of some of the plays preceding the great tragedies one point has become clear: that even in plays where the political interest is most evident, it is never exclusive or, as it were, self-contained. The implied question, What does this political action or attitude mean? is invariably reduced to personal terms: How does this affect relations between men? What kind of man acts in this way? How does he further make himself by so acting? Swift says of the party man, 'when he is got near the walls of his assembly he assumes and affects an entire set of very different airs; he conceives himself a being of a superior nature to those without, and acting in a sphere, where the vulgar methods for the conduct of human life can be of no use.'[5] It is Shakespeare's distinction that, when dealing with rulers and matters of state, he constantly brings us back to 'the vulgar methods for the conduct of human life', that he refuses to accept a closed realm of the political. Indeed, it is only by a deliberate focusing of our interest for a particular purpose that we can separate 'political' from 'non-political' plays, the two kinds being in fact linked by common themes and preoccupations. Thus in the Second Part of *Henry IV* Shakespeare's interests are plainly setting away from his ostensible subject towards a more fundamental exploration of the human condition that points towards the great tragedies;

---

[4] See *The Friend*, First Section, 'On the Principles of Political Knowledge'. I have dealt more fully with *Julius Caesar* in an article on 'Shakespeare and Political Wisdom', *Sewanee Review*, lxi. 1. (1953)

[5] Swift is speaking of 'those, who in a late reign began the distinction between the personal and politick capacity'. *A Discourse of the Contests ... between the Nobles and the Commons in Athens and Rome* (1701), chap. v.

and *Julius Caesar* shares with later, non-political plays, a preoccupation with the ways in which men give themselves to illusion. So too, from *Julius Caesar* onwards, it is possible to trace Shakespeare's political themes only in plays that, with the exception of *Coriolanus*, are not primarily political plays.

*Troilus and Cressida, King Lear, Macbeth*—each of these, in one of its aspects, takes the political theme a stage further. *Troilus and Cressida* makes a simple but far-reaching discovery: it is that the sixteenth-century commonplace of the necessity for order and degree might mean much or little according as the reason that formulated it was, or was not, grounded in the responsiveness to life of the whole person. I refer especially to what might be called the dramatic status of Ulysses' well-known speech on 'degree'. In the context of the whole play—the clash of varied attitudes to life which forces us to a judgement—this speech appears as something other than the expression of an unquestioned standard: for the significant thing is that it is spoken by Ulysses, and Ulysses is the chief exponent of a reason and policy that do not, any more than Troilus' emotionalism, commend themselves to us. To put it simply, just as emotion, divorced from reason, is reduced to appetite ('And the will dotes that is inclinable / To what infectiously itself affects . . . '), so reason, divorced from intuition, is reduced to cleverness: statecraft, for Ulysses, is the manipulation of men. Political order and authority—so the play as a whole forces us to conclude—are not concepts to be accepted without question, independent of some prior ground from which they draw their justification.

That ground is explored in *King Lear*; it is taken for granted in *Macbeth* and *Coriolanus*. What I mean is this. *King Lear* is not a political play; it is a play about the conditions of being human, and it seeks to answer the great question put by Lear as Everyman, 'Who is it that can tell me who I am?' But at the same time it has marked political implications. A play in which 'the king *is* but as the beggar' was bound to raise the social question, and to do rather more than hint that 'distribution should undo excess'. It was almost bound to raise the question of justice: why should the half-witted vagrant be whipped from tithing to tithing, or the farmer's dog be an image of authority? But the political implications go further than that. In a lecture on 'the Politics of *King Lear*' Mr Edwin Muir has suggested that Goneril, Regan, and Edmund have in common a way of seeing people which lacks a dimension. For Edmund, as A. C. Bradley had remarked, men and women are 'divested of all quality except their relation to [his] end; as indifferent as mathematical quantities or mere physical agents'. So too, says Mr Muir, Goneril and Regan 'exist in this shallow present'; without memory, they are without responsibility, and their speech 'consists of a sequence of pitiless truisms . . . . Their shallowness is ultimately that of the Machiavellian view of life as it was understood in [Shakespeare's] age, of "policy" . . . . We need not shrink from regarding Edmund and his confederates as political types.'[6] This, if we do not push it too far, suggests one of the ways in which the group opposed to Lear may properly be regarded. And the converse also holds. *King Lear* establishes the grounds of any politics that claim to be more than a grammar of power. Behind hierarchy and authority, behind formal justice and public order, is a community of persons bound by 'holy cords . . . . Which are too intrinse t'unloose.' The basic political facts of this play are that men can feel for each other, and that this directness of relationship —expressing itself in the humblest of ways as well as in the most exalted forms of loyalty and sacrifice—is the only alternative to a predatory power-seeking whose necessary end is anarchy. Ulysses, it will be remembered, had foretold how chaos would follow the 'choking' of degree:

> Then everything includes itself in power,
> Power into will, will into appetite;
> And appetite, an universal wolf,
> So doubly seconded with will and power,
> Must make perforce an universal prey,
> And last eat up himself.

> (I. iii. 119–24)

In *King Lear*, Albany, envisaging the same state of chaos, significantly shifts the argument:

[6] E. Muir, 'The Politics of *King Lear*', *Essays in Literature and Society* (London, 1949), pp. 39–42. See also J. F. Danby's *Shakespeare's Doctrine of Nature: a Study of 'King Lear'* (London, 1949), especially, in this connection, p. 38.

That nature, which contemns its origin,
Cannot be border'd certain in itself;
She that herself will sliver and disbranch
From her material sap, perforce must wither
And come to deadly use . . .
If that the heavens do not their visible spirits
Send quickly down to tame these vile offences,
It will come,
Humanity must perforce prey on itself,
Like monsters of the deep.

(IV. ii. 32–50)

We hardly need to put each passage back in its context to see
that the later one draws on a far deeper sense of what it is that
sanctions the human order.[7] Lear's discovery of his kinship
with the naked poor is both a moral and a political discovery:
it is a king who says, 'O! I have ta'en too little care of this.'

That is what I meant by saying that *Macbeth* takes for
granted the ground established in *King Lear*. Evil in *Macbeth*
is more than tyranny; but tyranny is part of the evil, and it is
defined in terms of a violation of those bonds—the 'holy
cords'—that are essential to the being of man as man. We
cannot fail to be affected by the varied images of concord, of
mutual service and relationship, through which we are made
aware that behind the disintegration and dissolution of
Macbeth's state—of his 'single state of man' and of the state at
large—are contrasting possibilities of order. And it seems to
me that the conception of order—as we are given it, in the
play—draws on a different dimension of experience from that
envisaged in the 'degree' speech of Ulysses. In *Macbeth*
institutional life—all that is indicated and symbolized by
churches, castles, 'humane statute'—guards and guarantees a
living system of relationships ('honour, love, obedience . . . '),
which in turn are related to more than human sanctions. Thus

---

[7] In *The Allegory of Love* (Oxford, 1936) (p. 110) C. S. Lewis translates some lines
from the Latin *Architrenius* of Johannes de Altavilla which curiously sum up the
central movement of *King Lear*, including its political meaning:

This must I do—go exil'd through the world
And seek for Nature till far hence I find
Her secret dwelling-place; there drag to light
The hidden cause of quarrel, and reknit,
Haply reknit, the long-divided Love.

the evocation of the temple-haunting martlets, of the birds that securely build and breed, is an image of life delighting in life, and it subtly and powerfully contributes to our sense of the ideal presence of a life-bearing order in the human commonwealth—in what the play calls 'the gentle weal'.[8]

In *Coriolanus*, which is the last of the great tragedies and also the last overtly political play, Shakespeare takes up again from the earlier 'histories' the theme of the Governor. Those earlier plays were largely, though not exclusively, studies of rulers who failed because they were isolated within an arbitrary conception of power or privilege: and I think one could deduce from them that Shakespeare saw the good ruler as not merely set over the people whom he ruled (though rule is necessary), but linked with, and in some sense expressive of, the society for whose sake he performs his office.[9] In *Coriolanus* the main subject is the relation between a member of the ruling class, a Governor, and the political society to which he belongs; and the handling of it results in a breaking-down of any over-simple distinction we might be tempted to make between what is 'individual', on the one hand, and what is 'social' and 'political' on the other. It is clear that if individual qualities are partly the result of social pressure (behind Coriolanus is Volumnia, and behind Volumnia is the patrician class), the political crisis is, to say the least, exacerbated by the personal disorders that play into it. The isolation and over-development of one quality in the hero is not only analogous to the failure of connection and integration in the social group ('Rome and her rats'), the one is shown as having a direct bearing on the other. The play thus draws on the same established affirmations as *Macbeth*: the state is not simply an embodiment of power, it is society in its political or

---

[8] These values are of course positively present to our minds and imaginations even in the explicit denial of them by the protagonists —in Macbeth's great invocation of chaos in IV. i, for example.

[9] In the simple moralizing of the gardeners' scene in *Richard II* (III. iv) the King's function is explicitly to 'trim and dress' his land, 'as we this garden': that is, not to impose his mere will, but to foster what is given in accordance with the laws of its nature. We may compare Burgundy's speech in *Henry V*, v. ii. In *Measure for Measure* Escalus, unlike Angelo—and this helps to define the Deputy—has a side of himself open to the rather foolish Elbow: Angelo talks about abstract justice; Escalus patiently sifts the evidence in an apparently unimportant case.

public aspect; and society is a mutual relation of persons who, by and large, need each other if they are to come to anything like maturity. What the play emphasizes is the challenge of difference and diversity. There is no suggestion that the social distinctions between patricians and plebeians ought not to exist: it *is* suggested that the diversified social group, the body politic, is in danger of corruption to the extent that *what lies behind diversity* is lost sight of. 'What lies behind' is of course simple humanity. It is Coriolanus' defective humanity that makes him a defective governor.[10]

If I have spoken as though these plays offered us a simple political moral or message, my excuse must be that the necessary qualifications are sufficently obvious. Indeed it might be claimed that my simplifications have all been in the interest of a recognition of complexity. Shakespeare's political thought, I have insisted, is not a body of abstract principles to be applied and illustrated. It is part of a continuous exploration and assessment of experience: it grows and develops. And in any one play it is part of a complex organization whose very nature it is, as work of art, to challenge each individual reader to become imaginatively alive: the political meanings are only *there* to the extent that we do so respond. So long as we keep this clearly in mind, simplification may have its uses. What I most want to suggest, then, is that Shakespeare's political meanings—the things he tells us about politics—are inherent in and inseparable from his method, his way of presenting his political material. Aware as he is of the need for mutual relationships within society, he does not merely preach this: rather he explores—with a maximum of concreteness and immediacy—the nature of mutuality and its opposite. Thus the distrust that he shows, from first to last, for individualism —for the attitude expressed in Richard of Gloucester's 'I am myself alone'—is based on a sure grasp of the self-mutilation inherent in egotism and isolation, of the inevitable denaturing effect of an attitude that wilfully blinds itself to the fact that

[10] For a fuller exposition I must again refer to my article, 'Shakespeare's Political Wisdom', *Sewanee Review*, lxi. 1 (1953). In a valuable article on '*Coriolanus*, Aristotle and Bacon', *Review of English Studies*, NS i. 2 (1950), Mr F. N. Lees applies to the play Aristotle's remark in the *Politics* (1. ii. 14): 'He that is incapable of living in a society is a god or a beast.'

personal life only has its being in relationship: Macbeth as tyrant inevitably 'keeps alone',[11] The converse of this is the pervasive sense that we find in the plays that the foundations of political organization are in the realm 'beyond politics', in those varied relationships that are the necessary condition of individual growth: it is only a Caliban (and Caliban drunk at that) who can wish for an untrammelled 'freedom'.[12] What we may call the idea of the state in Shakespeare is thus fundamentally opposed to the Renaissance conception of the state as a work of art.[13] Nor can it be adequately expressed by the conventional analogy of the bees,

> Creatures that by a rule in nature teach
> The act of order to a peopled kingdom.

> (I. i. 188–9)

Shakespeare probed further and more subtly than the political Archbishop of *Henry V*. What he went on to ask—what, I think, he was already asking when he wrote *Henry V*—was, what are the foundations of a living order? Both *Macbeth* and *Coriolanus* confirm the maxims,

> If a man have not order within him
> He can not spread order about him . . .
>   And if the prince have not order within him
> He can not put order in his dominions:

the disordered man makes for disorder, not only in his more immediate circle but his wider social relations.[14] And the contrasting positive values? Shakespeare does not sum things up for us, but I think that a few sentences from Boethius' *De Consolatione Philosophiae* (in the English of Chaucer) come

[11] Shakespeare's egotists—Richard of Gloucester, Don John, Iago—all use a manner of speech that expresses a defensive hostility—the opposite of 'a free and open nature'—and that suggests a hard immaturity as well as will. Grace Stuart's *Narcissus: a Psychological Study of Self-Love*, dealing with the ways in which self-hatred disguises as self-love, has some apt illustrations from Shakespeare, whose moral realism is of course inseparable from psychological insight.

[12] My sense of the political implications of Caliban's 'Freedom, hey-day! hey-day, freedom!' (*The Tempest*, II. ii) is confirmed by Professor Peter Alexander: see his *Shakespeare's Life and Art* (London, 1939), pp. 214–15.

[13] See Burckhardt, *The Civilization of the Renaissance* (Oxford, 1945), Part I, 'The State as a Work of Art'.

[14] Ezra Pound (Canto XIII) puts these words into the mouth of a Chinese sage. The

close to the spirit of his political philosophy: ' . . . al this
accordaunce of thynges is bounde with love, that governeth
erthe and see, and hath also commandement to the hevene. . . .
This love halt togidres peples joyned with an holy boond, . . .
and love enditeth lawes to trewe felawes.'[15] The love that is in
question is not of course simply a matter of feeling; it includes
a neighbourly tolerance of differences and a sense of mutual
need; and in its openness to life, its willingness to *listen*, it is
allied to that justice which gives each man his due, looking
towards what he is, or can become; and there is delight
superadded.[16] Shakespeare's abundance, his feeling for
uniqueness and variety, his imaginative grasp of what makes
for life—these qualities ensure that when political issues are
handled in the plays we sense behind them a concern for the
'trewe felawes' (Boethius' *sodales*), for the living body politic
in all its variety. We are inevitably prompted to a clearer
recognition of the fact that a wholesome political order is not
something arbitrary and imposed, but an expression of
relationships between particular persons within an organic
society. The 'concord' that Shakespeare invokes as the
alternative to both tyranny and anarchy in *Macbeth*[17] has this
depth of meaning behind it.

II

In this last part of my lecture I want to look beyond
Shakespeare and to ask some questions. None of Shakespeare's
greater plays can be adequately 'explained' by anything
outside itself; each is its unique self, with its own virtually

idea, I suppose, is common in Western philosophy; my point is that Shakespeare
does not merely invoke the idea, valuable as it is, he makes vividly present the kind of
actuality from which the idea springs. Professor D. W. Harding, writing on the
psychological aspects of war in *The Impulse to Dominate* (London 1941), has
reminded us that a mass phenomenon like war is not something that simply *happens*
to a community, that in the last analysis it is rooted in individual habits that make
part of the texture of normal 'peaceful' existence.

[15] Book II, Metrum 8.

[16] Paul Tillich's *Love, Power and Justice* (London, 1954), describing the intrinsic
and necessary relation between these three concepts, will be found to clarify the
meaning of love in social—as well as in directly personal—relations. On listening as
a function of creative justice see especially pp. 84–85.

[17] *Macbeth*, IV. iii. 97–100.

inexhaustible depth of meaning—'so ramm'd with life / It can but gather strength of life with being'. But no work of art, above all no major work, is entirely original: promptings and insights from the past have helped to make it, so that to apprehend it is in some measure to apprehend them. Shakespeare, undoubtedly, was receptive to what his age had to offer, and we have had valuable studies showing his awareness of the current modes of political thinking.[18] But Shakespeare's politics cannot be defined simply in terms of the Tudor view of history and the commonplaces of order and degree. When he enquired most deeply into the nature of political life what incitements were offered him to the affirmation, or reaffirmation, of positives transcending the political?

I am not a medievalist, but even a slight acquaintance with earlier literature suggests that the characteristics of Shakespeare's political wisdom, which I have tried to define, had some correspondence with older forms of thinking about politics and social life.[19] There was, for example, the medieval habit of discussing politics in terms not of masses but of men, and of men not only in one specialized aspect but in relation to all their needs, spiritual as well as material, as human beings. Thus R. W. and A. J. Carlyle, writing of political theory in the thirteenth century, speak of the general conviction that 'the end and purpose of the state is a moral one—that is, the maintenance of justice, or, in the terms derived from Aristotle, the setting forward of the life according to virtue, and that the authority of the state is limited by its end—that is, by justice'.[20] Similar considerations

---

[18] For example, Alfred Hart's pioneering *Shakespeare and the Homilies* (Melbourne, 1934) and E. M. W. Tillyard's *Shakespeare's History Plays* (London, 1944).

[19] Professor F. P. Wilson says of Shakespeare, 'The evidence suggests that when a theme took possession of his mind, especially a theme with a long tradition behind it, he read widely—not laboriously, but with a darting intelligence, which quickened his invention . . . . Somehow, like all thinking men in his day, he acquainted himself with that vast body of reflection upon the nature of man and man's place in society and in the universe which his age inherited in great part from the ancient and medieval worlds' ('Shakespeare's Reading', in *Shakespeare Survey*, iii (1950), 18, 20). Professor Wilson well suggests the innumerable ways in which any one aspect of 'the tradition' might reach Shakespeare. Cf. also M. D. H. Parker, *The Slave of Life: a Study of Shakespeare and the Idea of Justice* (London, 1955), p. 196.

[20] R. W. Carlyle and A. J. Carlyle, *A History of Medieval Political Thought in the*

of course lie behind the medieval formulations of economic ethics, as Professor Tawney and others have shown. This I suppose is sufficiently well known. What I should like to add is that if medieval political thought is ethical through and through, what is in question is not the legalistic application of a formula but the bringing to bear of spiritual penetration and moral insight. If Dante in the *De Monarchia* is medieval in his use—and abuse—of formal logic, he is also, I suppose, representative when he insists on the necessary connection between love and justice:

Just as greed, though it be never so little, clouds to some extent the disposition of justice, so does charity or right love sharpen and brighten it . . . Greed, scorning the intrinsic significance of man, seeks other things; but charity, scorning all other things, seeks God and man, and consequently the good of man. And since, amongst the other blessings of man, living in peace is the chief . . . and justice is the chiefest and mightiest accomplisher of this, therefore charity will chiefly give vigour to justice; and the stronger she is, the more.[21]

Similarly St Thomas Aquinas, discussing the advantages of just rule and the basic weakness of tyranny, remarks, 'there is nothing on this earth to be preferred before true friendship'; but 'fear makes a weak foundation'.[22] The significance of such comments is that although they are in the highest degree relevant and acute, they spring from an insight that is spiritual, moral, and psychological rather than political in any limited sense.

It is the same with the medieval conception of the nature and purpose of the state. For Aquinas man is by nature a social and political animal, destined therefore to live in a

*West* (Edinburgh, 1903–36), vol. v, *The Political Theory of the Thirteenth Century*, p. 35.

[21] *De Monarchia*, Book I, Chap. 11, Temple Classics edn., p. 153. A similar passage is the opening of Book I. Chap. 13, where Dante shows 'that he who would dispose others best must himself be best disposed'—which is Duke Vincentio's

> He who the sword of heaven will bear
> Should be as holy as severe;
> Pattern in himself to know . . .
>
> (*Measure for Measure*, III. ii)

[22] Aquinas, *Selected Political Writings*, translated by J. G. Dawson, edited by A. P. d'Entrèves (Oxford, 1948), pp. 55, 59. The whole passage is relevant to *Macbeth* in its political aspect.

society which supplies his needs in far more than a merely material sense. Life in a community, he says, 'enables man to achieve a plentitude of life; not merely to exist, but to live fully, with all that is necessary to well-being.'[23] This way of thinking not only reminds us of the social character of politics, it helps to bring out the implications of the great traditional metaphor (which has behind it both Plato and the New Testament) of the body politic: the implication, above all, of co-operation and mutuality not as a vague ideal of universal benevolence but as the necessary condition, intimately felt, of individual development in its diversity. I think that John of Salisbury, in whose *Policraticus* (1159) the organic conception of the state is prominent,[24] gives life to the metaphor, reveals its sharp immediacy, when he tells how Philip of Macedon, advised to beware of a certain man, replied, 'What, if a part of my body were sick, would I cut it off rather than seek to heal it?'—or when, speaking of the prince's reluctance to adminster even necessary punishment, he asks, 'Who was ever strong enough to amputate the members of his own body without grief and pain?'[25] The temptation for the modern reader is to regard the metaphor simply as a rhetorical or conventional flourish. Taken in its context it does not seem to be so, but rather to spring from a perception of the foundations of political and social life in 'the real spirit of helpfulness'.[26]

Then and then only will the health of the commonwealth be sound and flourishing when the higher members shield the lower, and the lower respond faithfully and fully in like measure to the just demands of their superiors, so that each and all are as it were members one of another by a sort of reciprocity, and each regards

[23] *Selected Political Writings*, p. 191. On Aquinas' conception of the State as 'the highest expression of human fellowship' see Professor d'Entrèves's Introduction, p. xv.
[24] *The Statesman's Book of John Salisbury* (selections from the *Policraticus*), translated with an Introduction by John Dickinson (Political Science Classics Series, (New York, 1927). The editor speaks of 'the absence of any clear distinction in John's thought between the social and the political; abuse of public power is conceived simply in terms of a breach of personal morality' (p. lxvii).
[25] *The Statesman's Book*, pp. 37–8. 'It was [Trajan's] habit to say that a man is insane who, having inflamed eyes, prefers to dig them out rather than cure them' (p. 39).
[26] *The Statesman's Book*, p. 95.

his own interest as best served by that which he knows to be most advantageous for the others.[27]

The social and moral bias of medieval political thought also appears in the conception of the nature and duties of the ruler, who is ideally concerned not with his own power, nor simply with the power of the state, but with the common good: 'for albeit the consul or king be masters of the rest as regards the way, yet as regards the end they are their servants'.[28]

These are random examples, I know, but it does seem that Shakespeare, in his thinking about politics, is closer to John of Salisbury than he is, say, to Hobbes: closer not only when he speaks explicitly of 'the king-becoming graces' in the great traditional terms,

> As Justice, Verity, Temp'rance, Stableness,
> Bounty, Perseverance, Mercy, Lowliness,
> Devotion, Patience, Courage, Fortitude,
>
> (*Macbeth*, iv. iii. 92–4)

but also in his whole conception of a political society as a network of personal relationships, and of the health or disease of that society as ultimately dependent on the quality and nature of those relationships. If this is so, one question is how the great commonplaces of medieval political and social thinking were kept alive into the sixteenth century. By the great commonplaces I do not only refer to explicit political formulations. From the principles deriving from Greek, Roman, and Christian sources diverse political theories could be drawn; and although some of the explicit theories such as that of the ruler's responsibility to God and to his people were still alive in the sixteenth century,[29] there were also,

---

[27] Ibid., p. 244. In *English Literature in the Sixteenth Century* (Oxford, 1954), p. 36, C. S. Lewis gives an interesting summary of an aspect of Calvin's social thought which has a similar revealing power: 'a Christian must not give "as though he would bind his brother unto him by the benefit". When I use my hands to heal some other part of my body I lay the body under no obligation to the hands: and since we are all members of one another, we similarly lay no obligation on the poor when we relieve them.'

[28] Dante, *De Monarchia* (Temple Classics), i. 12, p. 159.

[29] On the general question of the continuity of political thought see A. P. d'Entrèves, *The Medieval Contribution to Political Thought* (Oxford, 1939); J. W. Allen, *A History of Political Thought in the Sixteenth Century* (London, 1828), Part

with the changing circumstances of the age, major shifts of emphasis and direction. I refer also, and perhaps above all, to a manner of approach, and to a cast of mind. Mr Christopher Morris says of Tudor Englishmen that they did not find it easy to think of politics except in terms of persons: they 'were still medieval enough to persist in discussing political matters in what to us are not political terms'.[30] So that our enquiry would not only take the form of an investigation into the number of times that medieval formulations reappear in political tracts and the like. It would be less concerned, for example, with the elaboration of correspondences between the individual and the state than with habits of mind implying a direct perception of mutual need, of what Hooker called 'a natural delight which man hath to transfuse from himself into others, and to receive from others into himself especially those things wherein the excellency of his kind doth most consist',[31] it would be concerned with those habits of mind without which the commonplaces remain lifeless. The great metaphors ('the body politic'), the great moral sentences ('Without justice, what are states but great bands of robbers?') not only provoke thought; for their fullest efficacy at any time they demand a habit of active apprehension. An important part of our enquiry, then, would be into the tradition of vividness and particularity in the handling of social and political questions: a tradition of which the tendency was to transform the political into the social, and the social into the religious—the tradition (shall we say?) of *Piers Plowman*.[32]

Of the habits helping to constitute the tradition something, clearly, was due to the characteristic features of communities

---

II, Chap. III ('A Very and True Commonweal'); and Christopher Morris, *Political Thought in England: Tyndale to Hooker.*

[30] *Political Thought in England*, pp. 1–2.

[31] *Of the Laws of Ecclesiastical Polity* (Everyman edition, London, 1907), I. x. 12

[32] Of that poem it can be said, as Coleridge said of religion in *The Statesman's Manual*, that it acts 'by contraction of universal truths into individual duties, as the only form in which those truths can attain life and reality'. It would be interesting to know who bought and read *Piers Plowman* in the various editions put out by Robert Crowley in 1550—'the sense', it was thought, 'somewhat dark, but not so hard, but that it may be understood of such as will not stick to break the shell of the nut for the kernel's sake'. There were three impressions in 1550; a further edition appeared in 1561. See Skeat's edition of the poem (Oxford, 1886), vol. ii. pp. lxxii–lxxvi.

not yet large enough to obscure direct dealing between men with impersonal forms.[33] But social life alone did not make the tradition: it was made by proverbs and preachings, by ballads and plays, by words read and listened to; in Elizabethan England it was largely made by the Bible.

Shakespeare's contemporary, Richard Hooker—who is also, like Shakespeare, a great representative figure—may help to direct our thoughts. In Hooker, so far as I am acquainted with him, there is not only the familar 'medieval' insistence on the subordination of politics to ethics and religion; not only the sense that civilization, 'a life fit for the dignity of man',[34] is based on 'the good of mutual participation'[35] (and co-operation is with the dead as well as among the living): there is a deposition of mind that springs from and fosters a lively responsiveness to the actual. Hooker's sense of history, for which he is so rightly admired, is a sense of being in a concrete situation: it is allied with and encourages an unruffled acceptance of complexity,[36] and his work is a permanent antidote to the doctrinaire, simplifying mind —puritan or other. Yet the insistence on change, on the element of convention in human undertakings, is balanced by a firmness of principle that springs from an assurance of the continuity of the great affirmations. Hooker's attitude to the Bible is of interest not only to theologians and students of church history. Completely free from what Professor d'Entrèves calls 'the narrow and intolerant scripturalism of the puritans',[37] Hooker's appeal to the Bible is that of a free and reasonable mind for which the Bible has a special authority. And the relevance of this fact to our enquiry into

[33] See my lecture 'Poetry, Politics and the English Tradition', in *Further Explorations*, (London 1965).
[34] *Of the Laws of Ecclesiastical Polity* (Everyman edition), i. x. i.
[35] 'Civil society doth more content the nature of man than any private kind of solitary living, because in society this good of mutual participation is so much larger than otherwise. Herewith notwithstanding we are not satisfied, but we covet (if it might be) to have a kind of society and fellowship even with all mankind' (i. x. 12).
[36] 'The bounds of wisdom are large, and within them much is contained . . . . We may not so in any one special kind admire her, that we disgrace her in any other; but let all her ways be according unto their place and degree adored' (ii. i. 4). As Hooker says elsewhere, 'Carry peaceable minds and ye may have comfort by this variety', 'A Learned Discourse of Justification', op. cit., vol. i. p. 75.
[37] *The Medieval Contribution to Political Thought*, p. 104.

the more-than-political tradition becomes clear when we recall *The Statesman's Manual* of Coleridge. The Bible, he said, was 'the best guide to political skill and foresight' because its events and prescriptions demand a response of the whole man, because they embody universal principles in the sharply particular. 'In nothing', he said, 'is Scriptural history more strongly contrasted with the histories of highest note in the present age, than in its freedom from the hollowness of abstractions': its symbolic actuality ('incorporating the reason in images of the sense') offers the strongest possible contrast to histories and political theories produced by the 'unenlivened generalizing understanding'.[38] Remembering this, we may perhaps understand why 'the strange immediacy of scriptural history'[39] in the age of Shakespeare had a very decided bearing on the way in which the best minds sought to understand political situations.

What bearing this, and the other matters I have touched on, had on the practice of the age would be a separate study. When we think in turn of the adult political wisdom of Shakespeare and the tradition informing that wisdom, then of certain aspects of Elizabethan–Jacobean political life, its greed, faction and unscrupulousness,[40] inevitably a question confronts us. A cynical answer would be out of place. The passion of Dante does not prove that he came from a just city: rather, as we know, the reverse. Yet how much it meant that Italy in the thirteenth century, even in the conditions we know, should produce a Dante! Mr T. S. Eliot, borrowing the term from Canon Demant, speaks of 'the *pre-political* area', where the imaginative writer exercises his true political function. 'And my defence of the importance of the *pre-political*', he says, 'is simply this, that it is the stratum down to which any sound political thinking must push its roots, and from which it must derive its nourishment.'[41] That in the

---

[38] See *The Statesman's Manual*, in *Political Tracts of Wordsworth, Coleridge and Shelley*, ed. R. J. White (Cambridge, 1953), pp. 18, 24, 28 and *passim*. Mr White's Introduction gives a valuable account of this aspect of Coleridge's thought.

[39] David Mathew, *The Jacobean Age* (London, 1938), p. 14. 'The biblical characters were very close and they overshadowed the chronicles and the heraldry' (p. 15).

[40] See, for example, the closing pages of Professor J. E. Neale's Raleigh Lecture for 1948, 'The Elizabethan Political Scene', *Proc. Brit. Acad.* xxxiv (1948), 97–117.

[41] *The Literature of Politics* (Conservative Political Centre), p. 22.

imperfect conditions of Elizabethan–Jacobean England something was kept alive in the pre-political area that was of the greatest importance for the health of a political society, Shakespeare's plays (and not these alone) are the living witness. When we try to define what it was that was kept alive we find ourselves with a renewed sense of the meaning and nature of a tradition whose significance for us today should need no arguing. Towards the end of the Third Satire Donne says,

> That thou mayest rightly obey power, her bounds know;
> Those past, her nature, and name is chang'd; to be
> Then humble to her is idolatry.

Shakespeare's political plays are creative explorations of conceptions such as power, authority, honour, order, and freedom, which only too easily become objects of 'idolatry'. Their real meaning is only revealed when political life is seen, as Shakespeare makes us see it, in terms of the realities of human life and human relationships. As Aristotle said long ago, 'Clearly the student of politics must know somehow the facts about soul.'[42]

---

[42] *Ethics* (translated by W. D. Ross), I xiii.

# 6.  PERSON AND OFFICE IN SHAKESPEARE'S PLAYS

## By Philip Edwards

We accept as an important part of Shakespeare's strength that he was not prepared to show man isolated in a conflict with himself or his family or with God, nor on the other hand to show him as exclusively a public or political being. He showed all the circles of man's life, communion with self, domestic life, and public career, and he showed them interlocking and interacting, each influencing and being influenced by the other. This is true not only of a play like *Antony and Cleopatra*, in which Antony's love-life and his political power are interdependent, but also of *Romeo and Juliet*; not only of *Troilus and Cressida* but also of *Measure for Measure*. Some comedies, like *The Tempest* and *As You Like It*, are strongly political, but even in those which aren't, it is not often one feels that the omnipresent Duke might just as well have been a horse-dealer, or a sculptor with independent means.

We imagine that Shakespeare thought of men in the same deep focus he presented them in, and not many people would agree with John Palmer's introduction to his *Political Characters of Shakespeare* (London, 1945), where he argued that Shakespeare found himself 'willy-nilly' writing political plays because the audience insisted on princes and generals, that he had 'small interest' in politics, and that it is 'a strange paradox that Shakespeare who, above all other dramatists, was preoccupied with the private mind and heart of the individual, should have written a group of plays unmatched in any literature for their political content' (pp. vi, viii).

Shakespeare belonged to the great tradition of Elizabethan and Jacobean political drama, a drama which, possibly more than any other, gives us a conviction of the unity of the world as it weaves all levels of experience into a single fabric. He and his fellow dramatists could perhaps not have created a drama which so beautifully balanced the political and the personal if they had not had the perfect instrument of their unlocalized stage, which hospitably provided for all locations a man lives his life in without giving any that apparent priority which Ibsen's parlour or Racine's palace-chamber gives. The freedom to move rapidly from a council-room to a battlefield or a bedroom, and then to the cave of a man's own mind, like the freedom to move rapidly from soliloquy to intimate conversation and to public rhetoric, seems essential for that characteristic texture of the Elizabethan personal–political play, of which Shakespeare is the greatest exponent.

It is easy enough to see the chains of cause and effect by which Shakespeare binds together the personal, the private, and the public.[1] But we enter a difficult and debatable ground when we ask questions about the continuity of the person as he moves through his various habitations, about the comparative value of the life lived in the different circles, and whether such terms as 'inner self' and 'public role' are appropriate in discussing Shakespeare's plays. There has been a marked tendency in Shakespeare criticism in recent years to see political or public life in the plays as involving some kind of falsification, to see it as a region of posturing, of assuming masks, playing roles; or as a region where a man's better nature is, simply, corrupted. It seems to be taken for granted that there is a distinction between a Shakespearian person and the public or political position he chooses or is forced into. I give just a few examples.

In 1961, John Holloway wrote that Hamlet, as a revenger, was 'a man engaged in a known career'.

In this play as in many other tragedies, the experience of the protagonist is not the deployment of a determinate character, but the assumption, and then the enactment, of a determinate *rôle*. Rôle predominates over character, because once it is assumed by an actor, it will be much the same whatever his nature may be. It overrides that nature: the play is its acting out.[2]

---

[1] An argument against Shakespeare's authorship of *Edward III* is that there is no connection, causal or moral, between the king's adulterous pursuit of the Countess of Salisbury in the first part of the play, and his martial and kingly prowess in France in the second part.

[2] *The Story of the Night* (London, 1961), p. 26. Compare Erving Goffman: 'A

In an important essay of 1963, 'Character and Role from Richard III to Hamlet',[3] Peter Ure countered John Holloway's notion of character disappearing into determinate role with the suggestion that the plays show what I suppose Erving Goffman would call 'role distance': that they show an 'inward self' adjusting to a role, reshaping it or being shaped by it. Characterization, said Peter Ure, is in 'the interplay between character and role'. Richard III, the great actor, paradoxically cannot live out the majestic role of king, 'the inward self [is] unable to find any way of adjusting itself to the role'. Richard II on the contrary so pours himself into his role that 'he exhausts the self': there is nothing left when the role is abandoned. 'In both characters', the argument goes on, 'it is plain that the inward man has miscalculated his relation to his assignment.'[4]

In connection with Richard II, it is worth noting that the conception of the King as actor is, according to the New Variorum edition,[5] a twentieth-century growth. Since the relation between the person of Richard and his office as king is a main topic of this lecture, I cite a recent phrasing of this conception from James Winny: 'He cannot realise that the splendid role with which he identifies himself has no more substance than an actor's part, and is not the basis of his individuality.'[6]

In 1965 Matthew Proser published a book called *The*

---

self . . . virtually awaits the individual entering a position'; 'To embrace a role is to disappear completely into the virtual self available in the situation' (*Where the Action is: Three Essays*, London, 1969, pp. 41, 60).

[3] *Hamlet* (Stratford-upon-Avon Studies, 5, edited by J. R. Brown and B. Harris; London, 1963) pp. 9–28.

[4] Peter Ure made a striking extension of his theory of self and role, and the dreamlike quality of public office, in his edition of Ford's *Perkin Warbeck*, published in 1968, the year before his early death. The pretender, he argued, treated his life before its end as a work of art, ignoring the delusion it was built on. He performed excellently his chosen role of Richard IV, and 'it really does not matter' that 'the hero strutting it out before us' is 'really' the son of John Osbek. 'We have known that all along, in much the same sense that we have know that Henry VII is not "really" Henry VII *but a member of the Phoenix company*' (my italics). The omission of the middle person in the trio of the public figure of the king, the private person, and the actor comes as a surprise.

[5] *Richard the Second*, ed. M. W. Black, New Variorum (Philadelphia and London, 1955), p. 545.

[6] *The Player King* (London, 1968), p. 54.

*Heroic Image in Five Shakespearean Tragedies*, in which he argued that the hero strove to enact 'a certain public role', which was in fact a simplification of 'the entire human reality', and he sacrificed his life to an illusion. 'Conduct becomes in part a series of symbolic acts, poses, stances, and gestures which seek to define the heroic image in action' (p. 4).

Perhaps the most thoroughgoing statement on the estrangement of Shakespearian man from his public activities is Terence Eagleton's *Shakespeare and Society* (London, 1967), which approaches the plays from the concepts not of role-theory but of existentialism. 'One major crisis' in Shakespeare's work, the author holds, is 'the tension between spontaneous life and society . . . a crisis which . . . we are especially well-placed to appreciate and understand' (p. 177). Time and again we are shown (it is argued), in such characters as Hamlet, Troilus, Coriolanus, men whose authentic selves can have no fulfilment in a false society, who therefore, since men cannot live except in society, destroy themselves. Of Hamlet, Terence Eagleton writes, 'A self which can know itself only in constant opposition to its context finally destroys itself. This is the savage irony of the authentic man in a false society' (p. 62).

It seems to me that the problem of Shakespeare's view of the relation between the self or the person and public or official life is one of the important problems which Shakespeare criticism has to face. I am going to suggest, as a possible way forward, that Shakespeare proposes two antithetical modes in which a person and his public office are related, and that the opposition of these ways is a major subject of his drama. I shall try to establish the first way by moving from the Roman plays to *Richard II* and *King Lear*; the second will be illustrated by Henry V as prince and king.

*Julius Caesar*, one of the least problematic of Shakespeare's plays, presents a fairly simple view of the relations between private and public selves as one of painful antagonism. The stuff of humanity is malleable: between his home and the place where power is exercised a man's nature is easily disguised or changed. Casca is a man of quick mettle, but he 'puts on' a 'tardy form'. Brutus worries that the crowning of Caesar will 'change his nature'. In his own house, Caesar transforms himself quickly from the husband who promises his wife that 'Mark Antony will say I am not well', to the ruler who intones 'Shall Caesar send a lie?' Cassius believes he can politicize Brutus into a shape of his own devising, and so (disastrously) he does, becoming a Frankenstein at the mercy of his own monster. Brutus, in his maladroit handling of affairs in the political and military scenes, is not just a fish out of water; we witness a noble and gentle nature growing coarser as it continues to mistake its way in the public world which it cannot escape from.[7]

If we were tempted from the evidence of *Julius Caesar* to see the worsening of the self as it is exposed to the storms of political commitment as a general position of Shakespeare, we might think that our best spokesman was Coriolanus, who makes much of the corruption which he risks by joining in the political life of the city which he serves so ably and willingly as a soldier. But I shall argue that the evidence of *Coriolanus* points us in quite another direction.

When asked to go back to the angry crowd and win their votes by eating his words and showing a humble front, Coriolanus shouts:

> Must I
> With my base tongue give to my noble heart
> A lie that it must bear? . . .
> I will not do't,
> Lest I surcease to honour mine own truth,
> And by my body's action teach my mind
> A most inherent baseness.
>
> (III. ii. 99–101; 120–3)

In spite of a subtle and persuasive gloss on this passage by D. J. Gordon,[8] the picture of an inner sincerity endangered by the demands of political expediency will not do, for Shakespeare takes pains in this same scene to make it clear that this 'self' which Coriolanus is reluctant to tarnish is not as spontaneous as it might seem. Coriolanus is unable to

---

[7] See the beautiful rendering of the two Brutuses in Roy Fuller's poems 'The Ides of March' (*Collected Poems* (London, 1962), p. 182).

[8] 'Name and Fame: Shakespeare's Coriolanus', *Papers Mainly Shakespearian*, ed. G. I. Duthie (Edinburgh, 1964), pp. 50–1.

understand why his mother has not applauded his denunciation of the common people, and when Volumnia enters, he
turns to her:

> Why did you wish me milder? Would you have me
> False to my nature? Rather say I play
> The man I am.

(III. ii. 14–16)

The paradox of 'play the man I am' is so extraordinary that
one might disregard it as a confusion if Volumnia did not
reinforce it.

> You might have been enough the man you are
> With striving less to be so.

(III. ii. 19–20)

Coriolanus' 'nature', which seemed to his friends a matter of
instinct,[9] is (shall we say) a second nature: something willed,
something fashioned. It is impossible to think of the play
*Coriolanus* as showing us the native honesty of the self
trapped in the snares of the political world; it is more a
question of a being fashioned for one kind of life looking with
disdain on another. At the end of Act IV, Aufidius wonders
what it was that brought Coriolanus down in Rome:

> whether nature,
> Not to be other than one thing, not moving
> From th' casque to th' cushion . . .

(IV. vii. 41–3)

We consent. We cannot separate Coriolanus's self or his
nature from his profession as a soldier. What he is is what he
does. His identity is only visible when we take his soldiering
into account. The fusion of the man in his profession is
wonderfully drawn by Shakespeare; if ever a man was
declared by his activities, it is Coriolanus. His nature,
conditioned by a mother who thought the breasts of Hecuba
not lovelier than Hector's forehead when it spit forth blood,
has its home on the battlefield, and he takes his name from a

---

[9] Cf. Menenius, III. i. 257–8: 'His heart's his mouth; What his breath forges, that
his tongue must vent.'

battle.[10] The alarming cracks which show up in him in the
forum are not seen in war. His tragedy is that the range of
activities he is capable of is too small and his being cannot
meet the new demands made on it. He recognizes his own
dissolution: Cominius reports of him:

> Coriolanus
> He would not answer to, forbade all names;
> He was a kind of nothing, titleless,
> Till he had forged himself a name i' th' fire
> Of burning Rome.

(v. i. 11–15)

The play of *Coriolanus* suggests to us that it may be better to
think not of an inner or private self in antagonism to its life in
society, but the identification of a person and a particular
office in a unity so complete that a challenge to alter the offce
may destroy the person. It is worth remembering that when
Othello, whose being is also surely defined by his profession
as soldier, fears that his marriage has broken down, he makes
a long apostrophe to his martial life, which ends, 'Farewell,
Othello's occupation's gone!' It seems a curious note at such a
moment, but it illustrates his feeling of the unity of the inner,
the private, and the public lives. He is not what he was; and
what was he if not a soldier?

However trite or commonplace the idea that man is a unity
of being and doing, that he is defined by his activities, I
believe that Shakespeare's conception of it is foreign to
modern ways of thinking and I believe that awareness of it
greatly helps one's understanding of many plays. The play
which most fully demonstrates the conception is *Richard II*,
which must be read in the light of the important study of
'medieval political theology' which E. H. Kantorowicz
published in 1957, *The King's Two Bodies.*

Kantorowicz opened his work with the strange christo-
logical definitions which Tudor jurists were using concerning
the dual nature of a king. For example:

He has not a Body natural distinct and divided by itself from the

---

[10] Cf. N. Rabkin, *Shakespeare and the Common Understanding* (New York, 1967),
pp. 130, 132.

Office and Dignity royal, but a Body natural and a Body politic together indivisible; and these two Bodies are incorporated in one Person, and make one Body and not divers. (p.9)

Sixteenth-century England had, amazingly, revived a mystical concept of the personality of the king which had existed in the early Middle Ages, but which later times had made more common-sensical and matter-of-fact. Kantorowicz amply demonstrates that *Richard II* is steeped in the remarkable Athanasian theorizing about kingship which was preoccupying the English, but, because at bottom he seems to take the plain man's view that the 'monistic formula' of the fusion of an eternal and a temporal nature in one person is 'an ultra-fanciful maxim' (pp. 438–9), I don't think he realizes how deeply both Richard and his creator are immersed in the doctrine. *Richard II* is a tragedy only if both protagonist and audience share the view that the king is a mystical being, a man of flesh and blood whose humanity is transfigured and exalted by his office. The sacramental notion of the king's person is so strongly and movingly presented that it is perverse to see it as a peculiar infatuation of Richard's. The king is the figure of God's majesty, the sceptre is the outward mark of kingship, and even the handle of the sceptre is 'sacred' (III. iii. 80). The world 'sacred' appears more often in *Richard II* than in any other play of Shakespeare's; on each occasion, it refers to the king and each time it is used not metaphorically but in a strict liturgical sense, applied to that which has been consecrated.

At his anointing, the nature of the king is transformed; the change is final and cannot be reversed; the only way down is destruction. It is Richard himself who unsettles his own position by his carelessness and wilfulness, denying his own state by acts bordering on illegality, for only he who remained servant of the law could be master of the law.[11] Only as the rebellion against him gathers strength, and authority is slipping away from him does he begin to learn the true nature of his person and his office, that true nature being the identity of those two things.

From the ridiculous position that, because the balm cannot

---

[11] Cf. Kantorowicz, *The King's Two Bodies* (Princeton, 1957), p, 157.

be washed off from an anointed king and worldly men cannot depose the deputy elected by the Lord, he as a military commander is bound to defeat all his physical enemies, Richard flies to the other extreme. From a belief in a kind of angelic inviolability, he descends too rapidly to see himself as mere vulnerable man, fooled into accepting a role that is all illusion.

> Cover your heads, and mock not flesh and blood
> With solemn reverence; throw away respect,
> Tradition, form, and ceremonious duty;
> For you have but mistook me all this while.
> I live with bread like you, feel want,
> Taste grief, need friends; subjected thus,
> How can you say to me I am a king?
>
> (III. ii. 171-7)

It is necessary for Richard to assert his divine inviolability, and know it false in a physical sense; it is necessary for him, in reaction, to assert that he is merely human, and know that false also, if he is to understand, as more than an effort of reason or scholastic logic, that point of balance where the being of the two-natured king precariously exists. 'How *can* you say to me I am a king?' is a question that is in time answered.

But, still mistaken about himself, he initiates that impossibility, his deposition, and he pictures to himself the hermit or pilgrim he would be in his new life. Then he begins to understand that he is not mere man, forced out of office and bound to seek in poverty and humiliation some other life, but that his very being is his kingship; once he is not king, there is no being. It is this concept, which seems to be so central to so much in Shakespeare's writing, which is so hard to grasp.

> Single nature's double name
> Neither two nor one was called.
>
> ('The Phoenix and the Turtle', 39-40)

Impatience comes too easily to us in the world of jobs, where we believe either that a man has his own selfhood whatever he does to earn his bread and butter, or alternatively that a man receives a new self every time he changes his occupation.

Richard's problem is not an identity-crisis, nor the strain of role-conflict, nor the loss of status.

While he sees himself betrayed like Christ (who is the archetype of that which is at the same time inviolable and easily wounded), he also insists, as a man knowing his own guilt, on taking on himself the final treason of unkinging himself, with his own human tongue denying his sacred state (IV. i. 209), and so reducing himself to nothing.

> —Are you contented to resigne the Crowne?
> —I, no; no, I; for I must nothing bee.
>
> (IV. i. 200–1)[12]

That which has no being has no name:

> I have no name, no title,
> No, not that name was given me at the font,
> But 'tis usurped. Alack the heavy day,
> That I have worn so many winters out,
> And know not now what name to call myself.
>
> (IV. i. 255–9)[13]

Richard is a physical being who can be thrown out of office, but his deposition is sacrilege, the defilement of what is holy. 'Dust was thrown upon his sacred head' (V. ii. 30). It is also the annihilation of the king-man, and as the fragments that were Richard lie in prison, thoughts of possible modes of being chase themselves endlessly and fruitlessly, and the first part of his great soliloquy ends with a repetition of the word 'nothing' (V. v. 38–41).

As he hears a mysterious music, which begins to falter, he talks of men's lives as music, and is bitter that he did not detect the false sounds in his own life.

> And here have I the daintiness of ear
> To check time broke in a disordered string,
> But for the concord of my state and time
> Had not an ear to hear my true time broke.
> I wasted time, and now doth time waste me.
>
> (V. v. 45–9)

---

[12] The old spelling is given for the sake of the Ay/I pun.

[13] The great importance of this passage in the play has been at times obscured by the view which Dover Wilson supported that it contained an allusion to an imputation of Richard's illegitimacy.

It is at moments like this, when the imagery beautifully suggests the necessary unity of one's nature, one's position, and one's actions—the concord of one's state and time—that it is tempting to think of true kingship as a metaphor for a harmony of the personality, the unity of being and doing when private person and public office are one. Richard never achieves this, because the events which give him his knowledge are those which prevent him from putting his knowledge into action. But he has the understanding, and with it, a new dignity. Of course, in his greatest scene he is theatrical, he improvises a great ceremony for his humiliation; but kingship is for him no actor's part, put on and put off at will.

The play of *King Lear* reinforces the idea of kingship which *Richard II* suggests. In abdicating the 'power, / Pre-eminence, and all the large effects / That troop with majesty' while retaining 'the name, and all the additions to a king',[14] Lear tries to split his being where it cannot be divided.[15] The political inexpediency of the division of the kingdom is an outward reflection of the major crime, which is sacrilege. The name and the additions to a king are the outward and visible signs of the power of the king and the God-given grace to wield it. Detached from power, they are absurd. Lear tries to wear a crown without a head to put it on. As in *Richard II*, the hero becomes aware of the true balance of his being as that being suffers the destruction which his own act of denial invites. As with *Richard II*, it is I think a mistake to assume that Lear becomes a new person rejecting kingship in favour of humanity. He learns of the vanity of his old values, the ironies of authority, and sees the whole world anew, but I wonder how far, in this or in the other tragedies, it may be said that a second self supervenes upon the wrecking of the old. Tragedy forces the hero to find out—again or for the first

[14] *Lear*, I. i. 129–31, 134, following the Quarto's 'additions' instead of the Folio's 'addition'.

[15] Cf. lines from *I Henry VI*, v. iv. 133–7, quoted by Anne Righter, *Shakespeare and the Idea of the Play* (London, 1962), p. 117, where it is suggested that the French king should be viceroy to the English king, 'and still enjoy thy regal dignity'.

> Must he be then as shadow of himself,
> Adorn his temples with a coronet
> And yet, in substance and authority,
> Retain but privilege of a private man?
> This proffer is absurd and reasonless.

time—who he is. But though what he recognizes as the self is torn apart, though knowledge floods in and he sees for the first time the possibility of a different dimension in life, the only new resting-place is death. In tragicomedy it is different; Angelo in *Measure for Measure* and Leontes in *The Winter's Tale* survive disintegration and live on as changed men. Lear, who has helped to reduce himself to nothing, lives to recognize his mistakes and to recognize himself—'I am the king himself . . . Ay, every inch a king.' His old power is returned to him by Albany, but he is at the point of death.

Both *Richard II* and *King Lear* present the idea of unity of being, in which the person and his office, the private and the public being, are coextensive and inseparable. Within this conception, phrases like role-playing are irrelevant. But Shakespeare also presents an antithetical idea, a view of man as an amorphous self adapting to the social world, but never totally identified with his activities, never to be defined and limited as, say, king or soldier. Richard, as we saw, is often spoken of as playing a role—rather, playing *with* a role. But it is the man who supplants him, 'this king of smiles, this Bolingbroke' who is the actor, the man who makes a divorce between the tongue and the heart.[16] He 'stole courtesy from heaven' and 'dressed himself in humility'; he created an image to win the 'opinion' of the multitude and to maintain his authority. 'Thus did I keep my person fresh and new.'[17] Persona, perhaps, but the *person* of Bolingbroke is indeed uninteresting; at times he seems to be, as Osbert Lancaster once described someone, veneer all through. The true antithesis to Richard is Bolingbroke's complex and enigmatic son.

After Henry IV's death, Prince Hal speaks as follows:

> My father is gone wild into his grave,
> For in his tomb lie my affections;
> And with his spirits sadly I survive
> To mock the expectation of the world . . .
>
> The tide of blood in me
> Hath proudly flowed in vanity till now.

[16] Cf. Anne Righter, *Shakespeare and the Idea of the Play*, pp. 126–7.
[17] *I Henry IV*, III. i. 42, 50–1, 55.

> Now doth it turn and ebb back to the sea,
> Where it shall mingle with the state of floods
> And flow henceforth in formal majesty.
>
> (2 *Henry IV*, v. ii. 123–6, 129–33)

Hal says that he has doffed his nature and exchanged it for that of his father. To Falstaff he says, 'Presume not that I am the thing I was . . . I have turned away my former self.' These images which denote reformation in terms of change of the self are perhaps not in themselves important, but they become so as part of a consistent thread of references to the relation between the person of Hal and his public activities. On his accession, Hal says,

> This new and gorgeous garment, majesty,
> Sits not so easy on me as you think.
>
> (2 *Henry IV*, v. ii. 44–5)

It is a natural remark for the young new king; but it is also a part of a series of images which Shakespeare gives to Hal as prince and king, referring to kingship as integument, a covering to be worn. He has already called majesty 'a rich armour, worn in heat of day, That scalds with safety' (2 *Henry IV*, iv. v. 31–2). In the great soliloquy before Agincourt, Henry argues that kings are distinguished from private men only by the 'idol Ceremony', a god whom men foolishly worship.

> Art thou aught else but place, degree and form,
> Creating awe and fear in other men?
>
> (*Henry V*, iv. i. 242–3)

'Thrice-gorgeous ceremony' is featured by

> the balm, the sceptre, and the ball,
> The sword, the mace, the crown imperial,
> The intertissued robe of gold and pearl.
>
> (*Henry V*, iv. i. 256–8)

The royal robe is for Henry an appropriate image of kingship itself, an outward appurtenance adopted by the extraordinary ordinary man charged with governing his fellow men; though it has certain useful purposes, it is known by him for what it is and despised. The contrast here between Hal and Richard could hardly be more sharp. The balm and the sceptre were for Richard sacred; not externals, but outward expressions of the being who was to try to express God on earth; worship of them was not idolatry.

Having seen the stress on the exchanges of natures, and on kingship as integument, we are perhaps in a better position to appreciate the notorious first soliloquy of Prince Hal in the First Part of *Henry IV*. We may be less disposed to take it at its face-value, which is that Hal proposes to obscure his true self and indulge in what he considers offensive behaviour in order to surprise people into admiration when his real self is allowed to break through. Rather we shall ʹsee it as a triumphant (though very Lancastrian) jest,[18] a mischievous rationalization of self-indulgence: 'Why, the worse I behave, the better they'll think of me!' The speech relies not on the idea of a 'true self', but on the idea of an adjustable and compliant self, which can change when it is necessary from companion to king, and keep a certain detachment from either activity. Hal can always rise, magnificently, to the being which the occasion demands, in Eastcheap, at Shrewsbury, at Agincourt, or in the French court. Flexibly and successfully he deploys himself in a dozen roles. It is hard to say where he is most truly himself, because the self seems endlessly pliable. There could be no wedding of person and office where there is such versatility.

I argue, then, that Shakespeare presents two views of man: one, in which there is a continuum of the person and his public activities, an amalgam so complete that it is impossible to distinguish what a man is from what he is accustomed to do; the second, in which there is an autonomous and plastic self, urging itself forward and adapting to the various moulds available to it, in such a way that we are always aware of the separateness of the person and his office.

It is strange that the condition of unified being is usually shown as something unattainable, or discarded, or destroyed. Lear and Richard throw a pearl away, richer than all their tribe. Hamlet is denied that office which alone could define

---

[18] Cf. Morris Arnold's view of 1911 as cited in the New Variorum edition.

him and make him a whole man: there is never the 'doing' which can complete his 'being', so during the whole play he is a soul without a body, like a ghost. Macbeth, seeing a new unnatural office before him, shows us in a vivid sentence the concord of his life shattering. His 'single state of man' is so shaken:

> That function is smother'd in surmise
> And nothing is but what is not.
>
> (*Macbeth*, I. iii. 140–1)

Like Richard III, the arch-impostor dedicated to separateness of being, Macbeth in looking for a crown becomes the restless, unappeased and unappeasable self:

> —like one lost in a thorny wood
> That rents the thorns and is rent with the thorns
> Seeking a way and straying from the way,
> Not knowing how to find the open air,
> But toiling desperately to find it out.
>
> (3 *Henry VI*, III. ii. 174–7)

On the one hand we see unity of being as unattainable; on the other we see separateness of being as incipiently evil. Not that Prince Hal is a villain; but he is ominous even in his great abilities, as Yeats described him, with perception and charity, in those brilliant pages of *Ideas of Good and Evil* to which all the better criticism of the English history plays in this century is only an appendix.[19] But others are just bad men, who will, like Richard of Gloucester:

> Change shapes with Proteus for advantages
> And set the murderous Machiavel to school.
>
> (3 *Henry VI*, III. ii. 192–3)

They prey on those in the other camp, Iago on Othello, Edmund on Edgar, as Bolingbroke preys on Richard II.

How far do these two views on man represent Shakespeare's recognition of an historical change in the nature of the relation between the individual and society?

---

[19] Yeats, *Essays and Introductions* (London, 1961), pp. 102–9.

In a recent important study,[20] Alvin Kernan wrote,

In historical terms the movement from the world of Richard II to that of Henry V is the passage from the Middle Ages to the Renaissance and the modern world. In practical and social terms it is a movement from feudalism and hierachy to the national state and individualism. In psychological terms it is a passage from a situation in which man knows with certainty who he is to an existential condition in which any identity is only a temporary role.

It is certainly tempting to say that since Richard is so thoroughly medieval, his antithesis must be modern; it is tempting to see the play *Richard II* as a great elegiac lament for the old undivided cosmos as it is replaced by a world of brisk serviceability and opportunism. We may feel that in Richard II and his fellows, in Lear, Antony, Othello, Coriolanus, for example, there is a certain rigidity, an inability to respond to change, accompanying the appeal of their colourful if faulty characters, and that Shakespeare is playing a defunctive music for a creature which has had its time however much he regrets its passing. And on the other side, among those who demonstrate the discontinuity of self, the adventurers, there are some who characterize themselves as free from old-fashioned ways of thought, particularly Edmund, whose defeat at the end of *King Lear* by a knight in armour in formal medieval combat seems an interesting inversion of history. Shakespeare's plays do deal largely with supersession and replacement,[21] and the warfare between ineffective innocence and worldly-wise success seems inescapably not so much a timeless one as belonging to the particular period of transition which in their different ways Marlowe and Jonson also imaged.

If we accept that Shakespeare's bifold concept of the person shows his awareness of the 'true man' bewildered in the world of the 'new man', we must be very cautious indeed about going forward to accept related positions, which, I believe, impose a false modernity of outlook on an Elizabethan and Jacobean dramatist.

---

[20] 'The Henriad: Shakespeare's Major History Plays', *The Yale Review*, lix (Oct. 1969), 3–32. Cf. M. McLuhan, *The Gutenberg Galaxy* (London, 1962), pp. 11–17.
[21] Cf. Philip Edwards, *Shakespeare and the Confines of Art* (London, 1968), p. 5.

The helplessness of the Shakespearian hero in a world he cannot comprehend may possibly prefigure but it does not describe the necessary alienation of man from society, the illness of modern man. Certainly, as I have argued, it seems as though the principle of the unity of being is condemned to defeat. It seems practically impossible to live out a life in recognition of it. Shakespearian society is cruel and treacherous to many of its distinctive men, Henry VI, Richard II, Brutus, Hamlet, Troilus, for example. But defeat is not the same thing as alienation. Perhaps there is only a narrow divide between the difficulty which a number of Shakespeare's heroes have in reconciling themselves to an evil world and that total disaffection from organized society which most people mean when they talk of alienation and which perhaps received its classic fictional rendering years ago in Thomas Mann's *The Magic Mountain*. Yet the divide is there. Shakespeare does not show man lusting to escape and bury himself; the call of the contemplative life is almost nil in his plays. Kings, as a matter of course, envy those who have positions of less responsibility, shepherds, labourers, and wet sea-boys, but not even Henry VI thinks of the evasion of the hermit's cave. The world was inescapably there, to be lived in and fought with. Shakespeare could hardly foresee the sense of impersonality which many people feel themselves to be labouring under and which has led to the personification of the abstraction, 'society'. His concept of evil needed people. When we recognize in the bafflement or betrayal of a sensitive hero like Hamlet the crisis of estrangement of the modern world, we are not observing the play; we are once again paying tribute to the extraordinary fecundity of the myth.

Man's alienation from society is essentially an alienation from the work and the social roles forced on him by the highly developed division of labour of the modern industrial state, which gives little hope that what one takes up for a livelihood will engage one's whole being. The great majority of people, rich and poor, live shadow-lives in arbitrary and unfulfilling occupations. Hence the development of those major modern oppositions, inner and outer, private and public, the man and the mask. Writing of Dickens, W. J. Harvey spoke of 'the predicament of man in modern industrial society . . . the sharp division between public and private, the official and the person; one recalls Bucket the person and Bucket the detective, Vholes the lawyer and Vholes as parent and child'.[22] The word 'job', which until this century meant a brief casual task, became in twentieth-century America a word for one's career or profession. Shakespeare's fictional societies are not placed in this kind of world. We have to protest that the language won't serve when a critic (writing in 1949) says, 'If Lear had been more suited to his job or his job to him, he would have died peacefully.'[23] Even McLuhan's inspired suggestion that Lear in dividing his kingdom is moving from the world of roles to the world of jobs[24] is an uncertain trope. It is very hard indeed to translate Shakespeare's kings and generals into employers or employees, management or personnel, even when they are seemingly 'new men' in a new society. But this is not the only problem. Whether we speak of roles or of jobs we are liable to be importing into Shakespeare's world an assessment of the individual and society which belongs firmly to *our* world. The role-theory of modern sociology is born of a cynicism about one's involvement in the world which has pushed the personality of man to vanishing point. Some of this cynicism has brushed off on Shakespearian criticism. However strongly Shakespeare believed the stock idea that all the world's a stage, however much he recognized that there was something theatrical about every public speech or occasion, he did not accept a necessary disjunction between the inner self and the public self, nor did he show the self as the obedient creature of the adventitious social role. The self is a union of a man's nature with his profession, and this union is most forcefully shown in the imagery of the king as a single being compounded of two natures, one belonging to his mortal being and one to his superhuman office. The recognition of his true identity and of his responsibilities is forced on a man in a losing fight with a world which he cannot accommodate

---

[22] *Dickens and the Twentieth Century*, eds. Gross and Pearson (London, 1962), p. 156.
   [23] Albert Cook, *The Dark Voyage and the Golden Mean* (Cambridge, Mass., 1949), p. 11.
   [24] McLuhan, *The Gutenberg Galaxy*, p. 14.

himself to. His true activity, which Richard defined as a concord of music, is impossible because his defeat or supersession accompanies his recognition of himself. But there are others, better adapted to survive, though the play's ending may demolish them, who believe in their freedom to create their own lives, who move from one incarnation to another, men whose worldly success is moral failure, just as the worldly failure of the first group is moral success. It is in connection with this second group only that it seems to me proper to talk of their public lives as the assumption of roles and the acting out of parts. At all costs we must avoid attributing to Shakespeare *as a whole* our indwelling scepticism about social and political activity. It is difficult work, especially when Shakespeare seems sometimes to invite us to do so with the polarities of private and public in *Julius Caesar*, and with his constant subversion of 'the great image of authority'. But we run the risk of blurring the sharpness of his tragic vision if we are too affected by terminologies belonging to social conditions developing long after his time. It seems to us, from a distance of three and a half centuries, that in his political tragedies Shakespeare is recording something like a change in the very nature of man.[25] He may not have seen things so himself; he may have thought of the two kinds of personality as a sort of timeless opposition repeated in every generation rather than as a matter of historical development; he may have seen them as complementary types necessary in society— certainly he neither sentimentalizes the one nor entirely vilifies the other. But we see things in a different and rather melancholy perspective, and it is essential if we are to make the correct historical interpretation of the oppositions in his plays that we grasp firmly the quality of those oppositions as they relate to the nature of the individual and his relation with society.[26]

[25] See Alvin Kernan's study of the English history plays referred to on p. 120 above.

[26] I am grateful to Williams College, Massachusetts, for a visiting professorship in the autumn of 1969 which gave me time to think about the foregoing lecture. The interpretation of *Richard II* is developed from a lecture given to Birmingham University's Summer School at Stratford-upon-Avon in 1968; I saw the need to relate my ideas to the more general problems treated in the present lecture when discussing with Miss Rosamond Lomax her excellent proposals for a doctoral thesis on the theme of 'private and public' in Shakespeare.

# 7. HAMLET: THE PRINCE OR THE POEM?

By C. S. Lewis

A critic who makes no claim to be a true Shakespearian scholar and who has been honoured by an invitation to speak about Shakespeare to such an audience as this, feels rather like a child brought in at dessert to recite his piece before the grown-ups. I have a temptation to furbish up all my meagre Shakespearian scholarship and to plunge into some textual or chronological problem in the hope of seeming, for this one hour, more of an expert than I am. But it really wouldn't do. I should not deceive you: I should not even deceive myself. I have therefore decided to bestow all my childishness upon you.

And first, a reassurance. I am not going to advance a new interpretation of the character of Hamlet. Where great critics have failed I could not hope to succeed; it is rather my ambition (a more moderate one, I trust) to understand their failure. The problem I want to consider to-day arises in fact not directly out of the Prince's character nor even directly out of the play, but out of the state of criticism about the play.

To give anything like a full history of this criticism would be beyond my powers and beyond the scope of a lecture; but, for my present purpose, I think we can very roughly divide it into three main schools or tendencies. The first is that which maintains simply that the actions of Hamlet have not been given adequate motives and that the play is so far bad. Hanmer is perhaps the earliest exponent of this view. According to him Hamlet is made to procrastinate because 'had he gone naturally to work, there would have been an end to our play'. But then, as Hanmer points out, Shakespeare ought to have 'contrived some good reason' for the procrastination. Johnson, while praising the tragedy for its 'variety', substantially agrees with Hanmer: 'of the feigned madness of Hamlet there appears no adequate cause.' Rümelin thinks that the 'wisdom' which Shakespeare has chosen to hide under 'the wild utterances of insanity' is a 'foreign and disturbing element' as a result of which the piece 'presents the greatest discrepancies'. In our own time Mr Eliot has taken the same view: *Hamlet* is rather like a film on which two photographs have been taken—an unhappy superposition of Shakespeare's work 'upon much cruder material'. The play 'is most certainly an artistic failure'. If this school of critics is right, we shall be wasting our time in attempting to understand why Hamlet delayed.The second school, on the other hand, thinks that he did not delay at all but went to work as quickly as the circumstances permitted. This was Ritson's view. The word of a ghost, at second hand, 'would scarcely in the eye of the people have justified his killing their king'. That is why he 'counterfeits madness and . . . puts the usurper's guilt to the test of a play'. Klein, after a very fierce attack on critics who want to make the Prince of Denmark 'a German half-professor, all tongue and no hand', comes to the same conclusion. So does Werder, and so does Macdonald; and the position has been brilliantly defended in modern times. In the third school or group I include all those critics who admit that Hamlet procrastinates and who explain the procrastination by his psychology. Within this general agreement there are, no doubt, very great diversities. Some critics, such as Hallam, Sievers, Raleigh, and Clutton Brock, trace the weakness to the shock inflicted upon Hamlet by the events which precede, and immediately follow, the opening of the play; others regard it as a more permanent conditon; some extend it to actual insanity, others reduce it to an almost amiable flaw in a noble nature. This third group, which boasts the names of Richardson, Goethe, Coleridge, Schlegel, and Hazlitt, can still, I take it, claim to represent the central and, as it were, orthodox line of *Hamlet* criticism.

Such is the state of affairs; and we are all so accustomed to it that we are inclined to ignore its oddity. In order to remove the veil of familiarity I am going to ask you to make the imaginative effort of looking at this mass of criticism as if you had no independent knowledge of the thing criticized. Let us suppose that a picture which you have not seen is being talked about. The first thing you gather from the vast majority of the speakers—and a majority which includes the best art critics—is that the picture is undoubtedly a very great work. The next thing you discover is that hardly any two people in the room agree as to what it is a picture of. Most of them find something curious about the pose, and perhaps even the anatomy, of the central figure. One explains it by saying that it is a picture of the raising of Lazarus, and that the painter has cleverly managed to represent the uncertain gait of a body just recovering from the stiffness of death. Another, taking the central figure to be Bacchus returning from the conquest of India, says that it reels because it is drunk. A third, to whom it is self-evident that he has seen a picture of the death of Nelson, asks with some temper whether you expect a man to look quite normal just after he has been mortally wounded. A fourth maintains that such crudely representational canons of criticism will never penetrate so profound a work, and that the peculiarities of the central figure really reflect the content of the painter's subconsciousness. Hardly have you had time to digest these opinions when you run into another group of critics who denounce as a pseudo-problem what the first group has been discussing. According to this second group there is nothing odd about the central figure. A more natural and self-explanatory pose they never saw and they cannot imagine what all the pother is about. At long last you discover—isolated in a corner of the room, somewhat frowned upon by the rest of the company, and including few reputable *connoisseurs* in its ranks—a little knot of men who are whispering that the picture is a villainous daub and that the mystery of the central figure merely results from that fact that it is out of drawing.

Now if all this had really happened to any one of us, I believe that our first reaction would be to accept, at least provisionally, the third view. Certainly I think we should consider it much more seriously than we usually consider those critics who solve the whole *Hamlet* problem by calling *Hamlet* a bad play. At the very least we should at once perceive that they have a very strong case against the critics who admire. 'Here is a picture', they might say, 'on whose meaning no two of you are in agreement. Communication between the artist and the spectator has almost completely broken down, for each of you admits that it has broken down as regards every spectator except himself. There are only two possible explanations. Either the artist was a very bad artist, or you are very bad critics. In deference to your number and your reputation, we choose the first alternative; though, as you will observe, it would work out to the same result if we chose the second.' As to the next group—those who denied that there was anything odd about the central figure—I believe that in the circumstances I have imagined we should hardly attend to them. A natural and self-explanatory pose in the central figure would be rejected as wholly inconsistent with its observed effect on all the other critics, both those who thought the picture good and those who thought it bad.

If we now return to the real situation, the same reactions appear reasonable. There is, indeed, this difference, that the critics who admit no delay and no indecision in Hamlet have an opponent with whom the corresponding critics of the picture were not embarrassed. The picture did not answer back. But Hamlet does. He pronounces himself a pro-crastinator, an undecided man, even a coward: and the ghost in part agrees with him. This, coupled with the more general difficulties of their position, appears to me to be fatal to their view. If so, we are left with those who think the play bad and those who agree in thinking it good and in placing its goodness almost wholly in the character of the hero, while disagreeing as to what that character is. Surely the devil's advocates are in a very strong position. Here is a play so dominated by one character that 'Hamlet without the Prince' is a byword. Here are critics justly famed, all of them for their sensibility, many of them for their skill in catching the finest shades of human passion and pursuing motives to their last hiding-places. Is it really credible that the greatest of dramatists, the most powerful painter of men, offering to such an audience his consummate portrait of a man should produce something which, if any one of them is right, all the rest have in some degree failed to recognize? Is this the sort of thing that happens? Does the meeting of supremely creative with supremely receptive imagination usually produce such results? Or is it not far easier to say that Homer nods, and Alexander's shoulder drooped, and Achilles' heel was vulnerable, and that Shakespeare, for once, either in haste, or over-reaching himself in unhappy ingenuity, has brought forth an abortion?

Yes. Of course it is far easier. 'Most certainly', says Mr Eliot, 'an artistic failure.' But is it 'most certain'? Let me return for a moment to my analogy of the picture. In that dream there was one experiment we did not make. We didn't walk into the next room and look at it for ourselves. Supposing we had done so. Suppose that at the first glance all the cogent arguments of the unfavourable critics had died on our lips, or echoed in our ears as idle babble. Suppose that looking on the picture we had found ourselves caught up into an unforgettable intensity of life and had come back from the room where it hung haunted for ever with the sense of vast dignities and strange sorrows and teased 'with thoughts beyond the reaches of our souls'—would not this have reversed our judgement and compelled us, in the teeth of a priori probability, to maintain that on one point at least the orthodox critics were in the right? 'Most certainly an artistic failure.' All argument is for that conclusion—until you read or see *Hamlet* again. And when you do, you are left saying that if this is failure, then failure is better than success. We want more of these 'bad' plays. From our first childish reading of the ghost scenes down to those golden minutes which we stole from marking examination papers on *Hamlet* to read a few pages of *Hamlet* itself, have we ever known the day or the hour when its enchantment failed? That castle is part of our own world. The affection we feel for the Prince, and, through him, for Horatio, is like a friendship in real life. The very turns of expression—half-lines and odd connecting links—of this play are worked into the language. It appears, said Shaftesbury in 1710, 'most to have affected English hearts and has perhaps been oftenest acted'. It has a taste of its own, an all-pervading relish which we recognize even in its smallest fragments, and which, once tasted, we recur to. When we want that taste, no other book will do instead. It may turn out in the end that the thing is not a complete success. This compelling quality in it may coexist with some radical defect. But I doubt if we shall ever be able to say, sad brow and true maid, that it is 'most certainly' a failure. Even if the proposition that it has failed were at last admitted for true, I can think of few critical truths which most of us would utter with less certainty, and with a more divided mind.

It seems, then, that we cannot escape from our problem by pronouncing the play bad. On the other hand, the critics mostly agreeing to place the excellence of it in the delineation of the hero's character, describe that character in a dozen different ways. If they differ so much as to the kind of man whom Shakespeare meant to portray, how can we explain their unanimous praise of the portrayal? I can imagine a sketch so bad that one man thought it was an attempt at a horse and another thought it was an attempt at a donkey. But what kind of sketch would it have to be which looked like a *very good* horse to some, and like a *very good* donkey to others? The only solution which occurs to me is that the critics's delight in the play is not in fact due to the delineation of Hamlet's character but to something else. If the picture which you take for a horse and I for a donkey, delights us both, it is probable that what we are both enjoying is the pure line, or the colouring, not the delineation of an animal. If two men who have both been talking to the same woman agree in proclaiming her conversation delightful, though one praises it for its ingenuous innocence and the other for its clever sophistication, I should be inclined to conclude that her conversation had played very little part in the pleasure of either. I should suspect that the lady was nice to look at.

I am quite aware that such a suggestion about what has always been thought a 'one man play' will sound rather like a paradox. But I am not aiming at singularity. In so far as my own ideas about Shakespeare are worth classifying at all, I confess myself a member of that school which has lately been withdrawing our attention from the characters to fix it on the plays. Dr Stoll and Professor Wilson Knight, though in very different fasions, have led me in this direction; and Aristotle has long seemed to me simply right when he says that tragedy is an imitation not of men but of action and life and happiness and misery. By action he means, no doubt, not what a modern producer would call action but rather 'situation'.

What has attached me to this way of thinking is the fact that it explains my own experience. When I tried to read

Shakespeare in my teens the character criticism of the nineteenth century stood between me and my enjoyment. There were all sorts of things in the plays which I could have enjoyed; but I had got it into my head that the only proper and grown-up way of appreciating Shakespeare was to be very interested in the truth and subtlety of his character drawing. A play opened with thunder and lightning and witches on a heath. This was very much in my line: but oh the disenchantment when I was told—or thought I was told— that what really ought to concern me was the effect of these witches on Macbeth's character! An Illyrian Duke spoke, in an air which had just ceased vibrating to the sound of music, words that seemed to come out of the very heart of some golden world of dreamlike passion: but all this was spoiled because the meddlers had told me it was the portrait of a self-deceiving or unrealistic man and given me the impression that it was my business to diagnose like a straightener from Erewhon or Vienna instead of submitting to the charm. Shakespeare offered me a King who could not even sentence a man to banishment without saying

> The sly slow hours shall not determinate
> The dateless limit of thy dear exile.
>
> (*Richard II*, i. iii. 150–1)

Left to myself I would simply have drunk it in and been thankful. That is just how beautiful, wilful, passionate, unfortunate kings killed long ago ought to talk. But then again the critic was at my elbow instilling the pestilential notion that I ought to prize such words chiefly as illustrations of what he called Richard's weakness, and (worse still) inviting me to admire the vulgar, bustling efficiency of Bolingbroke. I am probably being very unjust to the critics in this account. I am not even sure who they were. But somehow or other this was the sort of idea they gave me. I believe they have given it to thousands. As far as I am concerned it meant that Shakespeare became to me for many years a closed book. Read him in *that* way I could not; and it was some time before I had the courage to read him in any other. Only much later, reinforced with a wider knowledge of literature, and able now to rate at its true value the humble little outfit of prudential maxims which really underlay much of the talk about Shakespeare's characters, did I return and read him with enjoyment. To one in my position the opposite movement in criticism came as a kind of Magna Charta. With that help I have come to one very definite conclusion. I do not say that the characters—especially the comic characters—count for nothing. But the first thing is to surrender oneself to the poetry and the situation. It is only through them that you can reach the characters, and it is for their sake that the characters exist. All conceptions of the characters arrived at, so to speak, in cold blood, by working out what sort of man it would have to be who in real life would act or speak as they do, are in my opinion chimerical. The wiseacres who proceed in that way only substitute our own ideas of character and life, which are not often either profound or delectable, for the bright shapes which the poet is actually using. Orsino and Richard II are test cases. Interpretations which compel you to read their speeches with a certain superiority, to lend them a note of 'insincerity', to strive in any way against their beauty, are self-condemned. Poets do not make beautiful verse in order to have it 'guyed'. Both these characters speak golden syllables, wearing rich clothes, and standing in the centre of the stage. After that, they may be wicked, but it can only be with a passionate and poetic wickedness; they may be foolish, but only with follies noble and heroical. For the poetry, the clothes, and the stance are the substance; the character 'as it would have to be in real life' is only a shadow. It is often a very distorted shadow. Some of my pupils talk to me about Shakespeare as if the object of his life had been to render into verse the philosophy of Samuel Smiles or Henry Ford.

A good example of the kind of play which can be twisted out of recognition by character criticism is the *Merchant of Venice*. Nothing is easier than to disengage and condemn the mercenary element in Bassanio's original suit to Portia, to point out that Jessica was a bad daughter, and by dwelling on Shylock's wrongs to turn him into a tragic figure. The hero thus becomes a scamp, the heroine's love for him a disaster, the villain a hero, the last act an irrelevance, and the casket story a monstrosity. What is not explained is why anyone should enjoy such a depressing and confused piece of work. It seems to me that what we actually enjoy is something quite different. The real play is not so much about men as about metals. The horror of usury lay in the fact that it treated metal in a way contrary to nature. If you have cattle they will breed. To make money—the mere medium of exchange—breed as if it were alive is a sort of black magic. The speech about Laban and Jacob is put into Shylock's mouth to show that he cannot grasp this distinction; and the Christians point out that friendship does not take 'a breed of barren metal'. The important thing about Bassanio is that he can say, 'Only my blood speaks to you in my veins', and again, 'All the wealth I had ran in my veins'. Sir Walter Raleigh most unhappily, to my mind, speaks of Bassanio as a 'pale shadow'. *Pale* is precisely the wrong word. The whole contrast is between the crimson and organic wealth in his veins, the medium of nobility and fecundity, and the cold, mineral wealth in Shylock's counting-house. The charge that he is a mercenary wooer is a product of prosaic analysis. The play is much nearer the *Märchen* level than that. When the hero marries the princess we are not expected to ask whether her wealth, her beauty, or her rank was the determining factor. They are all blended together in the simple man's conception of Princess. Of course great ladies are beautiful: of course they are rich. Bassanio compares Portia to the Golden Fleece. That strikes the proper note. And when once we approach the play with our senses and imaginations it becomes obvious that the presence of the casket story is no accident. For it also is a story about metals, and the rejection of the commercial metals by Bassanio is a kind of counterpoint to the conquest of Shylock's metallic power by the lady of the beautiful mountain. The very terms in which they are rejected proclaim it. Silver is the 'pale and common drudge 'twixt man and man'. Gold is 'hard food for Midas'—Midas who, like Shylock, tried to use as the fuel of life what is in its own nature dead. And the last act, so far from being an irrelevant *coda*, is almost the thing for which the play exists. The 'naughty world' of finance exists in the play chiefly that we may perceive the light of the 'good deed', or rather of the good state, which is called Belmont. I know that some will call this 'far-fetched'; but I must ask them to take my word for it that even if I am wrong, 'far-fetched' is the last epithet that should be applied to my error. I have not fetched it from far. This, or something like it, is my immediate and spontaneous reaction. A wicked ogre of a Jew is ten thousand miles nearer to that reaction than any of the sad, subtle, realistic figures produced by critics. If I err, I err in childishness, not in sophistication.

Now *Hamlet* is a play as nearly opposite to the *Merchant* as possible. A good way of introducing you to my experience of it will be to tell you the exact point at which anyone else's criticism of it begins to lose my allegiance. It is a fairly definite point. As soon as I find anyone treating the ghost merely as the means whereby Hamlet learns of his father's murder—as soon as a critic leaves us with the impression that some other method of disclosure (the finding of a letter or a conversation with a servant) would have done very nearly as well—I part company with that critic. After that, he may be as learned and sensitive as you please; but his outlook on literature is so remote from mine that he can teach me nothing. Hamlet for me is no more separable from his ghost than Macbeth from his witches, Una from her lion, or Dick Whittington from his cat. The Hamlet formula, so to speak, is not 'a man who has to avenge his father' but 'a man who has been given a task by a ghost'. Everything else about him is less important than that. If the play did not begin with the cold and darkness and sickening suspense of the ghost scenes it would be a radically different play. If, on the other hand, only the first act had survived, we should have a very tolerable notion of the play's peculiar quality. I put it to you that everyone's imagination here confirms mine. What is against me is the abstract pattern of motives and characters which we build up as critics when the actual flavour or tint of the poetry is already fading from our minds.

This ghost is different from any other ghost in Elizabethan drama—for, to tell the truth, the Elizabethans in general do their ghosts very vilely. It is permanently ambiguous. Indeed the very word 'ghost', by putting it into the same class with the 'ghosts' of Kyd and Chapman, nay by classifying it at all, puts us on the wrong track. It is 'this thing', 'this dreaded sight', an 'illusion', a 'spirit of health or goblin damn'd', liable at any moment to assume 'some other horrible form' which reason could not survive the vision of. Critics have disputed whether Hamlet is sincere when he doubts whether the apparition is his father's ghost or not. I take him to be perfectly sincere. He believes while the thing is present: he doubts when it is away. Doubt, uncertainty, bewilderment to almost any degree, is what the ghost creates not only in Hamlet's mind but in the minds of the other characters. Shakespeare does not take the concept of 'ghost' for granted, as other dramatists had done. In his play the appearance of the spectre means a breaking down of the walls of the world and the germination of thoughts that cannot really be thought: chaos is come again.

This does not mean that I am going to make the ghost the hero, or the play a ghost story—though I might add that a very good ghost story would be, to me, a more interesting thing than a maze of motives. I have started with the ghost because the ghost appears at the beginning of the play not only to give Hamlet necessary information but also, and even more, to strike the note. From the platform we pass to the court scene and so to Hamlet's first long speech. There are ten lines of it before we reach what is necessary to the plot: lines about the melting of flesh into a dew and the divine prohibition of self-slaughter. We have a second ghost scene after which the play itself, rather than the hero, goes mad for some minutes. We have a second soliloquy on the theme 'to die . . . to sleep'; and a third on 'the witching time of night, when churchyards yawn'. We have the King's effort to pray and Hamlet's comment on it. We have the ghost's third appearance. Ophelia goes mad and is drowned. Then comes the comic relief, surely the strangest comic relief ever written—comic relief beside an open grave, with a further discussion of suicide, a detailed inquiry into the rate of decomposition, a few clutches of skulls, and then 'Alas, poor Yorick!' On top of this, the hideous fighting in the grave; and then, soon, the catastrophe.

I said just now that the subject of the *Merchant* was metals. In the same sense, the subject of *Hamlet* is death. I do not mean by this that most of the characters die, nor even that life and death are the stakes they play for; that is true of all tragedies. I do not mean that we rise from the reading of the play with the feeling that we have been in cold, empty places, places 'outside', *nocte tacentia late*, though that is true. Before I go on to explain myself let me say that here, and throughout my lecture, I am most deeply indebted to my friend Mr Owen Barfield. I have to make these acknowledgements both to him and to other of my friends so often that I am afraid of their being taken for an affectation. But they are not. The next best thing to being wise oneself is to live in a circle of those who are: that good fortune I have enjoyed for nearly twenty years.

The sense in which death is the subject of *Hamlet* will become apparent if we compare it with other plays. Macbeth has commerce with Hell, but at the very outset of his career dismisses all thought of the life to come. For Brutus and Othello, suicide in the high tragic manner is escape and climax. For Lear death is deliverance. For Romeo and Antony, poignant loss. For all these, as for their author while he writes and the audience while they watch, death is the end: it is almost the frame of the picture. They think of dying: no one thinks, in these plays, of *being dead*. In *Hamlet* we are kept thinking about it all the time, whether in terms of the soul's destiny or of the body's. Purgatory, Hell, Heaven, the wounded name, the rights—or wrongs—of Ophelia's burial, and the staying-power of a tanner's corpse: and beyond this, beyond all Christian and all Pagan maps of the hereafter, comes a curious groping and tapping of thoughts, about 'what dreams may come'. It is this that gives to the whole play its quality of darkness and misgiving. Of course there is much else in the play: but nearly always, the same groping. The characters are all watching one another, forming theories about one another, listening, contriving, full of anxiety. The world of *Hamlet* is a world where one has lost one's way. The Prince also has no doubt lost his, and we can tell the precise moment at which he finds it again. 'Not a whit. We defy augury. There's a special providence in the fall of a sparrow. If it be now, 'tis not to come: if it be not to come, it will be now: if it be not now, yet it will come: the readiness is all: since no man has aught of what he leaves, what is't to leave betimes?'[1]

---

[1] I think the last clause is best explained by the assumption that Shakespeare had come across Seneca's 'Nihil perdis ex tuo tempore, nam quod relinquis alienum est' (Epist. lxix).

If I wanted to make one more addition to the gallery of Hamlet's portraits I should trace his hesitation to the fear of death; not to a physical fear of dying, but a fear of being dead. And I think I should get on quite comfortably. Any serious attention to the state of being dead, unless it is limited by some definite religious or anti-religious doctrine, must, I suppose, paralyse the will by introducing infinite uncertainties and rendering all motives inadequate. Being dead is the unknown $x$ in our sum. Unless you ignore it or else give it a value, you can get no answer. But this is not what I am going to do. Shakespeare has not left in the text clear lines of causation which would enable us to connect Hamlet's hesitations with this source. I do not believe he has given us data for any portrait of the kind critics have tried to draw. To that extent I agree with Hanmer, Rümelin, and Mr Eliot. But I differ from them in thinking that it is a fault.

For what, after all, is happening to us when we read any of Hamlet's great speeches? We see visions of the flesh dissolving into a dew, of the world like an unweeded garden. We think of memory reeling in its 'distracted globe'. We watch him scampering hither and thither like a maniac to avoid the voices wherewith he is haunted. Someone says 'Walk out of the air', and we hear the words 'Into my grave' spontaneously respond to it. We think of being bounded in a nut-shell and king of infinite space: but for bad dreams. There's the trouble, for 'I am most dreadfully attended'. We see the picture of a dull and muddy-mettled rascal, a John-a-dreams, somehow unable to move while ultimate dishonour is done him. We listen to his fear lest the whole thing may be an illusion due to melancholy. We get the sense of sweet relief at the words 'shuffled off this mortal coil' but mixed with the bottomless doubt about what may follow then. We think of bones and skulls, of women breeding sinners, and of how some, to whom all this experience is a sealed book, can yet dare death and danger 'for an eggshell'. But do we really enjoy these things, do we go back to them, because they show us Hamlet's character? Are they, from *that* point of view, so very interesting? Does the mere fact that a young man, literally haunted, dispossessed, and lacking friends, should feel thus, tell us anything remarkable? Let me put my question in another way. If instead of the speeches he actually utters about the firmament and man in his scene with Rosencrantz and Guildenstern Hamlet had merely said, 'I don't seem to enjoy things the way I used to', and talked in that fashion throughout, should we find him interesting? I think the answer is 'Not very'. It may be replied that if he talked commonplace prose he would reveal his character less vividly. I am not so sure. He would certainly have revealed *something* less vividly; but would that something be himself? It seems to me that 'this majestical roof' and 'What a piece of work is a man' give me primarily an impression not of the sort of person he must be to lose the estimation of things but of the things themselves and their great value; and that I should be able to discern, though with very faint interest, the same condition of loss in a personage who was quite unable so to put before me what he was losing. And I do not think it true to reply that he would be a different character if he spoke less poetically. This point is often misunderstood. We sometimes speak as if the characters in whose mouths Shakespeare puts great poetry were poets: in the sense that Shakespeare was depicting men of poetical genius. But surely this is like thinking that Wagner's Wotan is the dramatic portrait of a baritone? In opera song is the medium by which the representation is made and not part of the thing represented. The actors sing; the dramatic personages are feigned to be speaking. The only character who sings dramatically in *Figaro* is Cherubino. Similarly in poetical drama poetry is the medium, not part of the delineated characters. While the actors speak poetry written for them by the poet, the dramatic personages are supposed to be merely talking. If ever there is occasion to *represent* poetry (as in the play scene from *Hamlet*), it is put into a different metre and strongly stylized so as to prevent confusion.

I trust that my conception is now becoming clear. I believe that we read Hamlet's speeches with interest chiefly because they describe so well a certain spiritual region through which most of us have passed and anyone in his circumstances might be expected to pass, rather than because of our concern to understand how and why this particular man entered it. I foresee an objection on the ground that I am thus really

admitting his 'character' in the only sense that matters and
that all characters whatever could be equally well talked away
by the method I have adopted. But I do really find a
distinction. When I read about Mrs Proudie I am not in the
least interested in seeing the world from her point of view, for
her point of view is not interesting; what does interest me is
precisely the sort of person she was. In *Middlemarch* no
reader wants to see Casaubon through Dorothea's eyes; the
pathos, the comedy, the value of the whole thing is to
understand Dorothea and see how such an illusion was
inevitable for her. In Shakespeare himself I find Beatrice to be
a characer who could not be thus dissolved. We are interested
not in some vision seen through her eyes, but precisely in the
wonder of her being the girl she is. A comparison of the
sayings we remember from her part with those we remember
from Hamlet's brings out the contrast. On the one hand, 'I
wonder that you will still be talking, Signior Benedick',
'There was a star danced and under that I was born'. 'Kill
Claudio'; on the other, 'The undiscovered country from
whose bourne no traveller returns', 'Use every man after his
desert, and who should 'scape whipping?', 'The rest is
silence'. Particularly noticeable is the passage where Hamlet
professes to be describing his own character. 'I am myself
indifferent honest: but yet I could accuse me of such things
that it were better my mother had not borne me. I am very
proud, revengeful, ambitious.' It is, of course, possible to
devise some theory which explains these self-accusations in
terms of character. But long before we have done so the real
significance of the lines has taken possession of our imagination for ever. 'Such fellows as I' does not mean 'such fellows
as Goethe's Hamlet, or Coleridge's Hamlet, or any Hamlet':
it means *men*—creatures shapen in sin and conceived in
iniquity—and the vast, empty vision of them 'crawling
between earth and heaven' is what really counts and really
carries the burden of the play.

It is often cast in the teeth of the great critics that each in
painting *Hamlet* has drawn a portrait of himself. How if they
were right? I would go a long way to meet Beatrice or Falstaff
or Mr Jonathan Oldbuck or Disraeli's Lord Monmouth. I
would not cross the room to meet Hamlet. It would never be

necessary. He is always where I am. The method of the whole play is much nearer to Mr Eliot's own method in poetry than Mr Eliot suspects. Its true hero is man—haunted man—man with his mind on the frontier of two worlds, man unable either quite to reject or quite to admit the supernatural, man struggling to get something done as man has struggled from the beginning, yet incapable of achievement because of his inability to understand either himself or his fellows or the real quality of the universe which has produced him. To be sure, some hints of more particular motives for Hamlet's delay are every now and then fadged up to silence our questions, just as some show of motives is offered for the Duke's temporary abdication in *Measure for Measure*. In both cases it is only scaffolding or machinery. To mistake these mere *succedanea* for the real play and to try to work them up into a coherent psychology is the great error. I once had a whole batch of School Certificate answers on the Nun's Priest's Tale by boys whose form-master was apparently a breeder of poultry. Every thing that Chaucer had said in describing Chauntecleer and Pertelote was treated by them simply and solely as evidence about the precise breed of these two birds. And, I must admit, the result was very interesting. They proved beyond doubt that Chauntecleer was very different from our modern specialized strains and much closer to the Old English 'barn-door fowl'. But I couldn't help feeling that they had missed something. I believe our attention to Hamlet's 'character' in the usual sense misses almost as much.

Perhaps I should rather say that it *would* miss as much if our behaviour when we are actually reading were not wiser than our criticism in cold blood. The critics, or most of them, have at any rate kept constantly before us the knowledge that in this play there is greatness and mystery. They were never entirely wrong. Their error, on my view, was to put the mystery in the wrong place—in Hamlet's motives rather than in that darkness which enwraps Hamlet and the whole tragedy and all who read or watch it. It is a mysterious play in the sense of being a play about mystery. Mr Eliot suggests that 'more people have thought *Hamlet* a work of art because they found it interesting, than have found it interesting because it is a work of art'. When he wrote that sentence he must have been very near to what I believe to be the truth. This play is, above all else, *interesting*. But artistic failure is not in itself interesting, nor often interesting in any way: artistic success always is. To interest is the first duty of art; no other excellences will even begin to compensate for failure in this, and very serious faults will be covered by this, as by charity. The hypothesis that this play interests by being good and not by being bad has therefore the first claim on our consideration. The burden of proof rests on the other side. Is not the fascinated interest of the critics most naturally explained by supposing that this is the precise effect the play was written to produce? They may be finding the mystery in the wrong place; but the fact that they can never leave *Hamlet* alone, the continual groping, the sense, unextinguished by over a century of failures, that we have here something of inestimable importance, is surely the best evidence that the real and lasting mystery of our human situation has been greatly depicted.

The kind of criticism which I have attempted is always at a disadvantage against either historical criticism or character criticism. Their vocabulary has been perfected by long practice, and the truths with which they are concerned are those which we are accustomed to handle in the everyday business of life. But the things I want to talk about have no vocabulary and criticism has for centuries kept almost complete silence on them. I make no claim to be a pioneer. Professor Wilson Knight (though I disagree with nearly everything he says in detail), Miss Spurgeon, Miss Bodkin, and Mr Barfield are my leaders. But those who do not enjoy the honours of a pioneer may yet share his discomforts. One of them I feel acutely at the moment. I feel certain that to many of you the things I have been saying about *Hamlet* will appear intolerably sophisticated, abstract, and modern. And so they sound when we have to put them into words. But I shall have failed completely if I cannot persuade you that my view, for good or ill, has just the opposite characteristics—is naïve and concrete and archaic. I am trying to recall attention from the things an intellectual adult notices to the things a child or a peasant notices—night, ghosts, a castle, a lobby where a man can walk four hours together, a willow-fringed brook and a sad lady drowned, a graveyard and a terrible cliff above the sea, and amidst all these a pale man in black clothes (would that our producers would ever let him appear!) with his stockings coming down, a dishevelled man whose words make us at once think of loneliness and doubt and dread, of waste and dust and emptiness, and from whose hands, or from our own, we feel the richness of heaven and earth and the comfort of human affection slipping away. In a sense I have kept my promise of bestowing all my childishness upon you. A child is always thinking about those details in a story which a grown-up regards as indifferent. If when you first told the tale your hero was warned by three little men appearing on the left of the road, and when you tell it again you introduce one little man on the right of the road, the child protests. And the child is right. You think it makes no difference because you are not living the story at all. If you were, you would know better. *Motifs*, machines, and the like are abstractions of literary history and therefore interchangeable: but concrete imagination knows nothing of them.

You must not think I am setting up as a sort of literary Peter Pan who does not grow up. On the contrary, I claim that only those adults who have retained, with whatever additions and enrichments, their first childish response to poetry unimpaired, can be said to have grown up at all. Mere change is not growth. Growth is the synthesis of change and continuity, and where there is no continuity there is no growth. To hear some critics, one would suppose that a man had to lose his nursery appreciation of *Gulliver* before he acquired his mature appreciation of it. It is not so. If it were, the whole concept of maturity, of ripening, would be out of place: and also, I believe we should very seldom read more than three pages of *Gulliver* at a sitting.

# 8. HAMLET AND OPHELIA

## By HAROLD JENKINS

In the interpretation of *Hamlet* criticism has found many problems; but none has proved more puzzling than the hero's treatment of Ophelia in the so-called 'nunnery scene'. Dr Johnson saw in this Hamlet's 'useless and wanton cruelty' to one who was young and beautiful, harmless and pious. But Professor Dover Wilson defends Hamlet at some length by explaining how he must regard Ophelia as a jilt and a dissembler. It is usual to stress her playing the decoy, and to speak of her 'betraying' Hamlet. Sir Edmund Chambers may stand for many who deplore her weakness. Others have seen her as a light o' love; Dame Rebecca West tells us roundly that 'she was not a chaste young woman'; and there used to be a theory, favoured by some nineteenth-century German critics and still occasionally revived, that she was actually Hamlet's mistress. Yet Professor G. R. Elliott praises her 'religious strength' and perceives in her the symbol of 'the Christian charity . . . which Hamlet needs'. Professor Leo Kirschbaum, on the other hand, regards her as pitifully out of her depth in Hamlet's 'spiritual milieu'.[1] Amid such diverse opinions I feel nearly as bewildered as Ophelia herself. They do not encourage me to hope that anything I say about the problem will be universally acceptable; but at least they may excuse my wish to re-examine it.

The nunnery scene has its origin in the early versions of the Hamlet story. In Saxo and Belleforest, when Hamlet pretends to be mad, in order to test the genuineness of his madness the King employs a beautiful woman to try her charms upon him. This is the beautiful woman's role, and in Saxo and Belleforest it is the whole of it. In Shakespeare, however—with or

---

[1] Johnson (ed.), *The Plays of William Shakespeare* (1775), viii. 311; Dover Wilson, *What Happens in Hamlet* (Cambridge 1935), pp. 125 ff.; Chambers, *Shakespeare: A Survey* (London, 1925), pp. 187–8; R. West, *The Court and the Castle* (New Haven, 1957), p. 15; Elliott, *Scourge and Minister* (Durham, NC, 1951), pp. xxx–xxxi; Kirschbaum, 'Hamlet and Ophelia', *Philological Quarterly*, xxxv (1956), 388.

without the precedent of the lost English play of *Hamlet*—this single episode has become the middle of a story which has also a beginning and an end. And it is the beginning and the end which give the middle its significance.

The beginning of the story is that Hamlet loves Ophelia; and the character of his love is plainly told us by Ophelia herself in three short speeches to her father, who demands to know 'the truth'. Hamlet has made many 'tenders of his affection', 'in honourable fashion', and with 'holy vows of heaven'. Whatever doubts may be cast upon them, now or later, the memory of those 'holy vows of heaven' will stay with us throughout the play. Yet the end of Ophelia's story, when she drowns hanging garlands on a willow, is a death emblematic of forsaken love; and the flowers that should have decked her bridal-bed are strewed upon her grave. It is now that we get from the Queen the most explicit statement of what Hamlet's love had looked to: 'I hoped thou shouldst have been my Hamlet's wife.' But that this was also Hamlet's hope we may gather from those 'holy vows' at the beginning and the love so far beyond a brother's that he now at the end declares: 'I loved Ophelia. Forty thousand brothers Could not . . . Make up my sum.' Ophelia is the woman Hamlet had wished to marry. Yet the disastrous end of initial hope has come about through an encounter in which he has stormed at her to get her to a nunnery. This encounter is clearly the moment of crisis in Hamlet's relations with Ophelia; and that is why, if we would appreciate Ophelia's function in the play, we must try to understand its meaning.

The dramatic impact of the nunnery scene is very great; and the more so since it is most artfully prepared for. Remarkably enough, until it occurs, almost at the middle of the play, we are never allowed to see Hamlet and Ophelia meet, though we have known from the first that they inevitably must. This long deferment holds us in suspense, while everything is being done to enhance our curiosity and ensure that, when they do meet, their encounter will have the maximum effect.

Preparation begins from the moment that Hamlet's love is introduced. The first reference to it is when Ophelia's brother warns her to 'fear' Hamlet's 'trifling' with her chastity. This is before we hear anything of 'holy vows', which her father at once suspects of commending 'unholy suits'. The suspicions of Ophelia's father and brother arouse our apprehension that the course of love will not run smooth, and, with Shakespeare's flair for opening up a dramatic situation, this very scene, which tells of Hamlet's love, has Ophelia promising to give her lover up.

For her obedience to her father Ophelia has been much blamed. This was not, it is observed, the way of Juliet and Desdemona, who defied their fathers in the cause of love. But the simple answer to this is that Ophelia is in a different play—and a play to which the conventions of romantic love-story, where fathers exist in order to be circumvented, have singularly little relevance. The first premiss of *Hamlet* is that sons must avenge their fathers; and a play which required sons to avenge and daughters to flout their fathers would be in danger of moral chaos. Nor ought respect for a father to prove so hard to tolerate. The sixteenth century enjoined it, Shakespeare certainly approved of it, and instances of it are occasionally met with even at the present day. The natural bonds of the family are as strong for Ophelia as for Hamlet, as the play will show. It is not unimportant that the first words it gives Ophelia to speak assure her brother she will write to him; and when this admirable sister shows herself an obedient daughter by ceasing communication with Hamlet, we should not be surprised and should certainly not reproach her but should look forward to developments.

Developments are swift. For the next we see of Ophelia is when she enters terrified by Hamlet's strange apparition in her closet. The 'doublet all unbraced', ungartered stockings, and the rest Polonius immediately recognizes as the symptoms of love-madness, and they are in the play in order that he shall. But what Polonius sees as madness we are invited to regard as feigning. For Hamlet has already warned us that he will 'put on' some 'strange or odd' behaviour; and though the scholars tell us that two months have intervened, for an audience, who go by playing time, it is no longer ago than it takes to speak a mere eighty lines of verse since Hamlet made the promise which now seems to receive its QED. Yet this first account of 'strange or odd' behaviour disturbs us with its hints of something more mysterious and profound. That sign of Hamlet's, which Polonius ascribes to a distracted lover and we to a feigned madman, 'did seem to shatter all his bulk and end his being'. More has happened to Hamlet, as we know, than Ophelia's denying him. Yet it cannot be an accident that this first evidence of his so ambiguous madness is connected with Ophelia. Her description of how he went from her, finding his way 'without his eyes' and bending their light upon her to the last, haunts us. It is a parting reluctant yet of a spell-like compulsion; and it gives, of course, an image and foreshadowing of that later parting, which the nunnery scene will enact.

The closet episode, with its complex of suggestions, leaves us tantalized. And its effect is not diminished when we now find all the court in alarm about Hamlet's 'transformation' and Polonius arriving to expound his theory of it. To tell the court what Ophelia told him would be natural, but in drama tiresomely repetitive. So instead he reads a letter. We need not ask, as the commentators do, when Hamlet could have written this letter or Ophelia received it. What matters is its introduction at this point. Though this has been disputed, it is certainly a love-letter, but as certainly a strange one. The author of Shakespeare's sonnets could obviously have done better by Hamlet had he wished. The art of the letter, I take it, is neither to confirm nor yet dispel the notion of love-madness. It sustains mystification; and the touch of comedy in Polonius' fussy self-importance can be used to relax tension without surrendering suspense. Indeed comedy acquires an edge of irony as expectation grows that Polonius is due to be confounded. The more he insists that all is clear, the more we feel that all is yet to be explained. When he comes to his plot to confront Hamlet with Ophelia, we eagerly await the promised meeting.

There is ample excuse for the bad quarto to move on to it at once. But the authentic text of the second quarto shows Shakespeare still postponing it. Yet if we are still to be denied the expected encounter with Ophelia, what better could we have instead than an encounter with her father, who boasts of reading Hamlet's riddle? This will more than satisfy us for the moment by beginning his confounding, while raising interest even higher in what is still to come. When Hamlet enters for

Polonius to 'board' him, this is the first time that we see him since the 'transformation' of which we have heard so much. Immediate demonstration is essential, and is delightfully provided when Polonius' too pointed query, 'Do you know me, my lord?', wins the instant retort, 'You are a fishmonger.' Applied to Polonius in its literal sense, the word has a shattering incongruity, which its cant use for a wencher, if we know it, may redouble. Polonius disclaims it, Hamlet talks of the rarity of an honest man, goes on to a dead dog, and ejects, 'Have you a daughter?', thereby introducing with an agreeable shock the very topic the play requires them to discuss. All this confirms Polonius in his view that Hamlet is 'far gone', and on Ophelia's account, but permits us to suppose that Hamlet, like Touchstone and other licensed fools, is using his folly like a stalking-horse under cover of which to shoot his wit. Yet the role of the fool is one that Shakespeare often uses to hint at more than sanity can state, and with the line already blurred between the feint of madness and a genuine disturbance, we get glimpses through the mad talk of what is stirring deep in Hamlet's mind. Polonius' daughter comes into the dialogue in a context highly charged. Fishmongers were popularly associated with loose women, whether as their fathers or procurers, and 'honest' has a second meaning, with which women are concerned. A sudden leap brings us to polluted procreation. 'If the sun breed maggots in a dead dog, being a good kissing carrion—'. 'Carrion', too, has a second meaning, and from kissing and breeding to the woman who may do these a train of thought is clear. It is a pity Warburton perplexed it by emending to 'a *god* kissing carrion', which Johnson thought a 'noble' reading and which some scholars still defend. 'A good kissing carrion', like a good eating apple—to cite a parallel which I think was Percy Simpson's—is one well suited for the purpose. The dead dog which the sun embraces is prolific. The analogy with Polonius' daughter is not perhaps a pretty one; but at least it will be plain why Hamlet says, 'Let her not walk i' th' sun.' Knowing that Polonius is planning to 'loose' his daughter to the Prince, we may find the warning apt. That 'conception is a blessing' Hamlet punningly acknowledges; but with the maggots of the dead dog in mind we may have

our reservations, and we must be ready for Hamlet's recoil.
'As your daughter may conceive—friend, look to 't.' The
warning given to Polonius is to guard his daughter from the
destiny of her womanhood. This must be still in Hamlet's
mind when on Polonius' next appearance he addresses him as
Jephthah. For Jephthah too had a 'fair daughter', as Hamlet
indeed tells us by quoting a popular ballad. What he does not
tell us, but what the completed ballad would, and what in any
case we ought to know, is that Jephthah sacrificed his
daughter while she was still a virgin. And though Polonius,
along with most Shakespearian commentators, fails to see this
point, it does something to explain why Hamlet, when he
meets Ophelia, directs her to a nunnery. The Jephthah
allusion by itself would be enough to refute that queer theory
that Ophelia was Hamlet's mistress. What the play suggests is
not that Hamlet seduces her but that he condemns her to
virginity. This is what the nunnery scene does.

When now at last the lovers meet, for the first time in the
play, we are keyed up with expectancy. We know that
Ophelia has first accepted and then rejected Hamlet's love
addresses. We know that Polonius believes this has driven
Hamlet mad. We share Polonius' view that Hamlet's strange-
ness is connected with Ophelia. But I think we do not share
his view of what the connection is. When Ophelia now
repeats her rejection of Hamlet's love, on the stage before our
eyes, by giving him back his lover's gifts, the moment is
supremely tense. Yet whatever we expect from this, it will
hardly be what happens. For the first astonishing thing about
their conversation, though insufficiently remarked on, is that
the expected roles of the lovers are reversed. Ophelia, to be
sure, has denied Hamlet access to her; but it is she, not he,
who speaks of the 'many a day' since they have met. And
though she returns Hamlet's gifts, it is not she but he who
now repudiates their love. He does not complain of getting
his gifts back; he says he never gave them. It is not the
receiver but the giver of the gifts who proves 'unkind', so that
instead of his reproaching her with inconstancy, she reproaches him. This runs so much counter to what Polonius, at
least, would have led us to expect that many regard it as
duplicity on Ophelia's part. Professor Dover Wilson, for

example, says, 'She, the jilt, is accusing him of coldness towards her.'[2] But this is to ignore that Hamlet has just disowned the tokens of his love. It is not Ophelia only, it is the play itself which now presents the estrangement as of Hamlet's making. When Hamlet says, 'I never gave you aught', I cannot think it just for Professor Dover Wilson to put the stress on *you*—'I never gave *you* aught'—as though Hamlet charges a fickle Ophelia with having become another person. Her reply shows that she has not. It is true that some have heard in it the tones of calculation. Interpretation can be very subjective; and I am aware of that risk in my own. Yet I am fairly certain that a character in an Elizabethan play is not to be judged insincere for speaking in a rhyming couplet. The woman who returns the gifts is the same as first spoke of Hamlet's love. For her the gifts are 'remembrances', and when he chooses to deny them, she recalls the 'words of so sweet breath composed As made the things more rich', whose 'perfume' now is 'lost'. What *we* may recall is that her brother told her at the beginning to esteem Hamlet's love like a 'violet', with a 'perfume' 'sweet not lasting'. The ironic echo is poignant; and there will shortly be another. Her father warned her at the beginning, 'Do not believe his vows'; but now it is Hamlet himself who says, 'You should not have believed me.' The theory, whether Polonius' or ours, that what is troubling Hamlet is Ophelia's unkindness can hardly explain *this*. If the gifts which she holds out to him seem at first to image *her* denial of love, they stay on stage between them as the sign of *his*.

What then of the usual theory that Hamlet treats Ophelia as he does because she has betrayed him? Making Hamlet in our own image, we require him to resent her stopping the addresses she at first was ready to receive; but if he does, he never lets us know. The ways of madness, real or feigned, are legitimately extraordinary. Yet Hamlet's madness is at the dramatist's service, and if it serves him by being extra-ordinary, it must also be extraordinary in a significant way. And what I find both extraordinary and significant is that Hamlet reproaches Ophelia not for refusing his love but for

---

[2] *What Happens in Hamlet*, p. 130.

having once accepted it under the illusion that he gave it. We are perhaps at liberty to suppose that Ophelia's repelling him has contributed to this extraordinary behaviour; but that is something the play now chooses not to stress. What I think it comes to is that Ophelia's repelling Hamlet is a necessary part of the dramatic plot, which Shakespeare manipulates with customary dramatic skill. With Polonius's help it provides the occasion for the nunnery scene. But the use that is made of that occasion when it arrives suggests that Hamlet's imagination, and that of the dramatist who creates him, is involved with something deeper. And the conversations with Polonius have given dark hints of what it is.

Now certainly Hamlet distrusts Ophelia. In one of his sudden, bewildering questions he asks her, 'Are you honest?' If we think Ophelia has played him fast and loose, the question may seem pertinent. It comes just when she has returned his gifts. But it also comes just when she has shown how much she cherished them. This is what makes it particularly cruel. To Ophelia, whose beauty he has praised, Hamlet now maintains that beauty and honesty do not go together.

The power of beauty will sooner transform honesty from what it is to a bawd than the force of honesty can translate beauty into his likeness.

Ophelia's danger is apparent. Hamlet told her father to keep her from the sun; he tells her to 'admit no discourse' to her beauty. I take this to be less an accusation than a warning. But Ophelia has no fears of herself. She appears to believe that a woman's love may be pure. What Hamlet thinks about this, already glanced at in his talk about the carrion in the sun, about kissing, conception, and breeding, will now be more explicit. 'Why, wouldst thou be a breeder of sinners?' This question editors always punctuate in a way that seems to me mistaken. The 'why' is not, I think, an interrogative ('Why wouldst thou . . . ?'), as though Hamlet seeks a reason for a curious predilection on Ophelia's part. I take 'why' as an interjection. It is a favourite with Hamlet and conveys expostulation. 'Why, wouldst thou be a breeder of sinners?' There is one means other than Jephthah's to save Ophelia

from this fate. And I note that it is just at this point that
Hamlet first bids Ophelia to get her 'to a nunnery'.

Hamlet's objection to Ophelia, then, is that she is a woman,
and a woman he has loved. He has come to know what
women are, and Ophelia has to be shown. He does not accuse
her of having betrayed him; he implies that she inevitably
will. He lays out for her her character; but the sins for which
he reviles her—unfaithfulness, dissimulation, wantonness—
are less her own than the sins of all her sex. To the woman he
had hoped to marry he delivers a diatribe against marriage,
insisting that there shall be no more of it.

Yet there are two parties to marriage, and we must surely
think, as Hamlet does, of both. His protest, 'Wouldst thou be
a breeder of sinners?', when regarded merely as denunciation
of Ophelia, as it often is, is interpreted in too limited a sense.
Though Hamlet sees in Ophelia the nature of a woman and all
the sins that belong to it, his first speech to her in this
scene—and that means in the play itself—refers not to her
sins but to his.

> Nymph, in thy orisons
> Be all my sins remembered.

This is sometimes taken as sarcasm; but Johnson, with good
reason, thought it a 'grave and solemn' address; and if sarcasm
it is, like other of Hamlet's sarcasms it hides something
underneath. That Hamlet has in mind his condition of sinful
man will presently appear when he refers to the human stock
from which he springs. The Queen had hoped that Ophelia's
virtues would restore her ailing son; but Hamlet knows that
virtue itself cannot eliminate his taint. Is that not why he
could not love, and why Ophelia should not have received the
love he offered? In one significant speech these thoughts all
come together:

You should not have believed me; for virtue cannot so inoculate our
old stock but we shall relish of it. I loved you not.

Is it not because he is what he is that she should not have
believed him? It is now, when she twice confesses that she
has, that he breaks out, 'Get thee to a nunnery. Why, wouldst
thou be a breeder of sinners?' Though he has asked her if she

is honest and will presently proceed to her sins, it is again of his own sins that he first speaks.

I am myself indifferent honest, but yet I could accuse me of such things that it were better my mother had not borne me.

She should not have believed him, and she must not.

What should such fellows as I do crawling between earth and heaven? . . . Believe none of us. Go thy ways to a nunnery.

Far from valuing his love too little, she has valued it too well. So he not only denies his own love; he would also extinguish hers. It is not only herself that the nunnery is to save her from. If Hamlet cannot marry Ophelia, it is equally important that she must not marry him.

The nunnery scene, then, dramatizes with the utmost force and vividness Hamlet's parting from Ophelia and some complex reasons for it. The end of their interview confirms what the beginning of it suggested, that it is not Ophelia who has abandoned him but he who abandons her. Five times he bids her to a nunnery, and three times says 'Farewell', finally going off in rage while she is left solitary on the stage, 'deject and wretched', to recall once more those 'musicked vows' of which she has 'sucked the honey' and which we have just heard him disown. The scene has shown us that she has treasured Hamlet's love; it suggests that she has returned it; and may I not now add that she loves him still? The grief which she expresses is less for her plight than for his. When he poured abuse upon her, she prayed Heaven to restore him; and she says less of herself forsaken than of his noble mind now wrecked. The critic who pronounces her soliloquy 'all surface and starch'[3] may judge less well than Coleridge, who saw in it the exquisite unselfishness of love.[4] I do not think the play which gives her this soliloquy means to present Ophelia as a loose woman or a traitor.

But what are we to say about her famous lie? When Hamlet suddenly asks her, 'Where's your father?' and she replies, 'At home', we gasp. For those who see her as the betrayer, this is the climax of her treachery. Kittredge, however, in a very

---

[3] Kirschbaum, loc. cit.
[4] *Shakespearean Criticism*, ed. T. M. Raysor, Everyman edn. (London, 1960), i. 27.

interesting note, defends it as her only possible answer. She could hardly say, 'My father is behind the arras.' The lie is forced upon her, and we could add that she tells it plainly and without equivocation. But I do not find such arguments entirely satisfactory; for the play, had it wished to, could have saved her from her lie by sparing her Hamlet's question. Her answer is as staggering as the question, and that is one reason why Ophelia must give it. It forces upon our attention, and in the most sensational way, what we may by this time be in danger of forgetting, that Polonius is not 'at home', but close at hand. The crux, of course, is whether Hamlet is supposed to know this too. There is a well-known stage tradition for Polonius to betray his presence at this point, usually by peering through a curtain; and a common interpretation is that Hamlet seizes his opportunity to catch Ophelia out, and that his manner to her consequently changes from now on. His manner must be what the actor makes it, and if the actor exhibits mounting fury, the text will give him some support. But the text shows Hamlet making no more reference to Ophelia's lie than he has done to her repelling of his suit. I remember again that the ways of a suspected madman may be strange; but I may still observe that Hamlet does not say that women are liars, who betray their lovers to their fathers, and plot with their enemies against them. It is the critics who say this. What Hamlet says is that women are wantons, who give themselves faces God did not, and make cuckolds of their husbands—all of which has little to do with the lie Ophelia has just told but much to do with what he has been saying to her before. He has already put her honesty in question, maintained that beautiful women cannot be expected to stay chaste, and warned her against breeding sinners. He goes on to warn her against marriage. He has already recommended a nunnery twice; he now does so three times more. I have come across the proposal that when he first says, 'Get thee to a nunnery', he should speak the words with tenderness, as though anxious for her safety, and then, on discovering Polonius and the trick, he should change his tone to anger; and the scene could obviously be played in that way. But that the nunnery is first a literal one and then becomes a brothel,[5]

[5] Cf. *Hamlet*, ed. J. Q. Adams (Cambridge, Mass., 1929), pp. 258–60.

and that the actor's voice and gesture can convey this, is
something I take leave to doubt. When the nunnery, at
whatever stages, becomes a brothel, it becomes, I suspect, a
red herring.

The question, 'Where's your father?', interrupts the dialogue in Hamlet's characteristically disconcerting way; but it
does not deflect its course. That others before me have
perceived this is evident from the practice of some producers
of making Hamlet detect Polonius much earlier in the
scene—when he asks Ophelia if she is honest, or even when
she first offers to return the gifts. But this does not much
improve matters, since, as we have seen, the route which
brings us to the nunnery has come via Jephthah's daughter
from the carrion in the sun. If Hamlet is aware of Polonius'
trick at all, must he not be aware of it from the outset?
Professor Dover Wilson has some logic on his side in deciding
that Hamlet must overhear Polonius propose it, and he
invents a new stage-direction to enable him to do so.
Elizabethan play-texts being what they are, their stage-
directions are often insufficient. But they are only insufficient
when they fail to indicate some action which the dialogue
necessitates or implies. And an editor who supplements them
must be careful not to lead the dialogue when the dialogue
should lead him.

Now in the matter of overhearing on the stage the
Elizabethans had conventions, and an instructive article by
Miss Helen Gardner[6] has shown us what they were.
Shakespearian eavesdroppers declare themselves to us as such,
as indeed dramatic effect requires and as Polonius and
Claudius very elaborately do. They explain that they will be
'behind an arras' to 'mark the encounter' of Hamlet and
Ophelia; and when the encounter is over Polonius says, 'We
heard it all.' But Hamlet is less helpful. He does not say, 'I
heard it all.' He leaves Professor Dover Wilson to infer this.
In the converse situation, when a character who is spied on
has knowledge of the spies, he must likewise make it clear to
us. And that is another dramatic duty which Hamlet fails to
perform. Whatever we may think of the trick now being

---

[6] 'Lawful Espials', *Modern Language Review*, xxxiii (1938), 345 ff.

played on him, I find no evidence that Hamlet ever thinks, or knows, of it at all.

To the conventions which Miss Gardner has expounded, I should like to add another, best seen in an example. In *Henry IV* there is an episode in which Prince Hal and Poins arrange to spy on Falstaff with his whore. And no sooner have they taken up their places than Doll Tearsheet obligingly inquires, 'What humour's the Prince of?', with the result that the listeners hear something about themselves. Am I to suppose, as some indeed have done, that they are recognized by Doll Tearsheet, who deliberately leads Falstaff on? I am glad to find that the learned Variorum editor says I need not. In fact Doll asks about the Prince not because she knows, but because the audience know, that the Prince is within earshot. She requires no further motive for her question; the design it serves is not the speaker's but the play's. And dramatic convention readily permits this. Hamlet's question is no doubt less simple: while fixing on the unseen listener, it also exhibits the workings of Hamlet's mind. But the dramatic convention is fundamentally the same. Indeed it is precisely this convention that allows Hamlet to remind *us* of Polonius' presence and still be his surprising, incalculable self. Those critics and producers who make Hamlet discover where Polonius is provide him with so crude a reason for his question as to destroy half of its effect. That Polonius shall hear what Hamlet says is less Hamlet's purpose than the purpose of the play in which he figures.

It is to assist this purpose of the play that Ophelia must tell her lie. When she says her father is 'at home', Hamlet is able to retort, 'Let the doors be shut upon him, that he may play the fool nowhere but in's own house.' Whatever Hamlet has in mind by this, it is certain that the dramatist has more. For the play will show how Polonius, by not keeping to his own house, by playing the fool once more behind an arras, comes to grief. The fate of the second unseen listener is also now anticipated. We know that Hamlet must ultimately kill the King; and he gives us here the promise that he will. 'Those that are married already, all but one, shall live.' But again, what the play requires is not that Hamlet shall know, but that we shall know, that the King is there to hear it.

The opportunity for such dramatic piquancies was far too good for an accomplished dramatist to miss. But as Shakespeare's art exploits it, there is more than a brief thrill. The situation of Ophelia at the moment of her crisis is combined and involved with the other situations out of which Hamlet's tragedy develops. While Hamlet is announcing to Ophelia her fate, he foreshadows the fates of Polonius and the King; while he is bidding her to the nunnery, he reminds us of his duty of revenge. And the marriage that will not now take place is linked with one that has taken place already. The conjoining of these situations here is but one sign of the play's intense imaginative coherence. It is in the context of Hamlet's revenge and his mother's marriage that Ophelia's story is shaped, and it is of course within the larger drama of Hamlet's revenge and his mother's marriage—though I can speak of these but briefly—that Hamlet's relations with Ophelia have their deepest significance.

Before we know anything of Hamlet's vows to Ophelia, or indeed of Ophelia's existence, his revulsion from his mother's marriage is deeply impressed upon us. It is the marriage of one who, having hung upon a loving husband, accepts the embraces of his brother, posting with 'wicked speed' to 'incestuous sheets'. The Ghost that comes to tell Hamlet of his father's murder enlarges also on his mother's filthy lust; and these awful revelations will still be in our minds when we hear of Hamlet in Ophelia's closet looking like one 'loosed out of hell To speak of horrors'. His distracted state, which Polonius ascribes to disappointed love, is connected by the Queen with her 'o'er-hasty marriage'. 'Frailty, thy name is woman!' was Hamlet's bitter comment on what his mother's marriage showed him, and when at length we find him with Ophelia, it is of woman's frailty that he speaks and the sins that it engenders. The play represents him in the nunnery scene turning from Ophelia in anger and despair, and at once goes on, in its big central scene, where all its various actions intertwine, to show him for the first and only time with his mother and Ophelia together. The primary purpose of the play-within-the-play is no doubt to 'catch the conscience of the King'; but it also makes assault upon the conscience of the Queen. The imaging of her worthless love Hamlet watches, as the dialogue is at some pains to emphasize, from a place at Ophelia's feet. He draws Ophelia's attention to how cheerfully his mother sits by her new husband with her first one but just dead; and it is when the dumb-show has presented the fickleness of a royal wife that he taunts Ophelia with the brevity of woman's love. The re-enacting of his mother's story is framed by his bitter jests to Ophelia, which make her who has received his holy vows the object now of every lewd insinuation. For her share in this dialogue Ophelia's character has suffered much at the commentators' hands; but an examination of the dialogue will show, I think, that the obscene equivocations are all in Hamlet's part. The worst that we can say of her is that she appears to understand them. The explication of them, which editors forbear to give, I need not supply. It will be enough to say that they run all the time upon the sexual organs and their use in copulation. A final thrust about how women take their husbands is Hamlet's last word to Ophelia in the play.

To his mother he will speak further. For the play-scene is presently to be followed by a scene between Hamlet and his mother, just as it was preceded by a scene between Hamlet and Ophelia. These two scenes, in which he denounces each of them in turn, balance one another in the structure of the play, and set the marriage which is not to be against the marriage which is in being. In the interview with his mother Hamlet makes no mention of Ophelia; but the patterning of a play may often suggest to us what the dialogue cannot make explicit. It is impossible that we should not think of her. If 'hell' can mutiny 'in a matron's bones', Hamlet bursts out, the virtue of a youthful love may 'melt' in its own 'fire'. How should Ophelia be honest? Hamlet's mother has transformed marriage. She has done an act that

> takes off the rose
> From the fair forehead of an innocent love
> And sets a blister there, makes marriage vows
> As false as dicers' oaths, O, such a deed
> As from the body of contraction plucks
> The very soul.

>                           (III. iv. 42–7)

For the rose of love Hamlet sees the blister of the harlot; with the soul gone out of marriage, grossness alone remains. There must be no more marriage.

It is ironic that Gertrude, who feared that Hamlet's 'distemper' had to do with her marriage, should have hoped that Ophelia's virtues might help to cure him of it. It is still more ironic that the Queen at Ophelia's graveside should confess her hope that Ophelia should have been Hamlet's wife. And the description of the lovelorn maiden drowning beneath the willow acquires an extra poignancy from the fact that Gertrude speaks it. It is not usual for dramatists to make a royal personage the nuntius, and it cannot be an accident that Shakespeare does so here. Instead of asking whether the speech is out of character, or labelling it, with Kittredge, more lyrical than dramatic, should we not rather appreciate this sharp dramatic point?

In the dramatic ordering of the play the connection between Gertrude and Ophelia is everywhere implicit. Why is it to the King and Queen that Ophelia must sing her mad songs? But I must leave Ophelia for a moment to say something more of Hamlet.

By what his mother is he feels himself contaminated. Her union with her husband's brother, revolting as it is as a violation of natural law, is made still worse by the antithesis between the brothers. They are compared by Hamlet, when he first cries out upon the marriage, to Hyperion and a satyr. Before we know about the murder, the dead and living brothers may already appear in the imagination as something more than themselves. The god in man has died unmourned, and the beast usurps his place. The task imposed upon Hamlet, that of avenging his father, we may see, as I have suggested elsewhere,[7] as the reassertion of the god by the destruction of the beast. The strongest bonds of nature compel Hamlet to respond to the call of his father's spirit, but with his uncle ruling his father's kingdom and married to his mother, he finds himself in a world of grossness; and though his soul condemns it and he would isolate himself from it, he

---

[7] 'The Tragedy of Revenge in Shakespeare and Webster', *Shakespeare Survey*, xiv (1961), 47-8.

knows himself a part of it. He swears that the Ghost's commandment 'all alone shall live' within his brain 'unmixed with baser matter'. But from his lot of man the 'baser matter' can never be eliminated, as he does not long forget. He dedicates himself to his task, saying, 'I will go pray'; but even as he does so, he adds, 'for my own poor part', and thinking of 'so poor a man as Hamlet is', he knows that his noble mission is also his curse. When he shows his mother the pictures of her two husbands, he describes to her a wondrous man on whom 'every god did seem to set his seal', and whose 'empire' a 'vice of kings' has stolen. But hardly has he said this than his father's spirit, whom he has sworn to remember, reappears to warn him of forgetfulness. The 'tardy son' is chided for the deed he has neglected; while the corpse of Polonius lies there to show what he has done instead. The revenge plot, like the marriage plot, is a double one. The destined avenger of a father's murder becomes in a secondary action the killer of another's father and dies as the object of another son's revenge at the moment when he achieves his own. This paradox in the action of the play gives great dramatic tension to its catastrophe; but it also enlarges the whole revenge situation to symbolize that mysterious duality in man's nature upon which Hamlet continually reflects. It reveals to us how the same man may fulfil both parts, how he who is called to right wrong is also capable of perpetrating it. Hamlet requites Claudius for his crime; but he shares something of his guilt. When Hamlet at length resolves to kill the King he knows that it is 'perfect conscience' to remove 'this canker of our nature'. But is it not because the canker belongs to 'our nature' that the play cannot permit Hamlet to kill the King until the moment of his own death?

Hamlet's sense of the contamination in his nature, and in that larger nature of which his is a part, inspires in him a loathing for all the processes of life, of growth, of generation, and sexual union itself. In everything that engenders or nourishes life he sees the evil principle at work. The 'old stock', though virtue be grafted on to it, will still impart its taint. The world is a garden, but 'unweeded', possessed by 'things rank and gross in nature'; and he implores his mother not to 'spread the compost on the weeds / To make them ranker'. She, forgetting her union with the godlike man, sits cheerfully by her bestial husband's side, and lives

> In the rank sweat of an enseamed bed,
> Stewed in corruption, honeying and making love
> Over the nasty sty.
>
> (III. iv. 91–3)

Though Hamlet sees the god in man, he also sees how the beast everywhere transforms him. If he concedes that 'conception is a blessing', he thinks of the sun uniting with the carrion to bring forth living pollution. It is this sense of the pollution of life that destroys his joy in its loveliness. In the beauty of Ophelia he looks for the impurity of woman; in her innocent conversation he discovers sexual nastiness; and from the love that begins in 'holy vows' he foresees unholy issue. His renunciation of Ophelia expresses in the action of the play Hamlet's rejection of the beauty and nobility of life because of what must be inseparable from it.

We may see Ophelia as a decoy whom Polonius places in Hamlet's way; but what Hamlet sees, I think, is a temptress placed there by Nature. He puts the temptress behind him, but the violence with which he does so may suggest how vulnerable he feels himself to be. Remembering those eyes that bent their light upon Ophelia to the last, we know that what drives him from her has to struggle with what draws him to her. But though love would draw them together, he says 'We will have no more marriage.'

So Ophelia is left in the state of Jephthah's daughter. And if we recall, as Dowden did, that Jephthah's daughter, before she went to her death, spent two months bewailing her virginity, this may help to explain to us what Ophelia too will do. In forms given to her by madness, she sings of what she has not known. Her drowning under the willow, as I said, is emblematic. Where she sought to hang her garlands, 'an envious sliver broke'. And she is buried with those 'maimed rites' which Hamlet has to watch. But though a 'churlish priest' may begrudge them, she has, as the play insists, her 'virgin crants', her 'maiden strewments'; and as she is laid in the earth there is the wish that from her 'unpolluted flesh' 'violets' may 'spring'.[8]

Is it perhaps ironic that these words are spoken by Laertes, the brother who began her story by warning her to guard her chastity from Hamlet? That early scene in which she tells of Hamlet's love establishes her relationship with the father her lover will kill and the brother who will avenge him. In beginning the preparation for the nunnery scene, it also begins the design which links her fate with theirs. Polonius, who suspects Hamlet's love, afterwards brings his daughter to him; and Hamlet exhorts her to the nunnery and treats her father as a fool. When Hamlet has killed her father, the lamentations of forsaken love and sorrow for her father's death inextricably mingle in her disordered mind. 'She speaks much of her father', they say. And she says, 'My brother shall know of it.' Her brother indeed comes to avenge his father, but has first to follow his sister to her grave—which he does with a curse for the doer of the 'wicked deed' which has brought her to it. At Ophelia's grave Hamlet at last declares his love, and he and Laertes, as her lover and her brother, fight—in anticipation of their final contest, in which, as avengers of their fathers, both noble and both guilty, they will kill yet forgive one another.[9] Ophelia has died in her virginity. She has escaped life's contamination; she has also been denied its fulfilment. The pathos of her austere funeral preludes the catastrophe, upon which, however, she also sheds the brief fragrance of her innocence.

[8] Centring upon the nunnery scene, most interpretations of Ophelia ignore, and some wildly contradict, this very significant conclusion. A judgement on Hamlet's attitude to Ophelia is suggested by *Measure for Measure*, II. ii. 166–8, which observes that the sun in which the carrion corrupts brings the violet to flower.

[9] Laertes is usually thought of as some sort of villain. But Hamlet has more than his rank in mind when he calls him 'a very noble youth'. As the avenger of his father, he is comparable to Hamlet, as Hamlet indeed declares: 'By the image of my cause I see The portraiture of his.' Yet as the treacherous instrument of Claudius, Laertes no less than Hamlet dies through his own guilt at the moment of achieving his revenge.

# 9. THE NOBLE MOOR

## By Helen Gardner

Among the tragedies of Shakespeare *Othello* is supreme in
one quality: beauty. Much of its poetry, in imagery,
perfection of phrase, and steadiness of rhythm, soaring yet
firm, enchants the sensuous imagination. This kind of beauty
*Othello* shares with *Romeo and Juliet* and *Antony and
Cleopatra*; it is a corollary of the theme which it shares with
them. But *Othello* is also remarkable for another kind of
beauty. Except for the trivial scene with the clown, all is
immediately relevant to the central issue; no scene requires
critical justification. The play has a rare intellectual beauty,
satisfying the desire of the imagination for order and
harmony between the parts and the whole. Finally, the play
has intense moral beauty. It makes an immediate appeal to the
moral imagination, in its presentation in the figure of
Desdemona of a love which does not alter 'when it alteration
finds', but 'bears it out even to the edge of doom'. These three
kinds of beauty are interdependent, since all arise from the
nature of the hero. Othello's vision of the world expresses
itself in what Mr Wilson Knight has called the 'Othello
music'; the 'compulsive course' of his nature dominates the
action, driving it straight on to its conclusion; Othello
arouses in Desdemona unshakeable love. I am unable,
therefore, to accept some recent attempts to find meaning in a
play, which has to more than one critic seemed to lack
meaning, in its progressive revelation of the inadequacy of the
hero's nobility. Such an interpretation disregards the play's
most distinctive quality. It contradicts that immediate and
overwhelming first impression to which it is a prime rule of
literary criticism that all further analysis must conform.

A variety of critics in this century, while recognizing its
poignancy, human veracity, and dramatic brilliance, have
agreed in being unwilling to praise *Othello* without some
reservations. Bradley found in it 'a certain limitation, a partial

suppression of that element in Shakespeare's mind which unites him with the mystical poets and with the great musicians and philosophers'. Granville Barker said of Othello that he 'goes ignorantly to his doom'. 'The mere sight of such beauty and nobility and happiness, all wickedly destroyed, must be a harrowing one. Yet the pity and terror of it come short of serving for the purgation of our souls, since Othello's own soul stays unpurged .... It is a tragedy without meaning, and that is the ultimate horror of it.' Bradley's complaint that *Othello* is unphilosophic, and Granville Barker's, that it is 'without meaning', echo faintly the most famous of all attacks upon *Othello*. The absurd morals which Rymer found in it were a witty way of declaring it had no meaning, since Rymer equated meaning with general moral truth. The absence of general moral truth he made clear by his preposterously particular axioms. When Granville Barker adds, 'It does not so much purge us as fill us with horror and anger .... Incongruity is the keynote of the tragedy', we are hearing a polite version of Rymer's summary judgement: 'The tragical part is plainly none other than a Bloody Farce, without salt or savour.' And Mr T. S. Eliot, whose comments on Othello's last speech[1] gave the hint for subsequent discussions of the hero as a study in self-dramatization, self-idealization, and self-deception, remarked in a note to his essay on *Hamlet* that he had never seen 'a cogent refutation of Thomas Rymer's objections to *Othello*', thus implying that he found some cogency in Rymer's attack.

There are various reasons why *Othello* should seem more remote from us than the other tragedies. A feature of Shakespearian studies in the last twenty years has been the interest in the Histories and the comparative neglect of the Comedies. The social and political ideas of the Elizabethans: the Tudor conception of history as the realm of providential judgements, the ideas of natural order, the chain of being, and

---

[1] See 'Shakespeare and the Stoicism of Seneca', a lecture delivered in 1927, reprinted in *Selected Essays* (London, 1932). Mr Eliot was making a general comment on Elizabethan tragic heroes and took this speech as an extreme example. His comment touches, I think, all tragic heroes, and not merely Elizabethan ones. It raises the whole question of how the characters in a poetic drama present themselves, of the self-consciousness of the tragic hero by which he creates himself in our imagination.

'degree, priority and place', obviously relevant to the Histories, have also some relevance to *Hamlet, King Lear,* and *Macbeth*. They throw some light there, though perhaps rather 'a dim religious one', and on the periphery rather than on the centre. They cast no light upon *Othello,* whose affinities are with the Comedies. We must shut up the *Book of Homilies* and *The Mirror for Magistrates* and open the love poets for a change.

Then, again, the revival of interest in allegory, and indeed of the ability to read allegory, is one of the critical achievements of this century. This has naturally influenced the interpretation of Shakespeare's plays. Whether or not allegorical and symbolical interpretations hold in other plays, they are defeated in *Othello* by the striking human individuality of the characters. What Shelley rather intemperately called 'the rigidly-defined and ever-repeated idealisms of a distorted superstition' are not to be found in a play which abounds in 'living impersonations of the truth of human passions'. It is perhaps not wholly improper to see Cordelia as Truth. But Desdemona's truth is the devotion of her whole heart to the husband of her choice, and is quite consistent humanly, but not allegorically, with her marked tendency to economize with truth. And how can one attempt to allegorize a heroine whose companion is Emilia? The attempt to treat plays as if they were poems cannot succeed with a work which so signally exemplifies Ezra Pound's distinction: 'The medium of drama is not words, but persons moving about on a stage using words.'

It has been suggested that the frequent references to Heaven and Hell, angels and devils make a theological interpretation necessary. On the contrary, their very frequency deprives them of any imaginative potency. They are a part of the play's vivid realism, setting it firmly in the contemporary world. Because Macbeth so explicitly excludes 'the life to come', we may, I think, legitimately see in his tragedy a representation of 'judgement here', analogous to what men have thought the state of the lost to be, and say that *Macbeth* makes imaginatively apprehensible the idea of damnation. In the pagan world of *King Lear*, the sudden Christian phrase 'Thou art a soul in bliss' is like the opening of a window on to another landscape. For a moment analogy is suggested, and works upon the imagination. But Heaven and Hell are bandied about too lightly in *Othello* for the words to have any but a flat ring. The only great and moving lines which look beyond the grave are Othello's

> O ill-starr'd wench!
> Pale as thy smock! When we shall meet at compt,
> This look of thine will hurl my soul from heaven,
> And fiends will snatch at it.

(v. ii.   275–8)

Damnation and salvation are outside the field of reference of a play in which the Last Day is so conceived, as the confrontation of two human beings.[2] When Othello exclaims

> I look down towards his feet; but that's a fable.
> If that thou be'st a devil. I cannot kill thee.

(v. ii.   289–90)

And Iago tauntingly replies: 'I bleed, sir; but not kill'd', the point is too explicit to be suggestive. 'Devil' is a cliché in this play, a tired metaphor for 'very bad', as 'angel' is for 'very good'. Theological conceptions help us as little as do social and political ones.

But the fundamental reason, I think, for *Othello's* appearing of limited interest to many critics today is our distaste for the heroic, which has found little expression in our literature in this century, with the splendid exception of the poetry of Yeats. In *Othello* the heroic, as distinct from the exemplary and the typical: what calls out admiration and sympathy in contrast to what is to be imitated or avoided, the extraordinary in contrast to the representative, directly challenges the imagination. There are various ways in which, in discussing *Hamlet*, *King Lear*, and *Macbeth*, we can evade the challenge of the heroic. In *Othello* we cannot.

Othello is like a hero of the ancient world in that he is not a man like us, but a man recognized as extraordinary. He seems

---

[2] It is a little curious that members of a generation which has been so harsh to Bradley for inquiring about Lady Macbeth's children, and has rebuked Ellen Terry for speculating on how Sir Toby will get on with Maria as a wife, should pronounce so confidently on the eternal destiny of fictitious characters.

born to do great deeds and live in legend. He has the obvious heroic qualities of courage and strength, and no actor can attempt the role who is not physically impressive. He has the heroic capacity for passion. But the thing which most sets him apart is his solitariness. He is a stranger, a man of alien race, without ties of nature or natural duties. His value is not in what the world thinks of him, although the world rates him highly, and does not derive in any way from his station. It is inherent. He is, in a sense, a 'self-made man', the product of a certain kind of life whch he has chosen to lead. In this he is in sharp contrast to the tragic hero who immediately precedes him. Hamlet is son and prince. He is in the universal situation of man born in time, creature of circumstances and duties which he has not chosen. The human relation which arises from choice is the least important in the play, or rather it is important in its failure. Hamlet the son, Ophelia the daughter, are not free to love. The possibility of freedom is the very thing which is in question in *Hamlet*. The infected will, the dubieties of moral choice, the confusions of speculation are different aspects of our sense of bondage. The gate of death is barred in *Hamlet*; man, who has not chosen to be born, cannot choose to die. The choice of death is forbidden by religion in the first soliloquy; later it is seen as a choice made impossible by our ignorance of what we choose in choosing death, so that the puzzled will cannot be absolute for life or death. At the close the hero finds death at another's hand, and not by choice.

To this vision of man bound *Othello* presents a vision of man free. The past, whose claim upon the present is at the heart of *Hamlet*, is in *Othello* a country which the hero has passed through and left behind, the scene of his 'travels' history'. The ancestors of royal siege, the father and mother, between whom the handkerchief passed and from whom it came to him, have no claim upon him. His status in Venice is contractual. The Senate are his 'very noble and approv'd good masters' because he and they have chosen it should be so. His loyalties are not the tangle of inherited loyalties, but the few and simple loyalties of choice. His duties are not the duties of his station, but the duties of his profession. Othello is free as intensely as Hamlet is unfree, and the relation which fails to establish itself in *Hamlet* is the one relation which counts here, the free relation of love. It is presented in its more extreme, that is in heroic, form, as a relation between individuals, owing nothing to, and indeed triumphing over, circumstances and natural inclination. The universality of the play lies here, in its presentation of man as freely choosing and expressing choice by acts: Desdemona crossing the Senate floor to take her place beside her husband, Othello slaying her and slaying himself, Emilia crying out the truth at the cost of her life. *Othello* is particularly concerned with that deep, instinctive level where we feel ourselves to be free, with the religious aspect of our nature, in its most general sense. (This is why a theological interpretation seems so improper.) Othello's nobility lies in his capacity to worship: to feel wonder and give service.

Wonder is the note of Othello's greatest poetry, felt in the concreteness of its imagery and the firmness of its rhythms. Wonder sharpens our vision of things, so that we see them, not blurred by sentiment, or distorted by reflection, but in their own beautiful particularity. The services which he has done he speaks of at his first appearance as in his dying speech. He has taken service with the state of Venice. When it calls upon him on his marriage night he accepts, not merely without hesitation, but with alacrity: ''Tis well I am found by you.' This is the 'serious and great business' of his life, his 'occupation', source of his disciplined dignity and self-control. He is dedicated to the soldier's life of obedience and responsibility. The 'hardness' of his life gives to his sense of his own worth an impersonal dignity and grandeur. It is grounded in his sense of the worth of the life and the causes he has chosen. It is consistent with humility. This appears in the serious simplicity with which he lays before the Senate the story of his wooing, and later asks their permission, as a favour, to take his wife with him; for he is their servant and will not demand what in their need they could hardly refuse. It appears more movingly in his acknowledgement of his own 'weak merits' as a husband; and finally, most poignantly, in his image of himself as supremely fortunate, through no merit of his own stumbling upon a pearl. It is fitting that the word 'cause' should come to his lips at the crisis of his life. He has always acted for a cause. Othello is often spoken of as a man of action, in tones which imply some condescension. He is primarily a man of faith, whose faith has witnessed to itself in his deeds.

The love between Othello and Desdemona is a great venture of faith. He is free; she achieves her freedom, and at a great cost. Shakespeare, in creating the figure of her wronged father, who dies of grief at her revolt, sharpened and heightened, as everywhere, the story in the source. Her disobedience and deception of him perhaps cross her mind at Othello's ominous 'Think on thy sins.' If so, she puts the thought aside with 'They are loves I bear you.' She can no more confess herself wrong than John Donne, writing to his father-in-law: 'I knew that to have given any intimacion of it had been to impossibilitate the whole matter.' Heroic decision is seen in its rigour in the gentle Desdemona as well as in her husband.

That love as the union of free souls, freely discovering each in the other, is a mystery, inexplicable in terms of nature and society, is the assumption underlying the endless riddles, quibbles, paradoxes, and conceits of love poets, who in this age busied themselves with '*Metaphysical* Ideas and *Scholastical* Quidities' to explain, or more frequently to make more baffling, the mystery of how 'we two being one are it'.[3]

The famous double time, which has so vexed critics, though it does not trouble spectators, is in accord with this conception of love as beyond nature. That lovers' time is not the time of seasons is a commonplace. Shakespeare laughs at it in his comedies and Donne rings endless changes on the theme. *Othello* is like an illustration to the lecture which Donne read his mistress on Love's Philosophy, comparing the growth of their love to the course of the sun, the morning shadows wearing away until 'to brave clearnesse all things are reduc'd'. But the point of the lecture was that the analogy breaks down. There is no parallel between the shadows of afternoon and evening and the shadows which fall on love:

[3]Donne, 'The Canonization':

> The Phoenix riddle hath more wit
> By us, we two being one, are it.
> So, to one neutrall thing both sexes fit.

The morning shadowes weare away,
But these grow longer all the day,
But oh, loves day is short, if love decay.

Love is a growing, or full constant light;
And his first minute, after noone, is night.[4]

If love cannot perform the miracle of Joshua and make the sun stand still in the heavens, it will not suffer a slow decline. It is not in the nature of things: it has no afternoon. *Othello* is a drama of passion and runs to the time of passion; it is also a drama of love which, failing to sustain its height of noon, falls at once to night. To borrow Mr Edwin Muir's distinction, the long time belongs to the Story, the short belongs to the Fable.

*Othello* is also a drama of marriage. As the hero is more than a Homeric doer of great deeds, he is more than a lover; he is a husband. Desdemona is not only the 'cunning'st pattern of excelling nature' and the girl who 'saw Othello's visage in his mind'; she is his 'true and loyal wife'. Her soul and fortunes are 'consecrated' to him. The play is not only concerned with passion and love, but with what Montaigne and other experienced observers have thought incompatibles: love and constancy.[5]

My subject being the Noble Moor, I cannot spend as long as I should wish upon his Ancient. There is an assumption current today that Iago expresses in some way a complementary view of life to Othello's. His power over Othello is said to derive from the fact that 'into what he speaks are projected the half-truths that Othello's romantic vision ignored, but of which his mind held secret knowledge'. I am quoting Miss Maud Bodkin, since she has been much quoted by later writers. She also speaks of the reader 'experiencing the romantic values represented in the hero, and recognizing, in a manner secretly, the complementary truths projected into the figure of Iago'.[6] Professor Empson has put this view more breezily:

---

[4] Donne, 'A Lecture upon the Shadow'.

[5] 'It is against the nature of love, not to be violent, and against the condition of violence to be constant' (*Essays*, iii. 5). Cf. Iago's 'It was a violent commencement in her, and thou shalt see an answerable sequestration.'

[6] *Archetypal Patterns in Poetry* (London, 1934), pp. 223 and 333. When Miss Bodkin writes that as psychological critics we must note that the plot is built 'not

The thinking behind the 'melodrama' is not at all crude, at any rate if you give Iago his due. It is only because a rather unreal standard has been set up that the blow-the-gaff man can take on this extraordinary power. It is not merely out of their latent 'cynicism' that the listeners are meant to feel a certain sting of truth in Iago's claim to honesty, even in the broadest sense of being somehow truer than Othello to the facts of life.[7]

I cannot resist adapting some Johnsonian expressions and saying this is 'sad stuff': 'the man is a liar and there's an end on't.' What Iago injects into Othello's mind, the poison with which he charges him, is either false deductions from isolated facts—she deceived her father—and from dubious generalizations—Venetian women deceive their husbands—or flat lies. Whatever from our more melancholy experiences we choose to call the facts of life, in this play there is one fact which matters, upon which the plot is built and by which all generalizations are tested:

> Moor, she was chaste; she lov'd thee, cruel Moor.

> (v. ii. 252)

The notion that by striking a mean between the 'high-mindedness' of Othello and the 'low view' of Iago we shall arrive at a balanced view, one that is not 'crude', could only have arisen in an age which prefers to the heroic that strange idol of the abstracting intelligence, the normal, and for the 'beautiful idealisms of moral excellence' places before us the equally unattainable but far more dispiriting goal of 'adaptation to life'. But, in any case, the sum will not work out, for Iago has not a point of view at all. He is no realist. In any sense which matters he is incapable of speaking truth, because he is incapable of disinterestedness. He can express a high view or a low view to taste. The world and other people exist

merely on falsehoods . . . but also on partial truths of human nature that the romantic vision ignores' and cites as examples of such 'truths' that 'a woman, "a super-subtle Venetian", suddenly wedding one in whom she sees the image of her ideal warrior, is liable to experience moments of revulsion' and that 'a woman's love may be won, but not held, by "bragging and telling her fantastical lies" ', the irrelevance of psychological criticism, which generalizes and abstracts, where drama particularizes, is obvious. Whatever truth there may be in these two generalizations the plot is built on their untruth in this case.

[7] *The Structure of Complex Words* (London, 1951), p. 248.

for him only to be used. His definition of growing up is an interesting one. Maturity to him is knowing how to 'distinguish betwixt a benefit and an injury'. His famous 'gain'd knowledge' is all generalizations, information docketed and filed. He is monstrous because, faced with the manifold richness of experience, his only reaction is calculation and the desire to manipulate. If we try to find in him a view of life, we find in the end only an intolerable levity, a power of being 'all things to all men' in a very unapostolic sense, and an incessant activity. Iago is the man of action in this play, incapable of contemplation and wholly insusceptible to the holiness of fact. He has, in one sense, plenty of motives. His immediate motives for embarking on the whole scheme are financial, the need to keep Roderigo sweet, and his desire for the lieutenancy. His general motive is detestation of superiority in itself and as recognized by others; he is past master of the sneer. Coleridge has been much criticized for speaking of his 'motiveless malignity' and yet the note of glee in Iago confirms Coleridge's moral insight. Ultimately, whatever its proximate motives, malice is motiveless; that is the secret of its power and its horror, why it can go unsuspected and why its revelation always shocks. It is, I fear, its own reward.

Iago's power is at the beginning of the action, where he appears as a free agent of mischief, creating his plot out of whatever comes to hand; after the middle of the third act he becomes the slave of the passion which he has aroused, which is the source of whatever grandeur he has in our imagination. Othello's agony turns the 'eternal villain', the 'busy and insinuating rogue', the 'cogging cozening slave' of the first acts into the 'Spartan dog, more fell than anguish, hunger, or the sea' of the close. The crisis of the action comes when Othello returns 'on the rack', determined that he will not 'make a life of jealousy', and demands that Iago furnish him with proof. Iago's life is from now on at stake. Like Desdemona's it hangs upon the handkerchief. He must go forward, to everyone's ruin and his own.

Iago ruins Othello by insinuating into his mind the question, 'How do you know?' The tragic experience with which this play is concerned is loss of faith, and Iago is the instrument to bring Othello to this crisis of his being. His

task is made possible by his being an old and trusted
companion, while husband and wife are virtually strangers,
bound only by passion and faith; and by the fact that great
joy bewilders, leaving the heart apt to doubt the reality of its
joy. The strange and extraordinary, the heroic, what is
beyond nature, can be made to seem the unnatural, what is
against nature. This is one of Iago's tricks. But the collapse of
Othello's faith before Iago's hints, refusals, retreats, reluctant
avowals, though plausible and circumstantiated, is not, I
believe, ultimately explicable; nor do I believe we make it so
by searching for some psychological weakness in the hero
which caused his faith to fail, and whose discovery will
protect us from tragic experience by substituting for its
pleasures the easier gratifications of moral and intellectual
superiority to the sufferer. There is only one answer to Iago's
insinuations, the answer Othello made to Brabantio's
warning: 'My life upon her faith.' It is one thing to retort so
to open enmity; more difficult to reply so to the seemingly
well-meant warnings of a friend. That Othello does not or
cannot reply so to Iago, and instead of making the venture of
faith, challenges him to prove his wife false, is his tragic error.

Tragic suffering is suffering which a nature, by reason of its
virtues, is capable of experiencing to the full, but is incapable
of tolerating, and in which the excellencies of a nature are in
conflict with each other. The man of conscience suffers the
torment of confusion of conscience, the man of loving heart
the torment of love spurned and of invasion by the passion of
hatred. The one finds himself 'marshalled to knavery', the
other driven to bitter curses. The man of moral imagination
and human feeling will suffer the extremity of moral despair
and human isolation. The man of faith is most able to
experience what loss of faith is: but he is also unable to endure
existence in a world where faith is dead. Othello has known
'ecstasy', which doth 'unperplex'. The loss of that leaves him
'perplexed in the extreme' and conscious of sex and sex only
as 'what did move'.[8] He has seen Desdemona as his 'soul's

---

[8] Donne, 'The Extasie':

> This Extasie doth unperplex
>   (We said) and tell us what we love,
> We see by this, it was not sexe,
>   We see, we saw not what did move.

joy'. It is intolerable to be aware in her of only what 'the sense aches at'.

Until the end is reached drama looks always ahead. If Shakespeare has, in fact, presented his hero and his love as flawed, then he has done it so subtly that I do not see how any spectator can have been aware of it. As soon as his agony is upon him we look forward to its resolution, not backwards to find some imperfection in his nature to account for his error. What matters to the tragic dramatist is wherefore, not why: not what causes suffering, but what comes of it. We distract ourselves, and to no purpose, by asking insoluble questions such as: Why 'Seems it so particular' to Hamlet? Why does so small a fault in Cordelia seem so ugly to Lear? Why does a prophecy of 'things that do sound so fair' arouse in Macbeth not a glorious image of himself as a king, but a 'horrid image' of himself as a murderer? *Macbeth* is not a psychological study of ambition, or, if it is, it is a singularly unilluminating one. It is about murder. *Othello* is not a study in pride, egoism, or self-deception: its subject is sexual jealousy, loss of faith in a form which involves the whole personality at the profound point where body meets spirit.

The solution which Othello cannot accept is Iago's: 'Put up with it.' This is as impossible as that Hamlet should, like Claudius, behave as if the past were done with and only the present mattered. Or that Lear should accept Goneril and Regan's view of the proper meekness of the old and, in Freud's words, should 'renounce love, choose death, and make friends with the necessity of dying'. Or that Macbeth should attempt a tedious returning. The heroic core of tragedy is in this refusal of the hero to accommodate himself: it is why he can always be treated as a moral warning. Let Hamlet remember that 'Vengeance is the Lord's', allow the world to go its own way and mind the business of his own soul. Let Lear recognize that it is a law of life that the young should thrust out the old, and moderate his demands for love. Let Macbeth accept the human conditon that life is a 'fitful fever', the future always uncertain, and there is no possibility of being 'safely thus'. Let Othello remember that perfection is not to be looked for, that though two may at times feel one, at other times they will feel very much two. Desdemona is beautiful, whether she is true or not.

But to Othello loyalty is the very princple of his moral being. He cannot say tenderly with a modern poet

> Lay your sleeping head, my love,
> Human on my faithless arm;

and accepting that

> Certainty, fidelity
> On the stroke of midnight pass
> Like vibrations of a bell,

enjoy her as

> Mortal, guilty, but to me
> The entirely beautiful.[9]

Nor, since, far from being one who lives to himself alone, his nature goes out to seek value beyond itself, can he steel his senses against her beauty. He has not the invulnerability of the proud, and cannot armour himself with the thought of his own self-sufficient virtue, arguing that 'the Honour of a true heroique spirit dependeth not upon the carriage or behaviour of a woman', and remembering that 'the Gallantest men in the world were all Cuckolds' and 'made no stirre about it'.[10]

Tragic responsibility can only be savoured within a fixed field of moral reference. Mercy killings, honour slayings, and innocent adulteries are not the stuff of tragedy. But tragic responsibility is not the same as moral guilt. It shows itself in Hamlet's acceptance of the imperative to stay at his post, although this involves many deaths and his own commission of acts which outrage the very conscience which impels him; in Lear's flinging out into the storm to take upon himself the role of universal sufferer and universal judge; and in

---

[9] W. H. Auden, *Look Stranger* (1940), p. 43.

[10] 'The more descretion a man hath, the lesse shall hee bee troubled with these franticke fits: and seeing, as a certaine noble Gentleman sayth, the Honour of a true heroique spirit dependeth not upon the carriage or behaviour of a woman, I see no reason why the better sort should take this false playing of their Wives so much at the heart as they doe, especially, when it is their Destinie, and not Desert, to be so used. *Montaigne*, that brave French Barron, being of this minde; for saith he, the Gallantest men in the world, as *Lucullus, Cæsar, Anthony, Cato*, and such like Worthies, were all Cuckolds; yea, and (which was more) knew it, although they made no stirre about it: neither was there in all that time, but one Gull, and Coxcombe, and that was *Lepidus*, that dyed with the anguish thereof.' Marginal note by Robert Toft in his translation of Benedetto Varchi: *The Blazon of Jealousie* (1615), p. 29. The reference is to Montaigne, *Essays*, iii. 5.

Macbeth's perseverance in 'knowing the deed'. It shows itself in Othello's destruction of an idol, his decision to regain his freedom by destroying what he must desire, but cannot honour. That baser passions are mingled with this imperative to sacrifice, that in the final moment Othello kills his wife in rage, only means that in presenting man as 'an animal that worships', Shakespeare, keeping to 'the truth of human passions', presents both terms. But, in its mixture of primitive animality · and agonizing renunciation, the murder of Desdemona has upon it the stamp of the heroic. It has what Yeats saw in the Easter Rising, which neither his moral nor his political judgement approved, and one of whose leaders he had disliked and despised: a 'terrible beauty', contrasting with the 'casual comedy' of daily life.

The act is heroic because Othello acts from inner necessity. Although the thought of social dishonour plays a part in his agony, it has no place in this final scene. He kills her because he cannot 'digest the poison of her flesh',[11] and also to save her from herself, to restore meaning to her beauty. The act is also heroic in its absoluteness, disinterestedness, and finality. Othello does not look beyond it. It must be done. The tragic hero usurps the functions of the gods and attempts to remake the world. This *hubris*, which arouses awe and terror, appears in an extreme form in Othello's assumption of the role of a god who chastises where he loves, and of a priest who must present a perfect victim. He tries to confess her, so that in her last moment she may be true, and suffering the death of the body as expiation may escape the death of the soul. Her persistence in what he believes to be a lie and her tears at the news of Cassio's death turn the priest into the murderer. The heroic is rooted in reality here: the godlike is mingled with the brutal, which Aristotle saw as its true opposite, and Desdemona, love's martyr, dies like a frightened child, pleading for 'but half an hour' more of life.

---

[11] Cf. Adriana in *The Comedy of Errors*, II. ii. 144–8:

> I am possess'd with an adulterate blot;
> My blood is mingled with the crime of lust:
> For if we two be one and thou play false,
> I do digest the poison of thy flesh,
> Being strumpeted by thy contagion.

'I am glad I have ended my revisal of this dreadful scene. It is not to be endured,' said Johnson. And yet, this terrible act has wonderful tragic rightness. Only by it can the tragic situation be finally resolved and in tragedy it is the peace of finality which we look for. Living, Desdemona can never prove her innocence. There is nothing she can do to 'win her lord again'. She could, of course, save herself, and in so doing save her husband from crime, dishonour, and death. She could leave this terrifying monster and ask for the protection of her own countrymen, the messengers of Venice. This sensible solution never crosses her mind. She remains with the man her 'love approves', and since

There is a comfort in the strength of love,[12]

for all her bewilderment and distress she falls asleep, to wake to find her faith rewarded by death. But in death she does 'win her lord again'.

Emilia's silence while her mistress lived is fully explicable in terms of her character. She shares with her husband the generalizing trick and is well used to domestic scenes. The jealous, she knows,

are not ever jealous for the cause,
But jealous for they are jealous.

(III. iv.  160–7)

If it was not the handkerchief it would be something else. Why disobey her husband and risk his fury? It would not do any good. This is what men are like. But Desdemona dead sweeps away all such generalities and all caution. At this sight, Emilia though 'the world is a huge thing' finds that there is a thing she will not do for it. By her heroic disregard for death she gives the only 'proof' there can be of Desdemona's innocence: the testimony of faith. For falseness can be proved, innocence can only be believed. Faith, not evidence, begets faith.

The revival of faith in Othello which rings through his last speech overrides that sense of his own guilt which we have been told he ought to be dwelling on. His own worth he sees

---

[12] Wordsworth, 'Michael', line 248.

in the services he has rendered. It is right that he should be conscious of what has given his life value when he is about to take it, as he was conscious of her beauty when about to sacrifice that. His error he cannot explain. He sees it in an image which asserts her infinite value and his supreme good fortune, which in ignorance he did not realize, accepting and translating into his own characteristic mode of thought Emilia's characteristic 'O gull! O dolt! As ignorant as dirt!' The tears he weeps now are not 'cruel tears', but good tears, natural and healing. He communicates this by an image drawn from his life of adventure. Perhaps the Arabian trees come to his mind because in that land of marvels 'the Phoenix builds her spicy nest'. Then, as he nerves himself to end everything, there flashes across his mind an image from his past which seems to epitomize his whole life and will 'report him and his cause aright'; an act of suicidal daring, inspired by his chosen loyalty to Venice. With the same swiftness he does justice on himself, traducer and murderer of his Venetian wife. As, at their reunion, after the tempest, his joy stopped his speech, so now his grief and worship express themselves finally in an act, the same act: he dies 'upon a kiss'.

No circumstances point away from this close. No living Fortinbras or Malcolm, no dead Goneril and Regan allow us to speak of a purged realm or of the justice of the heavens. There is nothing but the 'tragic loading of this bed' and the comment of the generous Cassio: 'For he was great of heart.' Yet in this terrible end there is so solemn a sense of completeness that it might well be called the most beautiful end in Shakespearian tragedy.

Each of Shakespeare's great tragedies has its own design. The ground plan of the tragedy of *Othello* is that of a tragedy of fortune, the fall of a great man from a visible height of happiness to utter loss. This is not at all the shape the story has in the source; but this is how Shakespeare saw Cinthio's powerful but sordid story of a garrison intrigue. He spent his first two acts in presenting wonder great as content, and content that is absolute, delaying the opening of his tragic conflict until his third act. The design of the tragedy of fortune has a very different effect from the design of what may be called the tragedy of dilemma, in which, as in *Hamlet*, the hero is presented to us in circumstances not of his own making, confronted with another's crime; or from the design of the tragedy of error, where the hero's initial act releases evil forces and brings enormous suffering, or from that of the tragedy of crime and retribution. We never see Hamlet prosperous. Lear's rash and cruel act opens the action. Macbeth is no sooner before us than he is in temptation, 'rapt' in inner struggle. In plays with these designs, the conclusions have something of the nature of solutions: the end answers the beginning.

In its simplest form the tragedy of fortune cannot be rationalized. It takes man out of the realm of natural causality, the steady course which birth holds on to death, showing him as the victim of the illogical, what can neither be avoided nor foreseen. To achieve its effect it glorifies human life, displaying the capacity of the human heart for joy and leaving on the mind an ineffaceable impression of splendour, thus contradicting the only moral which can be drawn from it: *Vanitas vanitatum*. *Othello* has this in common with the tragedy of fortune that the end in no way blots out from the imagination the glory of the beginning. But the end here does not merely by its darkness throw up into relief the brightness that was. On the contrary, beginning and end chime against each other. In both the value of life and love is affirmed.

But *Othello* is also pre-eminently the tragedy of a deed. The 'deed of horror', *to deinon*, which in *Hamlet* lies behind the direct action, in *Macbeth* inaugurates it, and in *King Lear* is diffused through many acts of cruelty during the middle action, is, in *Othello*, the consummation of the action. Crime and catastrophe virtually coincide. Here again the shape of the play is quite different from the shape of the story in the source. The murder of Desdemona is not an act for which Heaven will in the end provide vengeance; it is a means of immediate revelation.

Fortune has been said to be the mistress of comedy, as opposed to Destiny, the mistress of tragedy. The vision of life which Shakespeare embodied in *Othello* cannot be analysed in terms of either destiny or fortune, and this is, I think, why more than one critic has complained that the play, although thrilling, lacks 'meaning'. The hero is a great individual, with all the qualities of a tragic hero, who expresses the strength of his nature in a terrible deed. But he finds the value of his life not within himself but without himself. He is the most obviously heroic of the tragic heroes, but he is unlike the great-hearted man of Aristotle, who is 'unable to make his life revolve round another' and is not 'given to admiration'. His nobility lies in his capacity to recognize value and give loyalty. The rhythm of pure tragedy is of a single life fulfilling itself and coming to an end in death. The rhythm of pure comedy is of relationships dissolved and reformed. The truth of tragedy is that each of us is finally alone. The truth of comedy is that man's final end is union with others, that he is 'in unitie defective'.

When, at the close of the *Symposium*, Socrates defended the wild paradox that 'the same person is able to compose both tragedy and comedy and that the foundations of the tragic and comic arts were essentially the same', his audience, who were so unfortunate as to live two thousand years before he was proved to be right, 'rather convicted than convinced went to sleep'. The foundation of Shakespeare's comedy and tragedy is the conception of man as finding his fulfilment in love, and therefore as not self-sufficient, but dependent upon others. In none of Shakespeare's great tragedies is the rhythm of fate felt in its purity, with the exception of *Macbeth*, whose hero rejects chance and chooses solitude. Over *Macbeth*, which is oracular, the future, the tense of destiny, lowers. Both 'fate' and 'fortune' are spoken of in *Othello*. In *King Lear* the word 'fate' does not occur, and its shockingly capricious end has poetic not dramatic logic. The presence of comedy 'universal, ideal and sublime' in *King Lear* made Shelley award it the palm over the masterpieces of the ancient world, the *Agamemnon* and the *Oedipus Rex*. For Shelley, though he does not make the connection, believed that the 'great secret of morals is love'.

In *Othello* the two rhythms are so finely poised against each other that if we listen to either without the other we impoverish the whole. Othello is the tragic hero, fulfilling his destiny, who comes to the limit, 'the very sea-mark of his utmost sail', expressing his whole nature in a tragic act. He is the comic hero, discovering at the close a truth he knew at the beginning, and so he appears, dazed and blundering beneath the scourge of Emilia's tongue, remote for the time from our sympathy. Should the course of his life be described as a pilgrimage to a goal, or is it a straying from a centre which he finds again in death? Such straying is of the essence of life, whose law is change. Failures and recoveries of faith are the rhythm of the heart, whose movement is here objectified and magnified for our contemplation. If the old saying is true 'Qui non zelat non amat', then the greater love is, the greater jealousy will be. Perfect love casts out fear; but beneath the moon, mistress of change, only in death can

> Beauty, truth, and rarity,
> Grace in all simplicity,

be safe from mistaking, and constancy find its true image. The close of *Othello* should leave us at peace, for

> Death is now the phoenix' nest;
> And the turtle's loyal breast
> To eternity doth rest.[13]

The significance of *Othello* is not to be found in the hero's nobility alone, in his capacity to know ecstasy, in his vision of the world, and in the terrible act to which he is driven by his anguish at the loss of that vision. It lies also in the fact that the vision was true. I cannot agree to find lacking in meaning this most beautiful play which seems to have arisen out of the same mood as made Keats declare: 'I am certain of nothing but of the holiness of the Heart's affections and the truth of Imagination.'

---

[13] 'The Phoenix and Turtle', 53 ff.

# 10.  OTHELLO AND COLOUR PREJUDICE

## By G. K. Hunter

It is generally admitted today that Shakespeare was a practical man of the theatre: however careless he may have been about maintaining consistency for the exact *reader* of his plays, he was not likely to introduce a theatrical novelty which would only puzzle his audience; it does not seem wise, therefore, to dismiss his theatrical innovations as if they were unintentional. The blackness of Othello is a case in point. Shakespeare largely modified the story he took over from Cinthio: he made a tragic hero out of Cinthio's passionate and bloody lover; he gave him a royal origin, a Christian baptism, a romantic *bravura* of manner and, most important of all, an orotund magnificence of diction. Yet, changing all this, he did not change his colour, and so produced a daring theatrical novelty—a black hero for a white community—a novelty which remains too daring for many recent theatrical audiences. Shakespeare cannot merely have carried over the colour of Othello by being too lazy or too uninterested to meddle with it; for no actor, spending the time in 'blacking-up', and hence no producer, could be indifferent to such an innovation, especially in that age, devoted to 'imitation' and hostile to 'originality'. In fact, the repeated references to Othello's colour in the play and the wider net of images of dark and light spread across the diction, show that Shakespeare was not only not unaware of the implication of his hero's colour, but was indeed intensely aware of it as one of the primary factors in his play.[1] I am therefore assuming in this lecture that the blackness of Othello has a theatrical purpose, and I intend to try to suggest what it was possible for that purpose to have been.

Shakespeare intended his hero to be a black man—that

[1] See R. B. Heilman, 'More Fair than Black; Light and Dark in *Othello*', *Essays in Criticism*, i (1951), 313-35.

much I take for granted;[2] what is unknown is what the idea of a black man suggested to Shakespeare, and what reaction the appearance of a black man on the stage was calculated to produce. It is fairly certain, however, that some modern reactions are not likely to have been shared by the Elizabethans. The modern theatre-going European intellectual, with a background of cultivated superiority to 'colour problems' in other continents, would often choose to regard Othello as a fellow man and to watch the story—which could so easily be reduced to its headline level: 'sheltered white girl errs: said, "Colour does not matter" '—with a sense of freedom from such prejudices. But this lofty fair-mindedness may be too lofty for Shakespeare's play, and not take the European any nearer the Othello of Shakespeare than the lady from Maryland quoted in the Furness New Variorum edition: 'In studying the play of *Othello*, I have always *imagined* its hero a white man.' Both views, that the colour of Othello does not matter, and that it matters too much to be tolerable, err, I suggest, by over-simplifying. Shakespeare was clearly deliberate in keeping Othello's colour; and it is obvious that he counted on some positive audience reaction to this colour; but it is equally obvious that he did not wish the audience to dismiss Othello as a stereotype nigger.

Modern rationalizations about 'colour' tend to be different from those of the Middle Ages and Renaissance. We are powerfully aware of the relativism of viewpoints; we distinguish easily between different racial cultures; and explicit arguments about the mingling of the races usually begin at the economic and social level and only move to questions of God's providence at the lunatic fringe.

The Elizabethans also had a powerful sense of the economic threat posed by the foreign groups they had daily contact with—Flemings or Frenchmen—but they had little or no continuous contact with 'Moors', and no sense of economic threat from them.[3] This did not mean, however, that they had no racial or colour prejudice. They had, to start

---

[2] I ignore the many treatises devoted to proving that he was of tawny or sunburnt colour. These are, however, very worthy of study, as documents of prejudice.

[3] See G. K. Hunter, 'Elizabethans and Foreigners', *Shakespeare Survey*, xvii ('Shakespeare in His Own Age') (1964), 37–52.

with, the basic common man's attitude that all foreigners are curious and inferior—the more curious the more inferior, in the sense of the proverb quoted by Purchas: 'Three Moors to a Portuguese; three Portuguese to an Englishman.'[4] They had also the basic and ancient sense that black is the colour of sin and death, 'the badge of hell, The hue of dungeons, and the Schoole of night' (as Shakespeare himself says).[5] This supposition is found all over the world (even in darkest Africa)[6] from the earliest to the latest times; and in the west there is a continuous and documented tradition of it.[7] It may be worth while giving some account of this. In Greece and Rome black was the colour of ill luck, death, condemnation, malevolence. The Roman feeling about the colour is well summed up in Horace's line:

hic niger est; hunc tu, Romane, caveto[8]

—on which the Delphin editor comments: 'Niger est] Homo pestilens, malus, perniciosus: contra est candidus, albus.' The soldiers of Brutus were dismayed to meet an Ethiop just before the battle of Philippi.[9] In Lucian's *Philopseudes* (§31) we hear of a ghost met in Corinth: 'when the Spirit appeared . . . he was squalid and long-haired and blacker than the dark' (μελάντερος τοῦ ζόφου). Suetonius tells us of a play, being rehearsed at the time of Caligula's death, in which the infernal connotations of the colour were used with self-conscious art. In this play Egyptians and Ethiopians played the parts of the inhabitants of the underworld.[10]

The coming of Christianity made no break in the tradition. Indeed, Christian eschatology seems to have taken over the black man from the underworld with great speed and

[4] See M. P. Tilley, *A Dictionary of Proverbs* (Ann Arbor, 1950), M. 1132.
[5] *Love's Labour's Lost*, iv. iii. 254 f.
[6] See V. W. Turner, 'Colour Classification in Ndembu Ritual', *Anthropological Approaches to the Study of Religion*, ed. M. Banton (1966); Arthur Leib, 'The Mystical Significance of Colours in . . . Madagascar', *Folk-lore*. lvii (1946), 128–33; Joan Westcott, 'The Sculpture and Myths of Eshu-Elegba, the Yoruba Trickster', *Africa*, xxxii (1962).
[7] See Hoffmann–Krayer and Bächtold–Stäubli, *Handwörterbuch des deutschen Aberglaubens*, s.v. Schwartz.
[8] Horace, *Satires*, I. iv. 85.
[9] Plutarch, *Brutus*, xlviii.
[10] Seutonius, *Caligula*, lvii.

enthusiasm. In the dream of Marcellus in the *Acts of Peter (c.* AD 200)[11] a demon appeared 'in sight like an Ethiopian . . . altogether black and filthy'. In the third-century *Acta Xanthippae* the devil manifested himself as the King of Ethiopia.[12] In the so-called 'Epistle of Barnabas' the devil is called ὁ μέλας.[13] In another early text the martyrdom of Perpetua is represented as a battle between the saint and a black-faced Egyptian—the devil, of course.[14] Among the visitors to the much-tried St Anthony was the Devil as a μέλας παῖς[15] in Cassian's *Collationes Patrum* the devil appears several times *in figura Aethiopis taetri.*[16] And so on; I have elsewhere given later examples of the same religious visions.[17] They went on, unchanging, into Shakespeare's own day.

The linguistic change from Greek or Latin to English did not free the word *black* from the associations that had formed round μέλας or *niger.* As *candidus* had combined the ideas of white skin and clear soul, so the word *fair* served to combine the ideas of beauty and whiteness. Black remains the adjective appropriate to the ugly and the frightening,[18] to the Devil and his children, the wicked and the infidel. In the medieval romances, the enemies of the knights are usually Saracens, often misshapen and monstrous (eyes in forehead, mouth in breast, etc.) and commonly black.[19] This is a tradition that

[11] M. R. James, *The Apocryphal New Testament* (Oxford 1924), p. 323 (Acts of Peter, 5 22).

[12] See M. R. James, *Apocrypha Anecdota (Texts and Studies,* ii. 3) (Cambridge, 1893), 54.

[13] Ed. Funk, *Patres Apostolici* (Tübingen, 1891), i. 48.

[14] *Passio Perpetuae,* ed. J. A. Robinson (*Texts and Studies,* ii. 1) (Cambridge, 1891), 76 f.

[15] See *Patrologia Graeca,* xxvi, col. 849 a.

[16] See *Corpus Scriptorum Eccl. Latinorum,* xiii (1886), 32, 55.

[17] G. K. Hunter, loc. cit.

[18] See Walter Clyde Curry, *The Middle English Ideal of Personal Beauty* (Baltimore, 1916). I have not been able to see J. E. Willms, *Über den Gebrauch der Farbenbezeichnungen in der Poesie Altenglands* (Munich, 1902). The kind of shock that could be produced by the association of blackness and beauty is illustrated by the Scottish tournament of 1505 in which James IV set up a negress as the Queen of Beauty, and himself as 'the wild knight' defended her honour. (See *Accounts of the Lord High Treasurer of Scotland,* III, xlviii ff., lii, 258 f.) The scandal that this caused can be discovered from Pitscottie.

[19] See, for example, *Cursor Mundi,* 8077; *Sir Ferumbras,* 2785; *Alisaunder,* B. 6402.

Shakespeare picks up in his description of Thomas Mowbray as a Crusader,

> Streaming the ensign of the Christian cross
> Against black pagans, Turks and Saracens.[20]

There was then, it appears, a powerful, widespread, and ancient tradition associating black-faced men with wickedness, and this tradition came right up to Shakespeare's own day. The habit of representing evil men as black-faced or negroid had also established itself in a pictorial tradition that persists from the Middle Ages through and beyond the sixteenth century. This appears especially in works showing the tormentors of Christ, in scenes of the Flagellation and the Mocking, though the tormentors of other saints are liable to have the same external characteristics used to show their evil natures. Thus in the south porch of the Cathedral of Chartres, the executioner of St Denis is shown as negroid. The alabaster tablets produced in England in the late Middle Ages, and exported to the Continent in large numbers, frequently have enough pigment remaining to show some faces coloured black. W. L. Hildburgh, writing in *Archaeologia*, xciii (1949), assumes that there is a link between this characteristic and the medieval drama: 'the very dark colour of the faces of the wicked persons [is] intended to indicate their villainous natures; in some tables the faces of the torturers and other iniquitous persons are black' (p. 76). E. S. Prior, *Catalogue of the Exhibition of English Medieval Alabaster Work* (London, 1913), had made the same point: 'the blackening of the faces of the ruffians and executioners and heretics as seen in many of the tables was no doubt a stage trick' (p. 21 n. 1). There is a good example in the Ashmolean Museum in Oxford, a crucifixion which the 1836 catalogue describes thus: 'the penitent thief looks towards Christ and the other has his face averted and is painted as a negro' (p. 146). Again, A. Gardner, writing of English medieval sculpture, tells us that 'In the martyrdom scenes the executioners are given hideous faces, which seem sometimes to have been painted black', *English Medieval Sculpture* (Cambridge, 1951), p. 310. He illustrates a

---

[20] *Richard II*, IV. i. 94 f.

good example showing the martyrdom of St Catherine (fig. 609, p. 309). Further examples are described in 'Medieval English Alabasters in American Museums', *Speculum*, xxx (1955), where the Scourging and the Resurrection are both marked by this feature. Wall-paintings in English churches preserve evidence of the same usage. A Massacre of the Innocents from Croughton (Northants.), illustrated in Borenius and Tristram, *English Medieval Painting* (1927) as plate 51, shows dark-faced soldiers. The Church of St Peter and St Paul at Pickering (N. Yorks.) has splendid fifteenth-century wall-paintings—not yet properly photographed— in which both Herod and the scourgers are given dark faces. Herod is represented in the same way, it may be noticed, in an alabaster tablet described in *The Archaeological Journal*, lxxiv (1917), plate xiii.

Among the sixteenth-century painted windows of King's College Chapel, Cambridge, the Scourging itself does not have this feature, but the window above (window X), intended as a typological comment on it ('Shimei cursing David'), gives a dark face to Shimei, the *vi sanguinum et vir Belial* (2 Samuel, 16: 7), as the legend tells us.

Among illuminated manuscripts, the Luttrell Psalter has a black scourger on fol. 92$^v$, and the Chichester Psalter, now in the John Rylands Library, has several full-page pictures of the Passion, in which the tormentors are black with grossly distorted features. The *Très-Belles Heures de Notre Dame* du Duc Jean de Berry has a full page Scourging, with two white tormentors and one black. Bodleian MS Douce 5—a Book of Hours of Flemish Provenance and fourteenth-century date— has a similar scene. The most celebrated picture in which this tradition appears is the Scourging by Giotto in the Arena Chapel in Padua. In this the negro scourger stands alone brandishing his rod above the head of Christ. Among the many monographs devoted to Giotto no one seems to have pointed to the tradition with which I am here concerned.

The latest picture which uses this tradition, so far as I know, is a martyrdom of St James, attributed to Van Dyck, sold by Weinmüller of Munich in 1958 (Catalogue 721, item 501).

It is suggested by several of the authorities cited here that the pictorial tradition was associated with theatrical usage. Certainly the drama of the Middle Ages seems to have used black figures to represent the evil of this world and the next. Creizenach[21] describes the European diffusion of the black faces. The surviving accounts of the Coventry cycle (which some think Shakespeare may have seen—and which he *could* have seen) retain the distinction between 'white (or saved) souls' and 'black (or damned) souls'.[22] The English folk-play describes St George's enemy as (*inter alia*) 'Black Morocco Dog', 'Black Prince of Darkness', or even 'Black and American Dog'.[23] In Thomas Lupton's *All for Money* (1558–77) 'Judas cometh in like a damned soul in black'.[24] Udall's *Ezechias*, acted in Cambridge in 1564, is stated to have represented the leader of the Assyrians as a giant and made his followers coal-black. As the reporter of the performance tells us:

> Dicta probat fuscis miles numerosus in armis
> Tam nullas tenebras dixeris esse nigras.[25]

In John Redford's *Wit and Science* (? 1530) we seem to have a moral transformation scene *coram populo*, expressed in terms of face colouring. Wit goes to sleep on Idleness's lap. Idleness then tells us:

> Well, whyle he sleepth in Idlenes lappe,
> Idleness marke on hym shall I clappe. (434 f.)[26]

When Wit awakens he is taken for Ignorance (child of Idleness); he looks in a glass and exclaims:

> hah, goges sowle,
> What have we here, a dyvyll?

---

[21] *Geschichte des neueren Dramas*, i (Halle, 1911), 201. An interesting detail appears in footnote 3 on this page: 'Wie intensiv die Bemalung war, ergibt sich den Summen, die in Frankreich den Barbarien und Badestubenbesitzern für Reinigung der Teufel bezahlt wurden.' (See also E. J. Haslinghuis, *De Duivel in het drama der Middeleeuwen* (Leiden, 1912), p. 182.)

[22] See Thomas Sharp, *A Dissertation upon the Coventry Mysteries* (Coventry, 1825), pp. 66, 70.

[23] E. K. Chambers, *The English Folk Play* (Oxford, 1933), p. 28.

[24] Ed. E. Vogel, *Shakespeare Jahrbuch*, xl (1904), l. 1439.

[25] See F. S. Boas, *University Drama in the Tudor Age* (Oxford, 1914), pp. 94 ff.

[26] Malone Society Reprints (1951).

This glas I se well hath bene kept evyll

.    .    .    .    .    .    .

Other this glas is shamefully spotted,
Or else am I to shamefully blotted.

.    .    .    .    .    .    .

And as for this face
Is abhominable as black as the devyll. (826–40)

Even in a proverbial title like 'Like will to like quoth the
Devil to the Collier' the widespread and universally accepted
point is exposed as part of the air that Englishmen of
Shakespeare's age breathed. Indeed, as late as Wycherley's
*The Plain Dealer* (1676) stray reference to the Devil's
blackness was supposed to be intelligible to a theatrical
audience ('like a devil in a play . . . this darkness . . . conceals
her angel's face').[27]

How mindlessly and how totally accepted in this period
was the image of the black man as the devil may be seen from
the use of 'Moors' or 'Morians' in civic pageants. 'Moors'
were an accepted part of the world of pageantry.[28] There were
Moors in London Lord Mayor's Pageants in 1519, 1521, 1524,
1536, 1541, 1551, 1589, 1609, 1611, 1624,[29] who seem to have
acted as bogey-man figures to clear the way before the main
procession. They were sometimes supplied with fireworks for
this purpose, and in this function seem to have been fairly
indifferent alternatives to green-men, wodewoses, devils. As
Withington has remarked,[30] 'it seems obvious that all these
figures are connected'; they are connected as frightening
marginal comments on the human state—as inhabitants of
those peripheral regions in the *mappae mundi* where Moors,
together with

Anthropophagi and men whose heads
Do grow beneath their shoulders,

[27] *The Plain Dealer*, IV. ii.
[28] Moors (like dwarfs and fools) were found also in the human menageries that the
courts of the Renaissance liked to possess. The Moors at the court of James IV of
Scotland appear often in the Treasurer's Accounts. One item there throws an
interesting light on their status: 'The nuris that brocht the Moris barne to see (i.e. to
be seen), be the Kingis command' (volume iii, p. 182).
[29] See Malone Society Collections, iii (1945).
[30] R. Withington, *English Pageantry*, i (Cambridge, Mass., 1918), 74.

rubbed shoulders (such as these were) with Satyrs, Hermaphrodites, salvage men, and others of the species *semihomo*.[31] An extreme example of this status of the Moor appears in the report of the pageant for the baptism of Prince Henry in 1594. It had been arranged that a lion should pull the triumphal car; but the lion could not be used, so a Moor was substituted.[32]

Renaissance scepticism and the voyages of discovery might seem, at first sight, to have destroyed the ignorance on which such thoughtless equations of black men and devils depended. But this does not prove to have been so. The voyagers brought back some accurate reports of black and heathen; but they often saw, or said they saw, what they expected to see—the marvels of the East.[33] In any case the vocabulary at their disposal frustrated any attempt at scientific discrimination. The world was still seen largely, in terms of vocabulary, as a network of religious names. The word 'Moor' had no clear racial status. The first meaning in the OED (with examples up to 1629) is 'Mahomedan'. And very often this

[31] The association of the negro with *semihomines* appears in a sixteenth-century sword-dance of 'Mores, Sauvages et Satyres', cited by Chambers (*Mediaeval Stage*, i. 199 n. 5), and in the decoration of the 'vasque de Saint Denis' (c.1180) decorated with sculptures of 'Sylvanus, satyr and negro' (see H. W. Janson, *Apes and Ape-lore* (London, 1952), p. 55). The *vasque* also uses a sculpture of an ape, and this may be associated with the others as a further illustration of the *semihomo*. The confusion of the age and the negro has a considerable history. The negress at the Court of James IV of Scotland who was set up as 'Queen of Beauty' (see above, n. 18) was compared to an ape; Dunbar tells us 'Quhou schou is tute mowitt lyk ane aep' ('of an blak-moir'). Joseph Glanvill, *Scepsis Scientifica* (1665), suggests that the apes (rather than the negroes) are the descendants of Cham. The confusion was a useful one for the defenders of negro slavery, and drew extra support from the often-repeated stories that orang-utangs frequently stole away and ravished black women. Thus Edward Long in his *History of Jamaica* (London, 1774) says that 'The equally hot temperament of their women has given probability to the charge of their admitting these animals [monkies or baboons] to their embrace' (ii. 383). Thomas Jefferson, in his *Notes on Virginia* (written in 1781), treats as an acknowledged fact 'the preference of the Oranootan for black women' (Question XIV).

[32] See *A True Reportary of the Baptisme of Frederik Henry, Prince of Scotland* (1594) (*STC* 13163).

[33] See R. Wittkower, 'Marvels of the East', *Journal of the Warburg and Courtauld Institutes*, v (1942), 159–97. See also L. Olschki, *Storia letteraria delle scoperte geografiche* (Florence, 1939), and R. Romeo, *Le scoperte americane nella coscienza Italiana* (Milan, 1954), who puts the idea expressed here with great clarity: 'Idee e valori preesistenti operano direttamente sui viaggiatori, spingendo a intendere in conformità ad essi testimonianze dubbie, discorsi in lingue sconosciute, fenomeni poco spiegabili' (p. 14).

means no more than 'infidel', 'non-Christian'. Like *Barbarian* and *Gentile* (or *Wog*) it was a word for 'people not like us', so signalled by colour. The word *Gentile* itself had still the religious sense of *Pagan*, and the combined phrase 'Moors and Gentiles' is used regularly to represent the religious gamut of non-Christian possibilities (see OED for examples). Similarly, *Barbary* was not simply a place in Africa, but also the unclearly located home of Barbarism, as in Chaucer (Franklin's Tale, 1451, Man of Law's Tale, 183).

I have suggested elsewhere that the discoveries of the voyagers had little opportunity of scientific or non-theological development.[34] And this was particularly true of the problems raised by the black-skinned races. No scientific explanation of black skins had ever been achieved, though doctors had long disputed it. Lodovicus Caelius Rhodiginus in his *Lectionum Antiquarum libri XXX* (1620) can cite column after column of authorities; but all without conclusive answers. We hear among the latest reports of Africa collected in T. Astley's *New General Collection of Voyages* (1745) that the blackness of the Negro is 'a Topic that has given Rise to numberless Conjectures and great Disputes among the Learned in Europe' (ii. 269). Sir Thomas Browne in three essays in his *Pseudodoxia Epidemica* (VI. x–xii) not only declared that the subject was 'amply and satisfactorily discussed as we know by no man' but proceeded to remedy this by way of amplitude rather than satisfactoriness. The theological explanation was left in possession of the field. Adam and Eve, it must be assumed, were white; it follows that the creation of the black races can only be ascribed to some subsequent *fiat*. The two favourite possibilities were the cursing of Cain and the cursing of Ham or Cham and his posterity—and sometimes these two were assumed to be different expressions of the same event; at least one might allege, with Sir Walter Ralegh, that 'the sonnes of Cham did possesse the vices of the sonnes of Cain'.[35] The Cham explanation had the great advantage that 'the threefold world' of tradition could be described in terms of the three sons of

---

[34] G. K. Hunter, loc. cit.
[35] *The History of the World*, I. vi. 2.

Noah—Japhet having produced the Europeans, Shem the Asiatics, while the posterity of Ham occupied Africa, or, in a more sophisticated version, 'the Meridionall or southern partes of the world both in Asia and Africa'[36]—sophisticated, we should notice, without altering the basic theological assumption that Cham's posterity were banished to the most uncomfortable part of the globe, and a foretaste of the Hell to come. This geographical assumption fitted in with the wisdom that the etymological doctors had in the Middle Ages been able to glean from the word *Ham*—defined as '*Cham: calidus*, et ipse ex praesagio futuri cognominatus est. Posteritas enim eius eam terrae partem possedit quae vicino sole calentior est.'[37] When this is linked to the other point made in relation to the Cham story—that his posterity were cursed to be slaves[38]—one can see how conveniently and plausibly such a view fitted the facts and desires found in the early navigators. Azurara, the chronicler of Prince Henry the Navigator's voyages, tells us that it was natural to find blackamoors as the slaves of lighter skinned men:

> these blacks were Moors (i.e. Mahomedans) like the others, though their slaves, in accordance with ancient custom which I believe to have been because of the curse which, after the Deluge, Noah laid upon his son Cain [*sic*], cursing him in this way: that his race should be subject to all the other races in the world. And from his race these blacks are descended.[39]

The qualities of the 'Moors' who appear on the Elizabethan stage are hardly at all affected by Elizabethan knowledge of real Moors from real geographical locations, and, given the literary modes available, this is hardly surprising. It is true that the first important Moor-role—that of Muly Hamet in Peele's *The Battle of Alcazar* (c.1589)—tells the story of a real man (with whom Queen Elizabeth had a treaty) in a real historical situation. But the dramatic focus that Peele manages to give to his Moorish character is largely dependent on the

---

[36] A. Willet, *Hexapla in Genesin* (1605), p. 119.

[37] Isidore of Seville, *Etymologiae*, VII. vi. 17. (Patrologia Latina, lxxxii, col. 276.)

[38] See St Ambrose, *Comment. in epist. ad Philippenses* (Pat. Lat. xvii, col. 432): 'servi autem ex peccato fiunt, sicut Cham filius Noe, qui primus merito nomen servi accepit.'

[39] *Discovery and Conquest of Guinea* (Hakluyt Society, xcv [1896], 54).

devil and underworld associations he can suggest for him—
making him call up 'Fiends, Fairies, hags that fight in beds of
steel' and causing him to show more acquaintance with the
geography of hell than with that of Africa. Aaron in *Titus
Andronicus* is liberated from even such slender ties as
associate Muly Hamet with geography. Aaron is in the play as
the representative of a world of generalized barbarism, which
is Gothic in Tamora and Moorish in Aaron, and unfocused in
both. The purpose of the play is served by a general
opposition between Roman order and Barbarian disorder.
Shakespeare has the doubtful distinction of making explicit
here (perhaps for the first time in English literature) the
projection of black wickedness in terms of negro sexuality.
The relationship between Tamora and Aaron is meant, clearly
enough, to shock our normal sensibilities and their black
baby is present as an emblem of disorder. In this respect, as in
most others, Eleazer in *Lust's Dominion* (c.1600)—the third
pre-Othello stage-Moor—is copied from Aaron. The location
of this play (Spain) gives a historically plausible excuse to
present the devil in his favourite human form—'that of a
Negro or Moor', as Reginald Scott tells us—but does not
really use the locale to establish any racial points.

These characters provide the dominant images that must
have been present in the minds of Shakespeare's original
audience when they entered the Globe to see a play called *The
Moor of Venice*—an expectation of pagan devilry set against
white Christian civilization—excessive civilization perhaps in
Venice, but civilization at least 'like us'. Even those who
knew Cinthio's story of the Moor of Venice could not have
had very different expectations, which may be summed up
from the story told by Bandello (III. xxi) in which a master
beats his Moorish servant, and the servant in revenge rapes
and murders his wife and children.[40] Bandello draws an
illuminating moral:

---

[40] Bandello, *Novelle*, Book III, novel xxi, derived from Pontanus (*Opera*, i. 25 b),
and translated by Belleforest, *Histoires tragiques*. The story was apparently
Englished in ballad form, in 1569, 1570, and again in 1624, 1675. See Hyder Rollins,
'Analytical Index' (*Studies in Philology*, xxi (1924) item 2542: 'a strange petyful novell
Dyscoursynge of a noble Lorde and his lady with thayre ij cheldren executed by a
blacke morryon.'

By this I intend it to appear that a man should not be served by this sort of slave; for they are seldom found faithful, and at best they are full of filth, unclean, and stink all the time like goats. But all this is as nothing put beside the savage cruelty that reigns in them.

It is in such terms that the play opens. We hear from men like us of a man not like us, of 'his Moorship', 'the Moor', 'the thicklips', 'an old black ram', 'a Barbary horse', 'the devil', of 'the gross clasps of a lascivious Moor'. The sexual fear and disgust that lies behind so much racial prejudice are exposed for our derisive expectations to fasten upon them. And we are at this point bound to agree with these valuations, for no alternative view is revealed. There is, of course, a certain comic *brio* which helps to distance the whole situation, and neither Brabantio, nor Iago nor Roderigo can wholly command our identification. None the less we are drawn on to await the entry of a traditional Moor figure, the kind of person we came to the theatre expecting to find.

When the second scene begins, however, it is clear that Shakespeare is bent to ends other than the fulfilment of these expectations. The Iago/Roderigo relationship of 1. i is repeated in the Iago/Othello relationship of the opening of 1. ii; but Othello's response to the real-seeming circumstance with which Iago lards his discourse is very different from the hungrily self-absorbed questionings of Roderigo. Othello draws on an inward certainty about himself, a radiant clarity about his own wellfounded moral position. This is no 'lascivious Moor', but a great Christian gentleman, against whom Iago's insinuations break like water against granite. Not only is Othello a Christian, moreover, he is the leader of Christendom in the last and highest sense in which Christendom existed as a viable entity, crusading against the 'black pagans'. He is to defend Cyprus against the Turk, the 'general enemy Ottoman'. It was the fall of Cyprus which produced the alliance of Lepanto, and we should associate Othello with the emotion that Europe continued to feel—till well after the date of *Othello*—about that victory and about Don John of Austria.[41]

Shakespeare has presented to us a traditional view of what

[41] See G. K. Hunter, loc. cit.

Moors are like, i.e. gross, disgusting, inferior, carrying the symbol of their damnation on their skin; and has caught our over-easy assent to such assumptions in the grip of a guilt which associates us and our assent with the white man representative of such views in the play—Iago. Othello acquires the glamour of an innocent man that *we* have wronged, and an admiration stronger than he could have achieved by virtue plainly represented:

> . . . as these black masks
> Proclaim an enshield beauty ten times louder
> Than beauty could, displayed
>
> (II. iv. 79–81)

(Is it an accident that Shakespeare wrote these lines from *Measure for Measure* in approximately the same year as he wrote *Othello*?) Iago is a 'civilized' man; but where, for the 'inferior' Othello, appearance and reality, statement and truth are linked indissolubly, civilization for Iago consists largely of a capacity to manipulate appearances and probabilities:

> For when my outward action doth demonstrate
> The native act and figure of my heart
> In compliment extern, 'tis not long after
> But I will wear my heart upon my sleeve
> For daws to peck at: I am not what I am.
>
> (I. i. 62–6)

Othello may be 'the devil' in appearance: but it is the 'fair' Iago who gives birth to the dark realities of sin and death in the play:

> It is engender'd. Hell and night
> Must bring this monstrous birth to the world's light
>
> (I. iii. 397–8)

The relationship between these two is developed in terms of appearance and reality. Othello controls the reality of action; Iago the 'appearance' of talk about action; Iago the Italian is isolated (even from his wife), envious, enigmatic (even to himself), self-centred; Othello the 'extravagant and wheeling stranger' is surrounded and protected by a network of duties, obligations, esteems, pious to his father-in-law, deferential to his superiors, kind to his subordinates, loving to his wife. To sum up, assuming that *soul* is reality and *body* is appearance, we may say that Iago is the white man with the black soul while Othello is the black man with the white soul. Long before Blake's little black boy had said

> I am black, but oh my soul is white.
> White as an angel is the English child,
> But I am black as if bereaved of light.

and before Kipling's Gunga Din:

> An' for all 'is dirty 'ide
> 'E was white, clear white inside . . .
> You're a better man than I am, Gunga Din!

Othello had represented the guilty awareness of Europe that the 'foreigner type' is only the type we do not know, whose foreignness vanishes when we have better acquaintance; that the prejudicial foreign appearance may conceal a vision of truth, as Brabantio is told:

> If virtue no delighted beauty lack
> Your son-in-law is far more fair than black.
>
> (I. iii. 289–90)

This reality of fairness in Othello provides a principal function for Desdemona in the play. Her love is of a spiritual intensity, of a strong simplicity equal to that of Othello himself, and pierces without effort beyond appearance, into reality:

> I saw Othello's visage in his mind.
>
> (I. iii. 252)

Her love is a daring act of faith, beyond reason or social propriety. Like Beauty in the fairytale she denies the beastly (or devilish) appearance to proclaim her allegiance to the invisible reality. And she does so throughout the play, even when the case for the appearance seems most strong and when Iago's power over appearances rides highest. Even when on the point of death at Othello's hands, she gives testimony to her faith (martyr in the true sense of the word):

Commend me to my *kind* lord.

(v. ii. 128)

*Othello* is then a play which manipulates our sympathies, supposing that we will have brought to the theatre a set of careless assumptions about 'Moors'. It assumes also that we will find it easy to abandon these as the play brings them into focus and identifies them with Iago, draws its elaborate distinction between the external appearance of devilishness and the inner reality.

Shakespeare's playcraft, however, would hardly have been able to superimpose these new valuations on his audience (unique as they were in this form) if it had not been for complicating factors which had begun to affect thought in his day.

The first counter-current I should mention is theological in origin and is found dispersed in several parts of the Bible. It was a fairly important doctrine of the Evangelists that faith could wash away the stains of sin, and the inheritance of misbelief, that the breach between chosen and non-chosen peoples could be closed by faith. The apostle Philip baptised the Ethiopian eunuch and thereupon, says Bede, the Ethiop changed his skin.[42] The sons of darkness could be seen to become the sons of light, or as Ephesians 5: 8 puts it:

For ye were sometimes darkness, but now are ye light in the Lord: walk as the children of light.

Jerome remarks on this (in Epistle xxii, § 1):

He that committeth sin is of the devil (John, 3: 8). Born of such a parent first we are black by nature, and even after repentance, until we have climbed to Virtue's height we may say *Nigra sum sed speciosa, filiae Hierusalem.*

Only after conversion, he goes on, will the colour be changed, as by miracle, and then will the verse be fitting: *Quae est ista, quae ascendit dealbata?* (Cant. viii. 5, translated from the Septuagint version).

Augustine hangs the same point on an interpretation of Psalm 73 (74 in the English Psalter), v. 14. The verse in the

---

[42] Bede, *Super Acta Apostolorum Expositio (Pat. Lat.* xcii, col. 962).

Authorized Version reads 'Thou brakest the heads of leviathan in pieces and gavest him to be meat to the people inhabiting the wilderness', but the Vulgate version has . . . *Dedisti eum in escam populis Ethiopibus.* Augustine[43] asks who are meant by the Ethiopians; and answers that all nations are Ethiopians, black in their natural sinfulness; but they may become white in the knowledge of the Lord. *Fuistis enim aliquando tenebrae; nunc autem lux in Domino* (Ephesians 5: 8). As late as Bishop Joseph Hall, writing one of his *Occasional Meditations* (1630) 'on the sight of a black-amoor', we find the same use of *nigra sum sed speciosa:*

This is our colour spiritually; yet the eye of our gracious God and Saviour, can see that beauty in us wherewith he is delighted. The true Moses marries a Blackamoor; Christ, his church. It is not for us to regard the skin, but the soul. If that be innocent, pure, holy, the blots of an outside cannot set us off from the love of him who hath said, *Behold, thou art fair, my Sister, my Spouse:* if that be foul and black, it is not in the power of an angelical brightness of our hide, to make us other than a loathsome eye-sore to the Almighty.

The relevance of this passage to Othello need not be stressed.

The grandest of all visual representations of this view that all men are within the scope of the Christian ministry ('We, being many, are one body in Christ', says St Paul in Romans 12: 5) is probably the portal of the narthex at Vézelay, displaying the relevance of the pentecostal spirit of evangelism even to the monsters on the verge of humanity—Cynocephali and long-eared Scythians, whose relation to the Christian world had been debated by St Augustine and other Fathers. But this monument has been treated with admirable fullness by Émile Mâle,[44] and it is not part of my function either to repeat or dispute what he has said.

Moreover, Vézelay does not touch on the colour question. And visual images are obviously of crucial importance here in establishing the idea of the black man as more than a patristic metaphor, as a figure that might be met with in real life. For the image of the black man, considered in relation to the

---

[43] St Augustine, *Enarrationes in Psalmos (Pat. Lat.* xxxvi, col. 938).
[44] Émile Mâle, *L'Art religieux du XII<sup>e</sup> siècle en France* (Paris, 1922), pp. 328 ff.

scheme of the Christian Evangel, we have to turn in the main to representations of the three Magi. In early Christian art there seems no evidence that the three kings were shown different from one another. As early as the eighth century,[45] however, the *Excerptiones Patrum*, attributed to Bede, had described Balthazar, the third king, in the following terms:

Tertius, fuscus, integre barbatus, Balthazar nomine, habens tunicam rubeam.[46]

I may quote Mâle on this description:

It should also be noted that . . . the term *fuscus* applied to Balthazar by the pseudo-Bede was never taken literally, and it was only in the fourteenth and still more in the fifteenth centuries that the king has the appearance of a Negro.[47]

It would be interesting to know what factors impeded the development of the black Balthazar in iconography. For as early as 1180, in the great typological sequence at Klosterneuburg, Nicholas of Verdun had represented the Old Testament type of the Epiphany—the visit of the Queen of Sheba to Solomon—with a Negro Sheba—a feature to be met with elsewhere.

It was another typological parallel, however, that probably did most to establish the black Balthazar—that between the three kings and the three sons of Noah. The genuine Bede makes this point in his commentary on Matthew:

Mystice autem tres Magi tres partes mundi significant, Asiam, Africam, Europam, sive humanum genus, quod a tribus filiis Noe seminarium sumpsit.[48]

and this view was given general diffusion in the *Glossa Ordinaria*.[49] If we suppose that Cham became the father of the black races, it follows that one of the Magi must represent these races. Balthazar carries on his face the curse of Cham,

---

[45] For the dating see P. Glorieux, *Pour revaloriser Migne* (1844), and J. F. Kenney, *Sources for the Early History of Ireland* (New York, 1929).
[46] Pseudo-Bede, *Excerptiones Patrum (Pat. Lat. xciv, col. 541).
[47] Émile Mâle, *The Gothic Image* (London and Glasgow, 1961), pp. 214–15.
[48] Bede, *In Matthaei Evangelium Expositio (Pat. Lat. xcii, col. 13).
[49] Walafridus Strabus, *Glossa Ordinaria (Pat. Lat. cxiv, col. 73).

but reveals the capacity for redemption through faith available to all races. And such another is Othello.

The sense that inferior and black-faced foreigners might in fact be figures from a more innocent world close to Christianity grew apace in the Renaissance[50] as the voyagers gave their accounts, not of highly organized Mahomedan kingdoms, but of simple pagans, timid, naked as their mothers brought them forth, without laws and without arms (as Columbus first saw them and first described them)[51] and perhaps having minds naturally prone to accept Christianity.[52] The old ideals and dreams of travellers, the terrestrial paradise, the fountain of youth, the kingdom of Prester John, assumed a new immediacy. And so the old impulse to bring the Evangel to all nations acquired a new primitivist dynamic. An interesting demonstration of this is supplied in a Portuguese picture of the Epiphany c.1505, sometimes attributed to Vasco Fernandes, where a Brazilian chief, in full regalia, replaces the black Balthazar. Alongside the view that such black pagans could only acquire Christian hope by enslavement grew an alternative vision of their innocence as bringing them near to God, by way of nature. Nowhere was the opposition between these two views more dramatically presented than in the famous debate at Valladolid between Sepúlveda and Las Casas.[53] Sepúlveda asserted that the American Indians were 'slaves by nature', since their natural inferiority made it

[50] There is an inconographic parallel in the use of negro figures to represent primitive innocence, in Bosch and perhaps elsewhere. Fränger, *The Millennium of Hieronymus Bosch* (London, 1952), notes (p. 108): 'This scene takes place in the presence of a Nubian girl, who is *nigra sed formosa* like the black bride of the Song of Songs (i. 5). We are doubtless justified in regarding these negresses, who appear so often in the picture, as embodiments of the innocence that had not yet vanished from the primal condition of tropical nature.'

[51] Quoted in R. Romeo, *Le scoperte americane nella coscienza italiana del Cinquecento*, p. 19; L. Olschki, *Storia letteraria delle scoperte geografiche* (Florence, 1937) pp. 11–22.

[52] So Columbus in the journal of his first voyage (16 October 1492): 'They do not know any religion, and I believe they could easily be converted to Christianity, for they are very intelligent.' The Bull *Inter cetera* of 1493 (which divided the New World between Spain and Portugal) speaks of the Indians as *'gentes pacifice viventes . . . nudi incedentes, nec carnibus vescentes . . . credunt unum Deum creatorem in celis esse, ac ad fidem catholicam amplexandam et bonis moribus imbuendum satis apti videntur'*.

[53] Described most fully in English in L. Hanke, *Aristotle and the American Indians* (London, 1959).

impossible for them to achieve the light of the gospel without enslavement.[54] Las Casas, on the other hand, dwelt on the innocence of the Indians, living *secundum naturam*, on their natural capacity for devotion, and on the appalling contrast between the mild and timid Indians and the inhumanity of their 'civilized' or 'Christian' exploiters. Of these two it was of course Las Casas who made the greatest impact in Europe. We should not forget that the Valladolid debate was decided in his favour; but it was not in Spain, but in France and England that primitivism grew most rapidly. Spanish claims to the New World and Spanish brutality in the New World combined the forces of jealousy, frustrated greed, and local self-righteousness so as to create (even if with initially polemical purpose) a whole new critique of European Christian pretensions. It could now be said that white European Christianity had been put to the test in America (the test being the salvation of souls) and had been found wanting. 'Upon these lambes', writes Richard Hakluyt (quoting Las Casas), 'so meke, so qualified and endewed of their maker and creator as hath bene saied, entred the spanishe, incontinent as they knew them, as wolves as lyons and as Tigres moste cruell of long tyme famished'.[55] Fulke Greville puts the same point even more categorically:

And in stead of spreading Christian religion by good life, [the Spaniards] committed such terrible inhumanities as gave those that lived under nature manifest occasion to abhor the devilry character of so tyrannical a deity [as the Christian God].[56]

The crown of all such Renaissance primitivism is Montaigne's *Essays*, and especially that on the Cannibals, where

---

[54] See Eric Williams, *Documents of West Indian History* (1963), item 155, discussing the view that a 'negro cannot become a Christian without being a slave'. Cf. the summary of Sepúlveda's position in Hanke, op. cit., pp. 44 f. The same views persist today, though with interesting modifications in the vocabulary: 'He (the Negro) requires the constant control of white people to keep him in check. Without the presence of the white police force negroes would turn upon themselves and destroy each other. The white man is the only authority he knows.' (Quoted in E. T. Thompson, *Race Relationships* (Durham, NC, 1939), p. 174.)

[55] *A Discourse on the Western Planting* (1584) printed in *The Writings of the two Richard Hakluyts*, vol. ii (Hakluyt Society [second series], lxxvii [1935], p. 258).

[56] Fulke Greville, *Life of Sir Philip Sidney* (1652), ed. Nowell Smith (Oxford, 1907), p. 116.

the criticism of Spanish Christianity has become a *libertin* critique of modern European civility. Shakespeare, in *The Tempest*, seems to show a knowledge of this essay,[57] and certainly *The Tempest* reveals a searching interest in the status of Western civilization parallel to Montaigne's, and a concern to understand the point of reconciliation between innocence and sophistication, ignorance and knowledge.

Of course, we must not assume that Shakespeare, because he had these concerns in *The Tempest*, must have had them also in *Othello*; but *The Tempest* at one end of his career, like *Titus Andronicus* at the other end, indicates that the polarities of thought on which *Othello* moves (if I am correct) were available to his mind.

I have spoken of 'polarities' in the plural because it is important to notice that Shakespeare does not present his *Othello* story in any simple primitivist terms. *Othello* is not adequately described as the exploitation of a noble savage by a corrupt European.[58] This is an element in the play, and it is the element that Henry James found so seminal for his own images of the relationship between American and European,[59] but it is not the whole play.

*Othello* has *something* of the structure of a morality play, with Othello caught between Desdemona and Iago, the good angel and the evil angel. Iago is the master of appearances, which he seeks to exploit as realities; Desdemona on the other hand, cares nothing for appearances (as her 'downright violence and storm of fortunes / May trumpet to the world'), only for realities; Othello, seeing appearance and reality as indissoluble cues to action, stands between the two, the object of the attentions and the assumptions of both. The play has something of this morality structure; but by giving too much

[57] Disputed in M. T. Hodgen, 'Montaigne and Shakespeare', *Huntington Library Quarterly*, xvi (1952), 23–42. Miss Hodgen finds a similarity of elements used to praise primitive life in Louis le Roy, Boemus, Vespucci, Mexia, etc.

[58] But Iago's Spanish name (and his nautical imagery) may represent Shakespeare's awareness of this potentiality in his play at some level of his consciousness. The relevance of the figure of Sant' Iago Matamoros (Moor-slayer) has been suggested by G. N. Murphy, 'A Note on Iago's name', *Literature and Society*, ed. B. Slote (Nebraska, 1964).

[59] See Agostino Lombardo, 'Henry James *The American* e il mito di Otello', *Friendship's Garland: Essays presented in Mario Praz*, ed. V. Gabrieli (Rome, 1966), pp. 107–42.

importance to this it would be easy to underplay the extent to which Othello becomes what Iago and the society to which *we* belong assumes him to be.

There is considerable strength in the anti-primitivist side of the great Renaissance debate (as that is represented in *Othello*) and this lies in the extent to which the whole social organism pictured is one we recognize as our own, and recognize as necessarily geared to reject 'extravagant and wheeling strangers'. I speak of the social organism here, not in terms of its official existence—its commands, duties, performances; for in these terms Othello's life is well meshed into the state machine:

> My services which I have done the Signiory
> Shall out-tongue his complaints.
>
> (I. ii. 17–18)

I speak rather of the unspoken assumptions and careless prejudices by which we all conduct most of our lives. And it is in these respects that Iago is the master of us all, the snapper-up of every psychological trifle, every unnoticed dropped handkerchief. It is by virtue of such a multitude of our tiny and unnoticed assents that Iago is able to force Othello into the actions he expects of him. Only the hermit can stand outside such social assumptions; but, by marrying, Othello has become part of society in this sense, the natural victim of the man-in-the-know, the man universally thought well of. And Iago's knowingness finds little or no resistance. We all believe the Iagos in our midst; they are, as our vocabulary interestingly insists, the 'realists'.

The dramatic function of Iago is to reduce the white 'reality' of Othello to the black 'appearance' of his face, indeed induce in him the belief that all reality is 'black', that Desdemona in particular, 'where I have garnered up my heart'

> ... that was fresh
> As Dian's visage, is now begrimed and black
> As mine own face.
>
> (III. iii. 390–2)

Thus in the bedroom scene (v.ii) Othello's view of Desdemona is one that contrasts

> that whiter skin of hers than snow
> And smooth as monumental alabaster
>
> (v. ii. 4–5)

with the dark deeds her nature requires of her.

> Put out the light, and then put out the light,
>
> (v. ii. 7)

he says; that is, 'let the face be as dark as the soul it covers';
and then murder will be justified.

This intention on Shakespeare's part is made very explicit at
one point where Othello tells Desdemona,

> Come, swear it, damn thyself; lest, being like one of heaven, the
> devils themselves should fear to seize thee; therefore be double
> damn'd—swear thou art honest. (IV. ii. 36 ff.)

What Othello is asking here is that the white and so
'heavenly' Desdemona should damn herself black, as Esdras
of Granada had done in Nashe's *The Unfortunate Traveller*,
with the result that:

> His body being dead lookt as blacke as a toad: the devill presently
> branded it for his own.[60]

It is, of course, to the same belief that Shakespeare alludes in
Macbeth's 'The devil damn thee black, thou cream-faced
loon'.

The dark reality originating in Iago's soul spreads across
the play, blackening whatever it overcomes and making the
deeds of Othello at last fit in with the prejudice that his face at
first excited. Sometimes it is supposed that this proves the
prejudice to have been justified. There is a powerful line of
criticism on *Othello*, going back at least as far as A. W.
Schlegel,[61] that paints the Moor as a savage at heart, one
whose veneer of Christianity and civilization cracks as the
play proceeds, to reveal and liberate his basic savagery:
Othello turns out to be in fact what barbarians *have* to be.

This view, however comforting to our sense of society and
our prejudices, does not find much support in the play itself.

---

[60] Nashe, *Works*, ed. McKerrow (London, 1904–10), ii. 326.

[61] August Wilhelm Schlegel, *Lectures on Dramatic Art* (1815), ii. 189.

The fact that the darkness of 'Hell and night' spreads from
Iago and then takes over Othello—this fact at least should
prevent us from supposing that the blackness is inherent in
Othello's barbarian nature. Othello himself, it is true, loses
faith not only in Desdemona but in that fair quality of himself
which Desdemona saw and worshipped: ('for she had eyes
and chose me'). Believing that she lied about the qualities she
saw in him it is easy for him to believe that she lies elsewhere
and everywhere. Once the visionary quality of *faith*, which
made it possible to believe (what in common sense was
unbelievable) that she *chose* him—once this is cancelled,
knowingness acquires a claim to truth that only faith could
dispossess; and so when Iago says

> I know our country disposition well;
> In Venice they do let heaven see the pranks
> They dare not show their husbands.
>
> (III. iii. 205–7)

Othello can only answer 'Dost thou say so?' Once faith is
gone, physical common sense becomes all too probable:

> Foh! one may smell in such a will most rank,
> Foul disproportion, thoughts unnatural.
>
> (III. iii. 236–7)

The superficial 'disproportion' between black skin and white
skin conquers the inward, unseen 'marriage of true minds'.
Similarly with the disproportion between youth and age: 'She
must change for youth'; being sated with his body she will
find the error of her choice. The tragedy becomes, as Helen
Gardner has described it, a tragedy of the loss of faith.[62] And,
such is the nature of Othello's heroic temperament, the loss of
faith means the loss of all meaning and all value, all sense of
light:

> I have no wife,
> O insupportable! O heavy hour!
> Methinks it should be now a huge eclipse
> Of sun and moon, and that the affrighted globe
> Should yawn at alteration.
>
> (v. ii. 100–4)

[62] Helen Gardner, 'The Noble Moor', *Proceedings of the British Academy*, xli
(1955) [No. 9 in this collection].

Universal darkness has buried all.

But the end of the play is not simply a collapse of civilization into barbarism, nor a destruction of meaning. Desdemona *was* true, faith *was* justified, the appearance was not the key to the truth. To complete the circle we must accept, finally and above all, that Othello was not the credulous and passionate savage that Iago has tried to make him, but that he was justified in his second, as in his first, self-defence:

> For nought I did in hate, but all in honour.
>
> (v. ii. 298)

The imposition of Iago's vulgar prejudices on Othello ('These Moors are changeable in their wills', etc.) is so successful that it takes over not only Othello but almost all the critics. But Iago's suppression of Othello into the vulgar prejudice about him can only be sustained as the truth if we ignore the end of the play. The wonderful recovery here of the sense of ethical meaning in the world, even in the ashes of all that embodied meaning—this requires that we see the final speech of Othello as more than that of a repentant blackamoor 'cheering himself up', as Mr Eliot phrased it.[63] It is in fact a marvellous *stretto* of all the themes that have sounded throughout the play. I shall only dwell on Othello's self-judgement and self-execution, repeating and reversing the judgement and execution on Desdemona and so, in a sense, cancelling them. Othello is the 'base Indian' who threw away the white pearl Desdemona, but he is also the state servant and Christian who, when the Infidel or 'black Pagan' within him seemed to triumph,

> Took by the throat the circumcised dog
> And smote him—thus.
>
> (v. ii. 358–9)

With poetic justice, the Christian reality reasserts its superior position over the pagan appearance, not in terms that can be lived through, but at least in terms that can be understood. We may rejoice even as we sorrow, catharsis is achieved, for

---

[63] T. S. Eliot, 'Shakespeare and the Stoicism of Seneca', reprinted in *Selected Essays* (London, 1932), p. 130.

What may quiet us in a death so noble,[64]

as this in the Aleppo of the mind?

It is often suggested that *Othello* is a play of claustrophobic intensity, painfully narrow in its range of vision. A. C. Bradley finds in it 'the darkness not of night, but of a close-shut murderous room'; he assumes that this is due to a limitation in its scope 'as if some power in his soul, at once the highest and the sweetest, were for a time in abeyance . . . that element . . . which unites him with the mystical poets and with the great musicians'. Elsewhere he refers to it as 'a play on a contemporary and wholly mundane subject'.[65] Many other notable critics have felt the same. Granville Barker believes that it is 'not a spiritual tragedy in the sense that the others may be called so . . . it is a tragedy without meaning, and that is the ultimate horror of it'.[66]

Given the approach to the play outlined in this essay I think it is possible to modify the view shared by these great critics. If we think of the action not simply in terms of the bad Iago's unresisted destruction of the good Othello, and of the bad Othello's unresisted destruction of Desdemona, but see these actions instead in terms of prejudice and vision, appearance and reality, indeed in terms of the whole question of civilization as canvassed, for example, in Montaigne's Essays —if we see these large questions as begged continuously by the action we may feel that some wider vision has been let into 'the close-shut murderous room'.

The domestic intensities of *King Lear* have been seen usefully and interestingly (by Theodore Spencer, for example) in relation to the intellectual history of the Renaissance.[67] The position of the king obviously calls on one set of traditional assumptions, while Edmund's doctrine of nature equally obviously draws on the views of the *libertins*, of Montaigne and Machiavelli. The pressure of these larger formulations may be seen to add to the largeness of scope in the play.

[64] Milton, *Samson Agonistes*, line 1724.

[65] A. C. Bradley, *Shakespearean Tragedy* (London, 1904), pp. 177, 185, 186.

[66] Harley Granville Barker, *Prefaces to Shakespeare*, fourth series (London, 1945), pp. 156, 175.

[67] Theodore Spencer, *Shakespeare and the Nature of Man* (Cambridge, Mass., 1943).

*Othello*, on the other hand, is thought not to be a play of this kind. 'The play itself is primarily concerned with the effect of one human being on another',[68] says Spencer. It is true that Iago operates in a less conceptualized situation than Edmund; but the contrast between his world view and that of Othello is closely related to the contrast between Edmund and Lear. On the one side we have the chivalrous world of the Crusader, the effortless superiority of the 'great man', the orotund public voice of the leader, the magnetism of the famous lover. The values of the world of late medieval and Renaissance magnificence seem compressed in Othello—crusader, stoic, traveller, believer, orator, commander, lover—Chaucer's parfit knight, Spenser's Red Cross, the Ruggiero of Ariosto. In Iago we have the other face of the Renaissance (or Counter-Renaissance), rationalist, individual, empirical (or inductive), a master in the Machiavellian art of manipulating appearances, a Baconian or Hobbesian 'Realist'.

In the conflict of Othello and Iago we have, as in that setting Edmund, Goneril and Regan against Lear and Gloucester, a collision of these two Renaissance views. Bradley points to a similarity between Lear and Othello, that they are both 'survivors of a heroic age living in a later and smaller world'. Both represent a golden age naïvety which was disappearing then (as now, and always). Lear's survival is across a temporal gap; his long life has carried him out of one age and stranded him in another. But Othello's travel is geographical rather than temporal, from the heroic simplicities of

> I fetch my life and being
> From men of royal siege
>
> (I. ii. 21–2)

into the supersubtle world of Venice, the most sophisticated and 'modern' city on earth, as it seemed to the Elizabethans.

Here, if anywhere, was the scene-setting for no merely domestic intrigue, but for an exercise in the quality of civilization, a contest between the capacities and ideals claimed by Christendom, and those that Christians were actually employing in that context where (as Marlowe says)

---

[68] Spencer, op. cit. (1961 edn.), p. 126.

. . . Indian Moors obey their Spanish lords.[69]

Othello's black skin makes the coexistence of his vulnerable romanticism and epic grandeur with the bleak or even pathological realism of Iago a believable fact. The lines that collide here started thousands of miles apart. But Shakespeare's choice of a black man for his Red Cross Knight, his Rinaldo, has a further advantage. *Our* involvement in prejudice gives us a double focus on his reality. We admire him—I fear that one has to be trained as a literary critic to find him unadmirable—but we are aware of the difficulty of sustaining that vision of the golden world of poetry; and this is so because *we* feel the disproportion and the difficulty of his social life and of his marriage (as a social act). We are aware of the easy responses that Iago can command, not only of people on the stage but also in the audience. The perilous and temporary achievements of heroism are achieved most sharply in this play, because they have to be achieved in *our* minds, through *our* self-awareness.

---

[69] Marlowe, *Doctor Faustus*, I i. 122.

# INDEX